Autopsy of a Crime Lab

Autopsy of a Crime Lab

EXPOSING THE FLAWS IN FORENSICS

Brandon L. Garrett

UNIVERSITY OF CALIFORNIA PRESS

University of California Press
Oakland, California

© 2021 by Brandon L. Garrett

Library of Congress Cataloging-in-Publication Data

Names: Garrett, Brandon, author.
Title: Autopsy of a crime lab : exposing the flaws in forensics / Brandon
  L. Garrett.
Description: Oakland, California : University of California Press, [2021] |
  Includes bibliographical references and index.
Identifiers: LCCN 2020043891 (print) | LCCN 2020043892 (ebook) |
  ISBN 9780520379336 (cloth) | ISBN 9780520976634 (ebook)
Subjects: LCSH: DNA fingerprinting—Law and legislation. | Evidence,
  Expert. | Criminal investigation. | Forensic sciences. | Forensic
  genetics.
Classification: LCC K5479 .G37 2021 (print) | LCC K5479 (ebook) |
  DDC 345/.064—dc23
LC record available at https://lccn.loc.gov/2020043891
LC ebook record available at https://lccn.loc.gov/2020043892

Manufactured in the United States of America

29 28 27 26 25 24 23 22 21
10 9 8 7 6 5 4 3 2 1

To Kerry, Alex, and Zack

Contents

PART I The Crisis in Forensics

Introduction

Imagine that you have been selected to sit on a jury in a criminal trial. An expert takes the stand. He emphasizes his credentials as a senior fingerprint examiner at the Federal Bureau of Investigation (FBI), in Quantico, Virginia, the preeminent crime lab in the country. A series of explosions had killed over 190 people in a terrorist attack. The expert proceeds to confidently describe a forensic hit, comparing a fingerprint of the defendant's to a print found on a bag of detonators in a white van parked near the scene. The expert explains that he studied high-resolution images of the prints on a computer screen, identified fifteen points they shared, and reached a firm conclusion: a "100 percent identification." Next, he asked two experienced colleagues to review the prints: the chief of his unit and a retired FBI examiner with thirty-five years of experience. Each of the three experts agreed 100 percent with his conclusion.

The judge instructs you, as a juror, to carefully observe all of the evidence in the case. The judge tells you that to convict you must be certain beyond a reasonable doubt that the defendant was the culprit. Would you convict?

"That's not my fingerprint, your honor," says the defendant, in response to this evidence.

"What . . ." the judge responds. "It wasn't your fingerprint?"

"If it is, I don't know how it got there," he insists. "It is not my fingerprint."

In the real case, Brandon Mayfield, a Portland, Oregon lawyer, pleaded for his freedom in an Oregon federal courtroom. Federal agents testified that they identified his fingerprint on a plastic bag with detonators found near the bombing of four commuter trains in Madrid, Spain, that killed 193 people and injured about two thousand more. The judge sided with the FBI and ordered Mayfield detained as a material witness to terrorism. Mayfield knew that he was innocent. He had never set foot in Spain. He had converted to Islam years earlier, and the FBI theorized that perhaps he had formed an allegiance to militant Islamic groups and traveled under a fake name. His case would come to reshape the course of forensics, but only after he faced the prospect of indefinite detention and the death penalty.

Would you convict a person if the only evidence in the case was a fingerprint comparison? What if it was a bite mark, a drug test, or a DNA test? Before making the momentous decision to convict a person, you should ask how reliable the evidence is. Forensic evidence refers broadly to evidence in legal matters that involves scientific methods; my focus in this book is on the wide array of forensic evidence used in criminal cases. What is most surprising is that many forensic examiners do not use methods that are based on solid scientific research. Indeed, with the exception of DNA testing, the experts who link evidence to particular defendants at criminal trials cannot give you a straight answer to the question, "How reliable is your evidence?" Techniques like fingerprinting have been used for over a hundred years. Surely, someone must know how reliable they are. Yet not only is reliability untested and unknown, but the experts do not candidly admit to the judge and the jury that deep uncertainty lies at the foundations of their work. They do not admit that no one has carefully tested the reliability of the methods they use or the work they do on routine cases. Nor do they admit that the crime lab where they work lacks a rigorous testing program. Instead, forensic analysts testify in court just like the actors on popular forensics shows: they claim to find a perfect match. Take, for example, an episode of the popular show *CSI: Miami*, where the investigators, like in Mayfield's case, had just a single fingerprint. Crack investigator Eric "Delko" Delektorsky looks at the image: "Got a tented arch." Delko runs the print through a computer, which displays a supposed 99.32 percent hit to a person they didn't expect: the victim's fiancé. Moments later, you see arresting officers escorting the fiancé out of the house. Case closed.[1]

The FBI analysts in Brandon Mayfield's case were even more certain: they were "100 percent" certain. They were so certain that when Spanish authorities issued a report with a negative conclusion, contrary to the FBI's fingerprint identification, the FBI fingerprint analysts forcefully disagreed and flew to Madrid, Spain, to present their findings, with blown-up photos illustrating their work. The FBI placed Mayfield under twenty-four-hour surveillance, and then they arrested him. Mayfield's lawyer counseled him that he could be detained indefinitely and might face the death penalty. Then, on May 20, 2004, the prosecutor stood up in court and told the judge something unexpected: that morning the government "received some information from Spain" which "casts some doubt on the identification." Spanish authorities "determined completely" that the print belonged to a known Algerian terrorist. The FBI agreed to release Mayfield, dropped all charges a few days later, apologized to Mayfield, and a federal investigation followed.[2]

Our crime labs need an autopsy. The episode profoundly harmed Mayfield and his family. The failure of these FBI agents brought home how little we know about the reliability of forensic evidence. We need to know why these errors occur. After all, fingerprints have been used in court for over a hundred years. Fingerprint examiners insisted for decades that they had an error rate of zero. If three experienced fingerprints experts could get it so badly wrong, in a high-profile case, then how reliable is fingerprinting? How about all of the other forensics? The problem cried out for a serious scientific inquiry. A mini-autopsy did occur in response to the Mayfield case itself, when the U. S. Department of Justice wrote a lengthy report identifying specific problems with the work done in Mayfield's case. However, the investigators did not try to answer the most fundamental question that you would want answered if you were sitting on a jury: How reliable is a fingerprint comparison? No scientific studies had been done on the question. The investigators briefly noted in their report that according to critics, the basic premises of fingerprint work remain scientifically unproven. They further noted that defense lawyers and academics had questioned whether one can reach a conclusion using fingerprints with absolute certainty, but then they said no more.[3]

A few lone voices, mostly in academia, had raised reliability concerns for years, but without any success in the courts. Particularly when DNA testing became more common in the 1990s, leading scientists, law professors, social scientists, and a few defense lawyers began to ask what research supported the traditional non-DNA forensics. They were ignored. In 1993, the U. S. Supreme Court issued its landmark decision in *Daubert v. Merrell Dow Pharmaceuticals, Inc.*, holding that federal judges must act as gatekeepers to ensure that experts use reliable methods. Lawyers expected that judges would finally scrutinize forensic science in court, particularly after many states adopted this federal rule. A few judges hesitantly raised reliability concerns about fingerprinting, but the FBI shut them down with confident assertions that such techniques were foolproof.

Slowly, revelations from cases like Mayfield's began to erode the wall of silence that law enforcement, forensic analysts, and prosecutors had built around forensic evidence. Part I of this book describes how lawyers, scientists, and investigators uncovered the full scope of this crisis. It was not only Mayfield who deserved answers. Not long after Mayfield was cleared, Keith Harward, a prisoner in Virginia, began to write letters seeking DNA testing. At trial, dentists claimed his teeth matched bite marks on the victim. He was innocent, but no one seemed to be listening until his letter reached the Innocence Project in New York, founded by lawyers Barry Scheck and Peter Neufeld. Meanwhile, a public defender in Washington, DC, Sandra Levick, had located a string of cold cases in which FBI agents gave highly overstated testimony about forensic hair comparisons. She too began to pursue modern DNA testing to prove innocence in old cases.

Researchers also began to pose new questions. Leading statisticians began to ask what probabilities exist for forensics, since there is no such thing as a 100 percent match; every conclusion has some degree of uncertainty. Itiel Dror, a psychologist, began to study the role cognitive biases play in forensics. Peter Neufeld and I began to examine the trial testimony in hundreds of cases of innocent people freed by DNA testing. We were surprised to find that in over half of the cases, forensic errors contributed to the original convictions.[4] A few dissenting forensic scientists began to cautiously ask questions from within their professional communities.

Entire crime labs now came under scrutiny. The same year that Mayfield was arrested, in 2004, the entire Houston crime lab was closed due to rampant errors. A well-known former prosecutor, Michael Bromwich, audited this mass disaster. Levick would soon learn that Bromwich had previously audited problematic testimony in FBI hair cases, including in her client's cases. Levick's persistence would trigger a new audit of thousands of old FBI cases. In 95 percent of the cases, FBI experts testified erroneously and misrepresented the reliability of the technique, including in death penalty cases. Other crises were brewing during this time, but without anyone detecting the problem. Sonja Farak and Annie Dookhan falsified massive amounts of work at labs in Massachusetts, until eventually they were caught and forty-thousand-plus cases were overturned. Labs in large and small cities, from Chicago, Illinois, to Cleveland, Ohio, to Amherst, Massachusetts, to entire state crime labs in West Virginia and Montana, all had audits, reviews, and cases reopened. Journalists began to pay attention to stories of botched forensic analysis. Some began to suspect that the authorities executed innocent people who had been based on flawed forensics.

Responding to a growing national problem, the U.S. Congress called on the preeminent scientific organization in the country, the National Academy of Sciences, to investigate and report. Federal appellate judge Harry Edwards, who co-chaired the committee of leading scientists, crime lab directors, judges, and lawyers, had, like many others, always assumed that forensics were foolproof evidence. Hearing about hundreds of cases like Mayfield's shocked the lawyers and the scientists in the group. It was as if everything stopped at the national meeting of the American Academy of Forensic Sciences (AAFS) on February 16, 2009, the day the report came out. The three-hundred-page tome could not have been clearer. A single sentence summed it up: "With the exception of nuclear DNA analysis, however, no forensic method has been rigorously shown to have the capacity to consistently, and with a high degree of certainty, demonstrate a connection between evidence and a specific individual or source." What did that mean? Only DNA testing, the scientists said, could reliably connect evidence to individuals. No other forensics were reliable enough to make a definitive hit. As crucial as forensics can be in criminal cases, much of forensic evidence used is "without any meaningful scientific validation."[5]

As that important report showed, many types of forensic comparisons lack reliability, but the problem becomes even more troubling when one looks at the entire process, from the crime scene, to the lab, and then to the courtroom. Part II of this book explores each of the ways that forensics can go wrong. Although forensic methods have error rates, including false hits and misses, the reliability of experts has rarely been carefully tested, even for long-standing and widely used techniques like fingerprint and firearms comparisons. When researchers do uncover error rates, forensic analysts often do not disclose them in court. We do not know how reliable particular forensics professionals are; most labs do not seriously test them. When judges deem them experts, they take the stand and use over-stated language and proclaim infallibility to the jury. Bias affects forensic examiners, who typically work as an arm of law enforcement.

When, despite the 2009 report, little had changed in our labs and courtrooms, a second group of top scientists, led by mathematician and geneticist Eric Lander, came together in response. In 2016, the President's Council of Advisors on Science and Technology (PCAST) issued a report that emphasized a simple message: If we do not know how reliable a forensic technique is, we should not use it until this fundamental question is answered. Lander and his fellow scientists said that some techniques, such as firearms and bite mark comparisons, lack validation. Other techniques, like fingerprint evidence, they found to be valid, but with error rates far higher than many people assume. Again, forensic experts, prosecutors, and judges largely ignored this scientific report. Although few new studies have been done to try to measure error rates, analysts continue to reach unsupported conclusions, prosecutors continue to rely on them, and judges have only grudgingly raised questions about evidence like firearms and bite mark comparisons.

Today, it is more important than ever that we get forensic evidence right. Part III turns from forensic experts to our crime labs. During this time of increasing scrutiny of forensics, crime labs did not shrink but grew in size. Demand for lab services and backlogs in testing have dramatically increased. Crime labs now process millions of requests every year, as more criminal cases depend on forensic testing. The FBI led efforts to expand massive forensic databases, which they search to generate new leads. Yet many labs lack sound quality controls. Many police lack sound protections against contaminating evidence at the crime scene. New technology can introduce new reliability concerns, as labs and police increasingly buy products from companies marketing rapid DNA machines, facial recognition algorithms, and other computer programs, many of which have unknown reliability.

All of us need answers, not least because what happened to Mayfield could happen to any of us. After all, he initially became a suspect due to a hit in a government forensic database. You may not know it, but you are in databases much like the one that his prints were found in. You do not need to be arrested or convicted of a crime to be searched in a database. Facial recognition databases contain millions of faces from airport footage, social media, passport photos, and driver's license photos. If you have any relatives who sent swabs of their DNA to ancestry websites, then you may be linked. We have all been placed in an all-encompassing and never-ending set of lineups, without our permission, and we are all at risk.

Joined by a new chorus of concerned scientists, lawyers, and forensic practitioners, people are working hard to bring more science into crime labs and courtrooms. Part IV of this book describes the path forward. Perhaps the most surprising center for reform is Houston, Texas, where the county shuttered its lab for pervasive quality control failures. Peter Stout, the self-professed "Crazy Nerd in Houston," took the helm of the new lab, the Houston Forensic Science Center, and transformed it into a model, where error testing and quality control is routine. Today, more scientists have taken up the challenge to replace the problematic concept of a "match" with sound statistics.

We can fix forensics. Forensics is like air travel or pharmaceuticals, which we carefully regulate because the consequences are great, and not like astrology, which we do not because we do not expect it to be reliable. We need national regulation of forensics. What smooth-talking actors tell you on TV, and what experts say in the courtroom is false. As Gil Grissom, the fictional CSI lab analyst, puts it, you have to "follow the evidence" because evidence "cannot lie." Once you understand the assumptions and the methods used in forensics, you can ask the right questions. Is an expert infallible, or is that just sci-fi CSI? How good are the experts? Why do

crime labs fail? Why do so many judges let in evidence of unknown reliability? After reading the chapters that follow, each dissecting the failures
of our crime labs, you will understand how to bring the system back to life.
The stakes could not be higher. Life and liberty hang in the balance, while
in our courtrooms and in our laboratories, lawyers and scientists wage a
battle to bring sound science to our system of justice.

1 The Bite Mark Case

In 1982, a murder trial in Newport News, Virginia dubbed "the bite mark case," turned into a media sensation, as the community heard dentists describe how they compared bite marks on the victim's legs to molds of the defendant's teeth. Police had struggled to solve the case, until the dentists stepped in. One of the dentists later recalled that "bite-mark analysis was new" at the time, which helped to explain the public fascination.[1] Twenty-five years later, I was looking through transcripts of old murder trials in Virginia, from dusty bound volumes pulled from law library shelves. I wanted to read how forensic experts testified in trials back in the 1980s and 1990s. I found two dozen trials, and while many had problematic forensic testimony, one stood out because it involved such unusual testimony. It was the bite mark case: the trial of Keith Allen Harward, a death penalty case in which six different dentists ultimately concluded that Harward bit the victim's legs repeatedly. They were all wrong.

In the early morning, a man broke into a home near the navy yards, in Newport News, Virginia. He beat a man inside to death with a crowbar, and then repeatedly raped his wife. During the assault, he bit her thighs and calves. She survived, called the police, and they swabbed and photographed the bite marks. She was unable to identify the person who

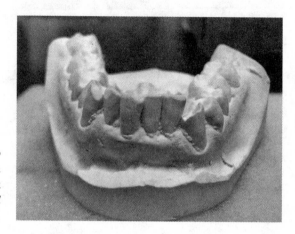

A dental mold was used to convict Keith Harward in 1982. Courtesy of Frank Green and the *Richmond Times-Dispatch*.

assaulted her—it was dark in the house at the time—but she described him as a white male wearing a white sailor's uniform with three nested V's, the insignia of an E-3 naval sailor. The *USS Carl Vinson*, a nuclear aircraft carrier, was under construction in the nearby yards—and it had thousands of E-3 sailors on board. Keith Harward was one of them.

In perhaps the most massive dental dragnet ever conducted, dentists examined the teeth of every one of the navy sailors on board the *USS Vinson*. About three thousand sailors took turns assembling in the mess hall, as two dentists shined flashlights in their mouths, looking for a telltale rotated tooth. The dentists examined Harward's teeth once, and they called him back to take a mold of his teeth, shown in the above figure. When they first compared his teeth to the marks on the victim, they excluded him. Tellingly, "the gauntlet," as Harward referred to that ordeal, turned up no leads.

Normally, we go to a dentist to clean and treat our teeth—not to solve crimes. But starting in the 1970s, a band of dentists started to sideline in criminal cases, for extra pay and a chance for a star turn in the courtroom. Dentists had long matched pristine molds of teeth to identify human remains. This new group of dentists, however, claimed to be able to match skin markings where an assailant bites a victim to a mold of a suspect's teeth. Because they testify in court and help with criminal cases, these dentists are known as forensic odontologists. The odontologists who testified in Harward's case could not have been more confident in their conclusions.

Although they cleared him during the shipboard "gauntlet," at trial the dentists reported that the bite marks all matched Harward's teeth.

THE METHODS OF FORENSIC DENTISTRY

One use of forensic dentistry is to identify human remains. Teeth are extremely durable, and even in terrible accidents they may be quite well preserved, when skin tissue, fingerprints, and facial features are not. Such postmortem forensic work can be far more reliable because the dentists may have a small, defined group of deceased people they are trying to tell apart. With complete sets of teeth to work with, dentists can conduct careful examinations, comparing X-rays of the deceased person's teeth with dental records of known people on file. Prior to the early 1970s, that is what forensic dentists did.[2] They did not examine bite marks on human skin, which are far more difficult to compare. We only bite with our front teeth. A bite makes marks on irregular surfaces. For those who have been around teething toddlers who had a "biter" phase, you know all too well that bites may not leave a clear mark; they can look like big red bruises. While few crimes involve macabre biting situations, murders, child abuse, and assault cases can sometimes have bite mark evidence.

The move toward using bite mark comparisons in the courts began with the case of *People v. Marx,* a California murder trial in 1974.[3] A UCLA School of Dentistry professor, along with two other experts, examined an oval-shaped laceration on the victim's nose. They believed it was a bite mark. The professor explained that he would not normally testify about a bite mark because it is so difficult to make a reliable comparison. This case was an exception, however, because the defendant's teeth were so unusual. The marks were particularly well preserved and defined in three dimensions, because nasal tissue is stretched so tightly. The professor said that this was the best bite mark he had ever seen.[4] The judge let the experts testify, even though it was novel to compare bite marks. The appeals judges agreed that this was appropriate expert evidence. That ruling was then relied on by judges in state after state, who more broadly agreed to let bite mark experts take the stand.[5] These experts did not limit their work to postmortem identification of remains or the rare case with an exceptionally well-defined bite mark. In 1976 they organized the American Board of Forensic Odontology (ABFO) as a professional group. Dentists began to testify that they could determine whether bite marks were a match.[6]

The most famous bite mark case was the trial of serial killer Ted Bundy. Bundy bit one of the three victims he raped and murdered at a sorority at Florida State University in 1987. He was largely convicted on the strength of the bite mark comparison, and then executed in 1989 by "Old Sparky," the Florida electric chair in 1989, after confessing to committing dozens of other murders. Apparently, Bundy had unusually crooked teeth, making his bite marks distinctive. The prosecutor showed the jurors blown-up photographs of the bite mark evidence at Bundy's trial. At the time of the trial, less than half of the states allowed bite mark evidence in court, but by the end of the 1990s, all fifty states permitted it. Yet there was more fiction than truth to what forensic odontologists were doing.

HOW TO COMPARE BITE MARKS

A bite mark comparison proceeds using fairly simple and commonsense steps. The examiner takes photographs of the bite marks themselves and then enlarges them. If the victim's body still has indentations from the bite marks, a mold of the bite mark may be made for a three-dimensional comparison. Today, a bite mark can be swabbed and DNA tested. However, if there is not enough saliva present, no DNA result may be possible, and a dentist may then examine the marks.

The dentist first examines the mark to determine whether it came from a human bite. That can be a challenging step. If it is a postmortem examination, there may be substantial contusions or bruising on the body, or decomposition, making it hard to determine whether some of the marks came from a bite. If the dentist concludes it was a human bite, the dentist then tries to determine whether it was upper or lower teeth that made the bite, and further to isolate which specific teeth made the bite.

Next, the dentist obtains a mold of the suspect's teeth. The dentist visually compares the two to look for similarities or differences. The dentist will sometimes overlay photos from the victim with the mold of the defendant's teeth. The dentist will sometimes look at the bite mark and dental mold side by side. The dentist will sometimes use computers to enhance or blow up images. There is no single accepted way for a dentist to do this comparison work.[7] In troubling cases, dentists have put the molds of the suspect's teeth on the victim's body, raising the question of whether they were creating new marks to match their target.

What do the forensic dentists look for when they are comparing the bite mark to the dental mold? They say that they are looking for features that are not apparent to the naked eye. They note that humans normally have thirty teeth, each with surfaces to compare, with an enormous amount of variation among them. People can also have features like missing teeth, braces, dentures or prosthesis, fillings, chips or cracks, or uneven bite motion. As a dentist explained in Keith Harward's trial, "you have acciden-tal characteristics, like wear patterns and breakage and things like that, which made the teeth unique and individual."[8]

There are several assumptions underlying this technique. First, there is the basic assumption that there is something unique about human denti-tion. Are all of our teeth different? How different? This question has never been empirically tested. There have never been analyses of large databases of teeth. No one has measured how common or rare it is to have any par-ticular features in teeth. There are no statistics on how often people share characteristics in their teeth. The National Academy of Sciences, in its important 2009 report, concluded that there needs to be more research "to confirm the fundamental basis for the science of bite mark compari-son." They said that it has "not been scientifically established" that human dentition is unique.[9]

Second, it has not been "scientifically established," the National Academy of Sciences explained, whether or not teeth can uniquely or reliably trans-fer information to human skin.[10] We bite with our front teeth. Those front teeth tend to have fewer features than the chewing and grinding teeth in back, which have more complicated crowns. The incisors in the very front tend to leave straight, rectangular-shaped marks. The neighboring canine teeth tend to make triangular bites. There is a question of how distinctly those front teeth can transfer a pattern to human skin. Most teeth do not make contact during a bite. In fact, there can be so little information in a bite mark that dentists face real challenges determining whether a given bite was made by a human or an animal. Researchers asked forensic dentists whether they could agree that a bite was human, and they rarely agreed. Human skin is very elastic. Bite marks on the skin "change over time and can be distorted by the elasticity of the skin, the unevenness of the bite surface, and swelling and healing."[11]

A third problem, as forensic dentists euphemistically put it, is that a biting situation can be "dynamic," with quite a bit of moving around by the biter and the bitten. There will be distortion, depending on movement, or the uneven surfaces involved. There will be differences between the shape of the teeth and the shape of the bite marks. How those differences should be interpreted is unknown. In fact, dentists have admitted that there will always be some differences between a bite mark and the biter's tooth molds. Yet there is no standard for how many differences it takes to say that a suspect could not have been the biter.

More fundamentally, there are no standards for the features that a bite mark examiner looks for. The method itself is not clearly defined. How many, and what quality of, individual characteristics must be observed to call the bite a "match" is unknown. Cases have cited as few as eight points of comparison to as many as fifty or more.[12] How much one has to see to declare a "match" is unknown. There had been an effort in the 1980s to come up with a scoring system to assess bite mark accuracy, but it was abandoned.

The entire process is vague, subjective, and depends on the experience and the judgment of the dentist. Yet the community of forensic dentists commonly testified with certainty that a single person's teeth made a mark: a "positive identification." For decades, the ABFO instructed that dentists could conclude that a bite mark matches a criminal defendant with a "virtual certainty; no reasonable or practical possibility that someone else did it." These guidelines did something even more remarkable. The ABFO actually put in writing that dentists could make their conclusions more aggressively if a lawyer tried to question them in court. The guidelines said that it was "acceptable to state that there is 'no doubt in my mind' or 'in my opinion, the suspect is the biter' when such statements are prompted in testimony."[13]

Despite manifest flaws, no judges meaningfully questioned this evidence.

BITE MARKS ON TRIAL

One dentist testified to "a very, very, very high degree of probability those teeth left that bite mark," referring to Keith Harward's teeth. Three times "very" must be a really good match. The prosecutor asked him to say more.

The dentist said, "My conclusion would be that with all medical certainty, I feel that the teeth represented by these models were the teeth that made these bite marks."

"There are no differences?" asked the prosecutor.

"I found absolutely no differences."

The prosecutor then asked him to tell the jury what "reasonable medical certainty" means.

The dentist explained, "I don't know what all of the teeth in the world look like, one to another. But we know from reading and studying that we've never had two people who have had the same teeth marks or same alignment of teeth, much less getting into the individualized characteristics within a tooth. So with that knowledge, we realized that from a practical standpoint, all medical certainty means that there is just not anyone else that would have this unique dentition."

Next, a second dentist testified that it was a "practical impossibility that someone else would have all [the] characteristics in combination." Again, the prosecutor asked him to elaborate. He said that he had found "with reasonable scientific certainty, Mr. Harward caused the bite marks on the leg."

"No discrepancies?" the prosecutor asked.

"No, sir. It's a practical impossibility that someone else would have all these characteristics in combination."

The prosecutor asked, "If you look hard enough, could you find someone with similar teeth, theoretically?"

"I sincerely doubt that," responded the dentist.[14]

This testimony was incredibly forceful. Studies suggest that people react very positively to experts who express great confidence in their conclusions. People tend to assume that confident experts must be correct. Indeed, jurors also focus on body language, or nonverbal cues, for confidence, such as whether an expert keeps fixed eye contact, good posture, remains positive, and uses assertive mannerisms like leaning forward. Jurors care about how trustworthy and likeable the expert appears.[15]

Credentials also really impress jurors. In one of the most realistic mock trial studies conducted on forensic experts, Jonathan Koehler, N. J. Schweitzer, Michael Saks, and Dawn McQuiston found that the expert's background and experience really mattered. Jurors cared more about the background and experience of the forensic expert than whether the method the expert was using was actually scientifically tested.[16]

The second dentist not only spoke with utter confidence and apparent deep knowledge but was internationally renowned. He had helped to convict Ted Bundy, and joined in the investigation of the assassination of President John F. Kennedy. He was a founding member of the ABFO, the professional group to which forensic dentists belong. The ABFO "certifies" forensic dentists as "diplomates" of the group. He served on a delegation to identify remains of Tsar Nicholas II and disappeared victims of the military regime in Argentina. More prominent still, he had been president of the American Academy of Forensic Scientists, which has 6,700 members.

"The jury was just slobbering, they were gone. (He) was like the Wizard of Oz. He levitated," said Harward, recalling what it was like when the dentist recounted his credentials.

The dentists said that Harward had unusual and distinctive characteristics on his teeth. One of his teeth "canted sideways" and there was a "hook type area" that seemed to match the bite mark. There was a "chipped area" and a "breakage" that aligned perfectly, they said. There were "no discrepancies."

The defense lawyer pointed out that there was a big discrepancy: a gap between two of Harward's teeth that was nowhere to be seen in the bite marks. The second dentist dismissed this out of hand. "What you're doing, you're making an error," he said, condescendingly calling it the type of mistake that, "you know, what I call well-meaning amateurs make."

Testimony like this does more than link evidence right to the defendant: it also dehumanizes the defendant. As Innocence Project lawyer Chris Fabricant puts it, a prosecutor can say that the defendant was an "animal" who "bit that poor victim, and science says so."[17]

In Harward's case, the prosecutor closed by telling the jurors that "doubt vanishes" when you have "experts who tell you, within reasonable scientific certainty, the teeth that made these molds made the bite on (the

victim's) legs." The jury convicted Harward in September 1982 and sentenced him to death. Due to a legal problem with the capital murder statute at the time, the Virginia Supreme Court sent the case back for a new
trial. In 1986, Harward was convicted at a second trial and sentenced to
life without parole.

DNA EXONERATION

At around the same time that I came across Keith Harward's records by
chance, he had written to the Innocence Project at Cardozo Law School in
New York City seeking DNA testing to prove the dentists wrong. Harward
had given up on appeals and post-conviction challenges twenty years
before; he had accepted that he would die in prison as an innocent man.
Another inmate, though, told him about the Innocence Project, and he
sent a letter. The Innocence Project took his case and obtained access to
crime scene material for DNA testing.

The swabs taken from the victim, in multiple places, all shared a single
male DNA profile. That profile belonged to another person, who also had
been a sailor on the USS Vinson. That man, the actual culprit, died in
prison in Ohio over a decade before, while serving time for burglary and
kidnapping. Harward was released in 2016, aged sixty, after thirty-three
years in prison. He saw his brothers in person, the day he was released, for
the first time in over thirty years.

What went wrong? We now know that not only were the dentists making exaggerated claims, but they were flat-out wrong that all of those
details matched Harward's teeth. What are the chances that six dentists
separately reached the same false conclusion? They may have all been
biased by pressure from police, and by each other. Before his first trial,
Harward had been arrested in an altercation with his girlfriend, where she
grabbed him and he bit her arm. She dropped the charges. But the police
and prosecutors clearly decided he was a "biter," and that may have
encouraged the dentists to change their story to fit what the prosecutors
wanted: a conviction. The dentists knew about each other's work. They
convicted an innocent man and let a murderer go free. Yet, at the time, the
"bite mark case" was celebrated as a triumph of forensics.

Harward is not the only person exonerated by DNA who had been convicted based on bite mark evidence—there have been ten so far. Roy Brown was convicted of murder in upstate New York, and suffered fifteen years in prison, before DNA exonerated him. At his trial, a bite mark examiner told the jury to "a reasonable degree of dental certainty" that his teeth made the mark, and called differences "[i]nconsistent but explainably so." Willie Jackson spent sixteen years in prison in Louisiana based on a bite mark match, before DNA testing finally exonerated him. Ray Krone was sentenced to death in Arizona after two dentists found a match; as one explained, "that tooth caused that injury" and "it was Ray Krone's teeth." Krone had his conviction reversed and then was convicted a second time based on the bite mark evidence; he was exonerated by DNA tests after ten years in prison.[18] He had been widely dubbed the "snaggle-toothed killer," and he did have distinctive teeth, but years later DNA testing identified the actual culprit, who had fairly normal-looking teeth.

THE DENTISTS RESPOND

In February 2017 Keith Harward attended the annual meeting of the American Association of Forensic Sciences. "I'm not here to make any friends," said Harward, at a workshop with forensic dentists titled, "Taking a Bite Out of Crime and Other Hairy Situations." Harward lashed out: "This bite mark stuff is bogus. Why even continue with it? It just doesn't make sense." "Thirty-four years thinking, 'Wow, what just happened?'" he said of his convictions. "You're taking people's lives in your hands and guessing, 'Well, I say it is so, so it's got to be.'"

Harward asked: "So why do it?" The only explanations that Harward could offer were "money and ego."[19] In 2018 the American Board of Forensic Odontologists did make a few changes to their guidelines. The dentists recommended the use of a "dental lineup" so bite marks are not compared only to a single suspect but rather to a series of dental samples. They said there should be independent verification by another dentist before making a final report.[20] They emphasized that the strongest conclusion a dentist can reach is whether the teeth can or cannot be excluded as having made a mark. Meanwhile, I will describe in this book how judges continue to let this evidence in.

In fact, some forensic dentists have branched out, providing immigration officers with conclusions, based on X-ray images, that a young person detained is in fact likely an adult and should be moved to adult detention. Young people arriving at the border may not have documentation. It really matters whether the person being detained is seventeen or eighteen, because minors are housed in shelters, to be reunited with family-member sponsors, and receive special legal protections, while adults are kept in prison-like detention centers. There is no research on statistics and the sizes of people's teeth that could actually allow one to tell the difference between a seventeen- and eighteen-year-old. In 2008, Congress enacted a law, the Trafficking Victims Reauthorization and Protection Act, forbidding use of bite mark forensics to determine age in immigration decisions. A federal audit emphasized: "Using radiographs of a person's bones or teeth . . . cannot produce a specific age due to a range of factors affecting an individual's growth." A few judges stepped in to reject decisions based on dental comparisons, noting how unsupported such analysis is; for example, in 2016 a federal judge found immigration officers were continuing to use dental X-rays alone to send children to detention. A new Immigration and Customs Enforcement (ICE) handbook says that dental exams should be used only as a "last resort." One dentist responded that the techniques being used by the dentists employed by ICE are "very subjective" and should not "be used in cases of life and liberty." To this day, however, young people may still be put into adult detention based on dental comparisons, and in 2019, lawyers challenged a number of additional cases in habeas proceedings.[21]

So, to summarize: Dentists in the 1970s began to say things never said before about human teeth. They reached aggressive conclusions, based on their subjective opinions, in life and death cases. One after another, judges fell into line and found the evidence admissible. To this day, dentists still make bite mark comparisons, although they may temper conclusions, and judges still let these comparisons in as evidence. Unfortunately, the same problems remain in a host of other types of forensic evidence. In the 1970s and 1980s, whether it was fingerprints, hair, fibers, toolmarks, or bite marks, experts would testify in court that they found a "match." They would claim 100 percent certainty in their conclusions. Yet they could not explain their methods in any detail, and no research supported their aggressive statements.

Keith Harward has this to say about the failure to seriously reform bite mark comparison forensics: "This is a warning—if I find out anybody's testifying in bite mark evidence cases I will come to the courtroom, I will contact the media, I will stand on the street corner in a Statue of Liberty outfit with a big sign saying 'This is Crap.'"[22]

2 The Crisis in Forensics

"In fact, it was the pursuit of a good story that has led me to the world of wrongful convictions," said John Grisham, the best-selling writer and attorney, speaking in the U. S. Senate. Grisham stumbled into the world of forensics when he happened to read the *New York Times* obituary of a man named Ron Williamson. "We were the same age, we both dreamed of being Major League baseball players, we both grew up in small towns in the Bible Belt, and we both came from the same religious backgrounds." Yet "Ron was convicted of a rape and a murder he did not commit, was sent to death row, went insane, and came within five days of being executed before receiving a miracle reprieve." Grisham began to write his first nonfiction book, *The Innocent Man,* to tell that story. The case provided his introduction to wrongful convictions and faulty forensics. In that case, the prosecutors had put forensic experts on the stand who gave faulty testimony about hair comparisons and blood typing.[1] Grisham recalled, "The most damaging testimony against Ron came from an expert—an analyst with the Oklahoma Bureau of Investigation. This expert testified that there were seventeen scalp and pubic hairs taken from the crime scene," and that the hairs were "microscopically consistent" with Williamson's. Eleven years later, each of those same hairs was DNA tested, and none came from Williamson, who was exonerated but died five years later of liver failure. After writing the book, Grisham became involved in work with the Innocence Project, and he soon realized the case was entirely typical. Unsound forensics "is a national problem."

"It is time to clean up the bad science," Grisham told the lawmakers, mincing no words, where "faulty science is rampant in American courtrooms." He called for urgent federal action to put a stop to the problem, including involvement of federal agencies to set binding scientific standards. We should not have fifty different definitions of "science" in each of the fifty states, he pointed out. During the hearing, Senator Amy Klobuchar asked: "Mr. Grisham, have you seen any ideas for books in this discussion here? Maybe you could do a thriller on the very slow process to get things done?" Grisham answered, "Well, everything is fair game for a book." Almost a decade later, very little has been done, and the federal government has not responded as he urged Congress to do.[2] The hearings on the Senate floor never would have happened, though, if a prominent scientific group had not issued a report in 2009 that detailed the flaws in much of the forensics used in our courts. In this chapter, I tell the story of how this crisis became the subject of such urgent concern, and then the aftermath of the report that exposed a national crisis in forensics.

THE JUDGE AND THE NATIONAL ACADEMY

Judge Harry Edwards, a prominent federal appellate judge, had "no preconceived views about the forensic science community." He had served on the law faculties at University of Michigan Law School and Harvard Law School, before serving on the board and then as chairman of Amtrak. He was appointed as a judge on the United States Court of Appeals for the District of Columbia and served as the chief judge. During his distinguished career, hearing appeals in complex and high-profile criminal matters, he "simply assumed," like most judges, that forensic science was "well grounded in scientific methodology."[3] He had written important judicial opinions and books, including on judicial process, legal ethics, and labor arbitration, but forensic science had never been a focus. Willing to take on a new challenge, Judge Edwards agreed to co-chair a National Academy of

Sciences committee that would study the challenges facing forensics. The judge soon realized that he had much to learn about the state of forensics and the aggressive defenders of the status quo.

At that time I had similarly unformed views of forensics, and like most lawyers, I did not have a science background. As a young lawyer, starting in 2002, I had worked on cases of DNA exonerees. In a Staten Island case, I toured the DNA unit of the New York Medical Examiner's lab to understand each step in the testing process that ultimately set our client free. The case involved a bite mark comparison, too, where the dentist had claimed our client's teeth were "consistent" with a bite on the victim. However, as part of the effort to obtain compensation for the exoneree, the focus was on the DNA test later done on the swabs from that bite. As a civil rights lawyer, I had never carefully looked at the work done by bite mark, fingerprint, or hair comparison experts. Like Judge Edwards, I assumed most of it was good science.

In 2009, now a law professor, I read stacks of criminal trial transcripts in the quiet comfort of my office. It is uncanny, in hindsight, that one of those records was from Keith Harward's trial. I coincidentally came across his case because of a call from the group Judge Edwards chaired. In 2008 I had just published my first article studying the cases of the first two hundred people exonerated by DNA testing.[4] Anne-Marie Mazza, senior director at the National Academy of Sciences (NAS), called me and described a committee of eminent scientists and lawyers who had gathered to examine the state of forensics. They wanted to learn about the role forensic testimony played in the cases of DNA exonerees. To study that question would require a massive research project; one would have to locate paper records of trial transcripts, read them, code them, and analyze the data. I was not sure I could take on a project that large. Before agreeing to produce the first-ever report on the role forensics played in DNA exonerations, I called my friend Peter Neufeld, co-founder of the Innocence Project. My first question to him: What is the National Academy of Sciences, exactly?

The National Academy of Sciences, established by an Act of Congress, signed by President Abraham Lincoln in 1863, is the leading organization of distinguished scholars in the sciences in the United States. It did not take long for Peter to explain that this was an august body and that this committee was engaged in a crucially important undertaking. Membership in the NAS is considered to be "one of the highest honors that a scientist can receive." One-hundred and ninety of the NAS members have received Nobel Prizes.[5] The committee formed to study forensic science had seventeen members, including several forensic scientists, leading research scientists, and prominent lawyers and judges. No one on the committee had ever criticized forensic methods in the past. In fact, six members had very close ties to forensic science. After hearing more about just how important this work was, I agreed to work with Peter to collect more information about what went wrong in DNA exoneree trials. We had just a few months to prepare an exhaustive report. Meanwhile, the committee's larger work would uncover a national crisis.

THE DNA REVOLUTION

When DNA testing arrived on the scene in the 1990s, it put all of forensics to the test. Before DNA testing became common, blood typing could sometimes be done in criminal cases, and it could readily *exclude* a suspect. If the blood at the crime scene was type A, then it definitely could not have been left by a person who secretes type O blood. Since many people share the common A, B, and O blood types, this was not often very useful evidence to *include* a suspect. An expert might be able to say that a person was among a group of 30 or 40 percent of the population that shared that blood type. Also, you needed quite a bit of blood or biological material to do blood typing. Most crime scenes did not have that quantity of material. Such testing was particularly useful in sexual assault cases or in cases where the culprit left a piece of saliva, or sweat, or blood-stained clothing.

DNA revolutionized forensic testing, but not right away. DNA was first identified in the 1860s. In 1953, James Watson and Francis Crick announced their discovery of the double-helix chemical structure of DNA. DNA resembles a twisted ladder, with the sides of the ladder made up of alternating sugar and phosphate groups, and with the middle rungs of the strand containing just four bases: adenine (A), guanine (G), cytosine (C), and thymine (T). The patterns in those base pairs encode the instructions that DNA provides to our cells; many thousands of those pairs may make up a single gene. Since its discovery, researchers have intensively studied the makeup of the human genome. DNA testing methods were developed in research laboratories, unlike much of forensic science, which was developed by police crime labs or assorted freelancers, like the dentists in Harward's case.

In the 1980s, British geneticist Sir Alec Jeffries pioneered the genetics research that made DNA testing possible in criminal cases by focusing on short repetitive sequences within the genome that are highly variable between individuals. Scientists like Jeffries developed ways to isolate those sequences. While nuclear DNA contains many genes that do important work, providing instructions for how to encode proteins, geneticists found that the vast majority of the sequences is "noncoding," sometimes called "junk DNA," although scientists are beginning to learn more about some purposes that it can serve. Early DNA testing required large quantities of biological material, however, so it was not commonly used in criminal cases.

The DNA revolution for criminal cases occurred by the mid-1990s, when a new technique called Short Tandem Repeat (STR) testing was developed. The key words are "short" and "repeat."[6] The entire DNA strand is six feet in length, yet each chromosome is packaged incredibly tightly in the nucleus of a cell, so it is only a few microns (or one millionth of a meter) wide. The STR technique tests short portions of the strand, which means that very small samples of DNA can be tested. The "repeat" part refers to the fact that those portions repeat a number of times, which vary widely from person to person. A second feature of this genetics revolution was Polymerase Chain Reaction (PCR) technology. Scientists developed enzymes that make copies, of copies, of copies, in a chain reaction that can produce billions of copies of the sample. Scientists developed rapid and largely computerized analysis of that genetic material as well. These STR and PCR tests were standardized in the 1990s and today they test over twenty portions of the DNA strand to produce a DNA profile.

Unlike traditional forensics, DNA testing relies on objective statistics. Researchers developed data on populations of people and the frequency of certain genetic characteristics, called alleles, that vary a great deal. The results of a DNA test do not provide a "match" but rather a probability. Using population statistics, scientists can determine whether one person in many millions, or even billions or trillions, could be expected to randomly match a particular DNA profile. In contrast, there are no population statistics for characteristics observed on bite marks, hair, fingerprints, or other objects like firearms and toolmarks. We have no idea how common or rare the details are that examiners rely upon for those forensics.

Companies began to market DNA technology to law enforcement, promoting "DNA FINGERPRINTING" as a way to get "CONCLUSIVE RESULTS IN ONLY ONE TEST!"[7] The FBI quickly took on a leading role, choosing its own protocols and building a new DNA Analysis Unit. The FBI became the go-to lab for DNA testing, although by the mid-1990s, more state and local labs began to test DNA as well. In 1993 Congress enacted legislation authorizing the FBI to assemble DNA samples in a national databank, the Combined DNA Index System (CODIS).[8]

Judges quickly ruled DNA evidence admissible evidence in criminal cases, although not without a fight. In its infancy, DNA experts sometimes would testify that DNA was a "match," or they used probabilities that were not based on careful calculations. In response, defense lawyers called serious researchers in academic molecular biology and genetics to testify.[9] High-profile disputes about the lack of transparency and potential subjectivity of DNA methods led to the "DNA Wars" of the 1990s. The National Academy of Sciences convened leading scientists to study the problem and settle on clear standards for forensic use of DNA testing.[10]

The impact of DNA on the criminal justice system quickly became apparent. The first innocence projects took off. Lawyers like Barry Scheck and Peter Neufeld, who founded the Innocence Project in New York City, realized that time is on the side of DNA testing. DNA material can remain intact for years, so decades after a conviction, evidence could be retested. In hundreds of cases, 370 and counting, post-conviction DNA testing has proved the innocence of convicts. The Innocence Project leads in the use of DNA testing to exonerate, but their work has also sparked a national and global network of innocence projects. Each year at the annual Innocence Network conference, exonerees take the stage to celebrate their hard-won freedom, and while the early conferences were smaller, today it can take more than an hour just to introduce all of the exonerees attending. These people spent on average over fifteen years in prison. For years, prosecutors and judges insisted on their guilt, and often it took years of fighting in the courts for lawyers to secure their freedom, although more recently some prosecutors have formed conviction integrity units and have themselves reinvestigated cases and secured exonerations. Much can be learned from studying these miscarriages of justice; my first book analyzed the cases of the first 250 DNA exonerees in detail.[11] I might never have begun that work had Anne-Marie Mazza not called from the NAS, asking me to report on the role that forensic science played in exoneration cases.

The U. S. Congress had asked scientists at the National Academy of Sciences to reexamine forensic science in part because the steady drumbeat of DNA exonerations increasingly called forensics into doubt. While great improvements in forensics had been made, and crime labs increasingly had larger and dedicated professional staffs, the scientific underpinnings of entire disciplines had been called into question. Moreover, crime labs were facing quality control scandals. For example, in chapter 11 I will describe an audit of the Houston crime laboratory that uncovered errors in hundreds of cases, including in the DNA unit, and ultimately shut down the lab.[12] As cases were reopened, labs investigated, and scandals proliferated, lawmakers called for a serious scientific review.

FLAWED FORENSICS IN DNA EXONERATION CASES

Forensic science itself needed an autopsy, to uncover what had gone wrong with the forensics in so many innocent people's trials. Fortunately, at the time that the committee reached out, the Innocence Project had recently digitally scanned its files. Peter Neufeld and I decided to work together on the postmortem: an analysis of the trial testimony of forensic analysts in DNA exonerees' cases. We planned to read and code these trials and then report our findings to the NAS committee. We also wanted to see whether the forensic expert testimony in these innocent people's cases was typical or not. That was why I was reading randomly pulled trials from Virginia, like Keith Harward's, as well as criminal trials from several other states.

We soon saw a clear pattern. While hundreds of innocent people had been freed by DNA technology, most had been convicted in the first place based on traditional forensic evidence, like hair, bite mark, and even fingerprint comparison. Peter Neufeld and I found that in the majority of these innocence cases, the forensic evidence was not just in error—analysts had overstated the evidence in court and given the jury an exaggerated picture. We found the same flawed testimony in the random trials that we picked. This suggested forensic misconduct was an ingrained feature of serious criminal trials. We told the committee that flawed forensic testimony in the DNA exoneree cases was extensive and it was just the beginning of a deep and disturbing problem. Author John Grisham, commenting on these findings, noted most DNA exonerees were convicted by forensics, "much of which was flawed, unreliable, exaggerated or sometimes outright fabricated." Our courts, Grisham said, "have been flooded with an avalanche of unreliable, even atrocious 'science.'"[13]

Today, 370 people have been exonerated by post-conviction DNA testing in the United States. The same troubling figures that I relayed to the National Academy of Sciences still hold true in this larger and still-growing group of innocent people. Of those 370 exonerees, at least 250 had forensic evidence in their cases. Some had forensic tests results that should have helped them prove innocence at the time of their conviction. Fifty-two of those exonerees, for example, had forensic evidence that outright excluded them and pointed to their innocence at the time they were convicted. In thirty cases, though, this forensic evidence of innocence, including DNA or fingerprint or other comparisons, was concealed from the defense. However, far more had prosecutors present forensic evidence that contributed to their false convictions. In my latest update of the data, I found 114 of the 250 had invalid presentation of forensic science at the time that they were convicted. Twenty more had vague testimony presented that did not explain the conclusions reached. In thirty-one cases, we know of serious errors made during the analysis. Thus, well over half of these exonerees were freed by DNA testing, but they were wrongly convicted in the first place based on flawed forensics.[14]

RESISTING SCIENCE

Leading scientists had never scrutinized most of the forensic disciplines—the non-DNA forensics that really needed it—apart from two very critical NAS reports on voice comparison and bullet lead comparison evidence. Fingerprints have been admitted in criminal cases in the United States since 1911, and handwriting and firearms comparisons have been used for a century or more.[15] Other techniques were more recent, like bite mark and bullet lead comparisons (the FBI stopped using the bullet lead comparison method after the NAS report debunked it). Nor were the problems with forensics unknown, as DNA exonerations mounted. Congress poured hundreds of millions of dollars into reducing DNA backlogs, creating DNA databanks, and expanding crime lab capabilities in DNA. The other forensics took a back seat.[16] Law enforcement tried to stymie efforts by scientists to study non-DNA forensics. In fact, the National Academy of Sciences planned to study non-DNA forensics earlier, in 2002. In a revealing editorial, the editor-in-chief of the scientific journal *Science* asked if forensic science was an "oxymoron." He described how the Department of Justice and Department of Defense insisted on "rights of review" before the NAS could publish their findings. Rightly concerned with this imposition on scientific integrity, the NAS refused to review forensics under such conditions.[17]

Finally, in 2005, Congress appropriated funding for a major NAS effort, and the committee began its work in fall 2006. The committee held meetings over many months. They began by inviting the entire forensics community to submit research and papers. The experience forever changed the views of these scientists and lawyers, as they became exposed to problems that they had never known to have existed. At the committee hearings, an expert fingerprint analyst was asked about the extent of research on how well a fingerprint examiner can make a conclusion about a smudged or partial print. The expert admitted: "Research has yet to be done."[18] One of my friends on the committee told me how you could practically hear a pin drop in the room when he made this admission.

Another forensic expert explained microscopic hair analysis to the committee. Judge Harry Edwards asked the expert, "If your daughter was falsely accused of a felony and the only evidence against her was a microscopic hair sample, how would you feel?" He responded that he would be very concerned. Judge Edwards was troubled to hear that the expert was "essentially conceding" that a person might be wrongfully convicted if hair evidence was the basis for a prosecution.[19]

In another telling exchange, Peter Neufeld and I told the committee about the case of Neil Miller, a DNA exoneree. At Miller's trial the forensic analyst had described how the blood type from the evidence collected from the rape victim was consistent with Miller's blood type. He testified that approximately "forty-five percent of the population" had type O blood, like Miller did. The analyst never explained that 100 percent of all men could match the evidence. At the time they could not separate or quantify the fluid from a male contributor to a sample; the victim's fluids could mask any contribution from the culprit. It was obvious to any competent expert that if nothing different from the victim's blood type was observed, then no conclusions could be reached at all about the culprit's blood type. Miller was convicted based on flawed forensic testimony, and yet this was not a junk science. ABO blood typing is highly reliable and based on sound population statistics. Instead, the problem was that the analyst gave misleading statistics to the jury. Over fifty DNA exonerees were convicted based on misleading testimony regarding traditional blood typing.

After reading this testimony to the committee, a crime lab director forcefully objected. He said that there was nothing unethical about the testimony that led to Miller's wrongful conviction, because it is the job of defense lawyers to bring out any problems with testimony, and it is not the job of the lab analyst to offer the right statistics. I could tell from their expressions that many in the room were aghast that the director of a lab viewed highly misleading forensic testimony as entirely appropriate. What made the moment still more telling was our next slide. In another case, that of DNA exoneree Marvin Mitchell, the same analyst testified, and this time, where it helped the prosecution's case, he explained why blood typing could be such a limited form of evidence. In Mitchell's case, the blood type observed matched the victim but not the defendant. This time, the very same lab analyst who testified in Neil Miller's case explained that the stain might have been "too diluted . . . to pick up Mr. Mitchell's blood type."[20] This lab analyst was selectively presenting misleading statistics to help the prosecutors to convict defendants, at least two of whom later turned out to be innocent.

SCIENTISTS TAKE A STAND

The forensic science community could talk about nothing else in the months before the National Academy of Sciences committee released its report. At the national conference of the American Academy of Forensic Sciences, which began on the day the report came out, lab analysts were asking: "What does it say? Have you read it?" On February 16, 2009, the report, *Strengthening Forensic Science in the United States: A Path Forward,* was published. The response by many forensic analysts, when they read the report, was "surprise, disbelief, resentment, anger, and indifference."[21] The report was "not fair," and ivory tower academics "don't get us," many responded. After all, one after another, forensic practitioners had told the committee they were positive that the work that they were doing was fine.

The committee produced a book-length three-hundred-page report, with thirteen main recommendations. The committee comprehensively reviewed the state of the research across a host of forensic techniques. Perhaps the most-quoted portion of the report concluded that much of forensic evidence used in criminal trials is "without any meaningful scientific validation." The committee described "major problems" in forensics, including where faulty forensic science led to wrongful convictions.[22] They described the need for more research. Many types of forensics work simply did not have reliable scientific methods or foundations. They noted that the judges and courts "will not cure the infirmities" of forensic science; the problems are too ingrained and judges have been "utterly ineffective."[23] That was a damning critique from a committee co-chaired by a prominent federal judge. Identifying major gaps in the research was a big part of the committee's job, but so was identifying solutions. They called for a national response to a national crisis: Congress needed to create a National Institute of Forensic Science to develop standards and ensure that forensic science work is done in a truly scientific manner.[24]

Thousands of media outlets reported on the findings; you can see the complete list of stories on the NAS website, and you just keep scrolling and scrolling, past stories in the *New York Times, Nature, Science,* and more. Television shows from *Nova* to *NCIS* to John Oliver's *Last Week Tonight* have covered the report. Commentators called the report a "blockbuster" and a "watershed."[25] Congress held hearings, and legislation was introduced to regulate forensics along the lines that the NAS proposed— none of that legislation passed. The U.S. Supreme Court promptly cited the report, with Justice Antonin Scalia noting that forensics have "serious deficiencies" and are not "immune from the risk of manipulation."[26] The president appointed a committee on forensic science.[27] Traditional forensics, however, had powerful defenders. One prosecutor, testifying before the Senate, called the report an "agenda-driven attack on well-founded investigative techniques." Then-senator Jeff Sessions said, "I don't think we should suggest that those proven scientific principles that we've been using for decades are somehow uncertain."[28]

THE DENTISTS RESPOND

The dentists that compare bite marks unwittingly give us a test case for how our system responds to a ringing statement from the scientific community that techniques used for decades lack support. The National Academy of Sciences report discussed bite mark comparison specifically, stating there was "no evidence of an existing basis" for using bite marks to identify an individual. The committee concluded that scientific research must be done to know whether a bite mark comparison can ever "provide probative value."[29] The forensic dentists were listening. In response, in 2009 the American Board of Forensic Odontology changed its rules for its members. They now stated that "terms such as unconditional identification of a perpetrator, or identification 'without doubt,' are not sanctioned as final conclusions in an open population case." They changed their wording.

THE WHITE HOUSE REPORT

Eric Lander, a mathematician and geneticist, founder of the Broad Institute of Harvard and MIT and a leader of the Human Genome Project that led the way in mapping our DNA, met with leadership at the Department of Justice. These federal prosecutors told him they needed a "grace period." Prosecutors would be "in a lot of trouble" if scientists called into question a host of forensic methods.[30] Yet this was over six years after the NAS report, and foundational work had not been done on many forensic techniques. Very little had changed, except perhaps for the wording of some forensic conclusions.

In fall 2015, the White House had convened a committee of the President's Council of Advisors on Science and Technology (PCAST), which focused more deeply on problems in a handful of important forensic disciplines: analysis of DNA mixtures, firearms comparisons, fingerprint comparisons, and bite mark comparisons. Like the NAS committee, this group brought together prominent scientists, including Lander. "We concluded it was not within our roles as scientists to grant grace periods," Lander recalled. They went ahead and released their report, which was very forceful. They stated unequivocally that unscientific forensics should no longer be used. There should be no grace periods, no extensions: such forensics should not be used until real studies were done to show they are reliable.

The scientists reviewed thousands of studies assessing the reliability of forensic methods, but found only a handful that had been adequately designed. An adequately designed study must include real tests of the technique, with large samples, independent researchers running the study, and open data that others can reproduce—in other words, they must be real scientific studies. For some techniques, like fingerprints, PCAST said there had been a minimally adequate number of real studies (at least two) done on the technique. PCAST described undocumented error rates, and how even for methods like fingerprinting, error rates were far higher than jurors and lawyers might assume. People needed to be fully informed about these error rates in criminal cases.

Techniques like firearms and bite mark comparisons were different: adequate studies had not been done. The PCAST report found: "Bite mark analysis does not meet the scientific standards for foundational validity and is far from meeting such standards." They said: "To the contrary, available scientific evidence strongly suggests that examiners cannot consistently agree on whether an injury is a human bite mark . . . with reasonable accuracy."[31] They concluded that techniques like bite mark and firearms comparisons should not be used in court.

The FBI promptly responded that it disagreed with "many of the scientific assertions and conclusions" in the report and that it failed to mention "numerous published research studies" that were sufficiently well designed.[32] In response, PCAST invited the FBI or any others to submit any published studies that they had somehow missed, that might speak to the reliability of these forensic methods. The DOJ concluded that there were in fact no additional studies for PCAST to consider.[33]

The loudest protests came from prosecutors, who roundly criticized the report. The Department of Justice said that they would ignore the report outright and would continue to use forensics the way they always had. Then-attorney general Loretta Lynch explained that the DOJ was "confident that, when used properly, forensic science evidence helps juries identify the guilty and clear the innocent." At a law school event on forensics, the DOJ's forensic science spokesperson, Ted Hunt, argued that a flexible and "holistic" test should be used to decide what is valid science. Lander responded that requiring studies be done with large samples, independent research supervision, and reproducibility is not too narrow a definition; it is what is "called science."[34]

The National District Attorneys Association accused PCAST of "pervasive bias" and called the report "scientifically irresponsible." This was not because of any flaws in the recommendations, but because adopting them would have a "devastating effect" on law enforcement.[35] The leading organization of fingerprint examiners said it stood behind the reliability of fingerprint evidence.[36] In 2016, the Texas Forensic Science Commission announced a moratorium on the use of bite mark evidence in the state. No other state has followed their lead and taken that step.

This story is like the movie *Groundhog Day*, in which Bill Murray relives the same day over and over again. We have seen the same plotline for other flawed forensics techniques, including some that have been discredited as far too unreliable to be used in court, and yet judges still let experts testify about the techniques in court. The NAS issued a scathing report concerning voice comparison in 1979. The FBI, to its credit, stopped using the technique in response, but state courts continued to let it in as if nothing had changed, including in the case of an innocent man, David Shawn Pope, who was later exonerated by DNA testing.[37]

For decades, the FBI used a technique called comparative bullet lead analysis to link bullets to a particular box of ammunition in evidence. The NAS finally reviewed the research and in 2004 wrote a report concluding that one cannot support any statement that "a crime bullet came from a particular box of ammunition."[38] People had been convicted, even executed, in cases relying on this bogus bullet matching technique. The FBI initially claimed that this technique was still usable. Over a year later, the FBI finally discontinued the technique, explaining that it had become too costly to maintain the equipment. Statisticians Drs. Karen Kafadar and Clifford Spiegelman examined an FBI database that it had refused to share with the NAS, but which it claimed had supported this technique. They found the database was riddled with errors and inconsistencies.[39] Hidden and flawed data, stubborn refusal to follow the science, and grave consequences: this has been the story of forensic evidence, time and time again.

A response to critical scientific reports, however, continues to be defensiveness, denial, and anger. As then–deputy attorney general Rod Rosenstein put it in a speech in 2018, forensic science is "under attack" and critics have an "erroneously narrow view" of forensics because they expect it to all be statistics and automated.[40] That is not so: experts do not need to be replaced by computers. Human experts can reach accurate judgments—but we need real evidence that the methods they use are in fact reliable.

GOOD SCIENCE

Stubborn resistance to criticism and hostility to scientific research is the very antithesis of good science. As the *New England Journal of Medicine* and other leading medical journals put it in a brief to the U. S. Supreme Court, the concept of "good science" is simple: it is "the scientific community's system of quality control," which protects us all from "unsubstantiated" analysis. Any proposition must "undergo a rigorous trilogy of publication, replication and verification before it is relied upon."[41] What leading scientists keep telling us is that, apart from the DNA area, no forensic techniques have undergone sufficiently rigorous testing. Error rates have been unknown, as the next chapter will describe. Simply put, we need to bring good science to forensics.

PART II Flawed Forensics

3 False ID

In the future-world depicted in the 1989 film *Back to the Future 2*, people use their fingerprints to access everything. Fictional high school student Marty McFly, played by Michael J. Fox, travels to the then-exotic year 2015, where people use fingerprints for identification, to unlock doors, and to pay for things. In that fictional future, bandits amputate fingers to gain access to the victim's homes and bank accounts. In our world, criminals hack computers rather than fingers. Our fingerprints do not control everything, because while fingerprints are reasonably effective for biometric identification purposes, they are not perfect. Fingerprints can unlock smartphones, and Apple Pay and Android Pay have used them. However, Apple researchers calculated an error rate of 1 in 50,000 for its iPhone fingerprint system.[1] Phones only capture partial prints, since the scanners are quite small. Users can experience errors if the screen is dirty, or if fingertips are wet. As a result, many people cannot open their phone on the first or second try. Due to the high incidence of errors, newer devices adopt face scans.

The stakes for such biometrics are usually small: a phone frustratingly does not open on the first try. In criminal cases, however, life and liberty are at stake, and unfortunately, it is not possible to "match" fingerprints.

In fact, the term "match" is misleading, if what is meant is a perfect hit: a certain conclusion that a pattern in fact came from a particular object. The word "match" is not used today by well-trained forensics professionals. Indeed, at the FBI, supervisors instructed hair and fiber examiners not to use the word "match" after the O. J. Simpson trial, where the judge barred an FBI examiner's use of the word regarding hair evidence.[2] Instead, examiners now use terms like "identification" with quite detailed accompanying definitions.

What the terminology obscures is that any comparison of fingerprint evidence, or any other pattern evidence for that matter, involves some degree of uncertainty. An examiner making a decision relies on objective information, like measurements, but also subjective judgments, like an "inner conviction" or a "personal point of certainty."[3] Any decision that a person makes has an error rate. You will learn that for many forensic techniques—even fingerprinting—error rates can be so high that if you had thought these were at least nearly perfect matches, you will be shocked. In this chapter I will tell the story of how fingerprinting evolved, from claims of infallibility to revelations of error. I tell the story of the fingerprint errors in Brandon Mayfield's case and unpack how errors can occur in fingerprinting generally. I conclude by arguing that examiners must always express uncertainty and present evidence using research-based probabilities. The notion of a perfect forensic identification must be exposed as a myth and discarded.

THE FARROW MURDERS

Fingerprints have been used for identification purposes for thousands of years. Clay tablets documenting business deals in ancient Babylon featured fingerprint impressions. In Qin Dynasty China, handprints were used in criminal investigations. In 1788 a German doctor, J. C. A. Mayer, was perhaps the first to conclude that fingerprints are "unique." He added a more cautious note, though, explaining: "Although the arrangement of skin ridges is never duplicated in two persons, nevertheless the similarities are closer among some individuals."[4] British colonial authorities began using handprints on a large scale in India as a tool to enforce their contracts. Fingerprinting then made its way to Scotland Yard.

The murder of shopkeepers Thomas and Ann Farrow in southeast London led in 1905 to the first murder trial using fingerprint evidence. The attackers bludgeoned the Farrows and one left a greasy fingerprint on the emptied cashbox to their store. A local milkman saw two young men near the store that day. He couldn't make an identification, but people in the neighborhood saw the brothers Albert and Alfred Stratton in the area. Inspector Charles Collins from Scotland Yard, which had just started using fingerprint identifications in 1901, said he found eleven points of similarity between the prints. As professor Simon Cole recounts, the inspector explained at trial that as few as four points of similarity would have been enough, based on his personal experience at Scotland Yard, where he had seen different fingerprints that shared three points of similarity but not four.[5] Just four points would be considered shockingly weak evidence today. The jury convicted the Stratton brothers, who were hanged that same day.[6] A few years later in the United States, the murder trial of Thomas Jennings hinged on a fingerprint. The examiner from the police department said Jennings, and Jennings only, could have left the prints. The appeals judges agreed this was proper evidence, because the method "is in such general and common use." Jennings was hanged.[7]

During that time, writers began to feature fingerprinting in their depictions of criminal investigations. As the Mark Twain character Pudd'nhead Wilson said in a fictional murder trial in small-town Mississippi: "Every human being carries with him from his cradle to his grave certain physical marks which do not change their character, and by which he can always be identified—and that without shade of doubt or question."[8] Twain was inspired by Arthur Conan Doyle's short stories in *The Adventures of Sherlock Holmes* to include fingerprinting in his story. Sherlock Holmes noticed a thumbmark on a letter in the early story "The Sign of the Four," but never conducted a fingerprint comparison.[9]

Since then, police have used fingerprints in thousands of cases around the world. By the 1940s, FBI agents kept over 100 million fingerprint cards in paper files. Today, far larger computerized databases of fingerprints are kept by local, state, and national law enforcement worldwide. Fingerprints have entered popular culture as the first forensic technique to "uniquely" identify individuals. Especially in the early days of DNA testing, people referred to it as DNA fingerprinting—such was the cultural power of fingerprints. Fingerprints became connected to the very idea of individuality. Elvis Presley said: "Values are like fingerprints. Nobody's the same, but you leave them all over everything you do." Or as David Sedaris put it with more snark, "All of us take pride and pleasure in the fact that we are unique, but I'm afraid that when all is said and done the police are right: it all comes down to fingerprints."[10]

A SINGLE PRINT

While our fingerprints are very detailed, we do not leave the same impression every time we touch something. If you have ever had to roll prints for a background check, you will be asked to roll them carefully. Sometimes they will ask you to roll the prints again, because you did not leave an acceptable image. Obviously, a person committing a crime is not trying to leave a good print, and is unlikely to neatly roll a finger from left to right to create a smooth pattern on a nice flat surface that preserves a print well. Fingerprints found at crime scenes are often not visible to the naked eye. Hidden prints are called latent prints: it can take dusting with powder, or other development techniques, to make them visible.

Although fingerprints have been used in major criminal investigations for over a hundred years, perhaps the most famous fingerprint image ever is the latent print that Spanish police found on the bag with seven detonators, inside an abandoned van near the May 2004 terrorist bombings of commuter trains in Madrid, Spain.[11] As you know from the introduction, the FBI searched government fingerprint databases and fixed on the fingerprint of a lawyer in Portland, Oregon, named Brandon Mayfield. The FBI did not just search fingerprints from criminal arrests, but also searched its databases of suspected terrorists, and its civil file, with fingerprints taken from government employees and military servicemembers. The FBI analyst ran the database search and received a list of twenty candidate prints. The analyst began with the first and best candidate, and when he reached the fourth print in the list, he decided that it looked good and stopped there. He then ordered a copy of Mayfield's inked tenprint card to get a better-quality version of the print for a further comparison.

It may surprise you to hear that today's computerized fingerprint databases do not claim to accurately determine the source of a print. If the operator enters your prints, the program will generate a list of prints that most resemble yours, according to the designer's parameters. How the search program works, and what measurements its algorithm uses, is typically not shared by the company that designed it, not even with the labs using it. Unlike what you see on TV, a hit is not displayed instantly on a screen. Instead, human experts must still do a lot of painstaking work. They must examine each of the candidate prints suggested by the database search. Sometimes none of the candidate prints offered by the database resemble the crime scene prints.

On crime shows, a whole team of experts spends all of their time on a single case, conveniently wrapped up at the end of an episode. In real crime labs, experts can struggle under serious backlogs, and may work on hundreds of cases at a time. The Madrid bombing investigation was so important, though, that the case proceeded more like on TV, in that three separate FBI examiners looked at the prints. When the first examiner looked at the ten-print card, he felt it confirmed his prior determination. Note that when he ran the Madrid bombing print in the database, Mayfield's print appeared fourth.[12] That might tend to indicate that he was not the best candidate. However, when the examiner looked at Mayfield's prints in more detail, he found fifteen points, or minute details, that corresponded to the latent print. Next, two examiners, a supervisor and a retired FBI examiner with over thirty years of experience, verified the conclusion. Normally there would be just one "verifier," but in a high-profile case like this, the FBI asked two people to verify the conclusion. There was an area to the upper left with some differences; this area gave one of the examiners "heartburn from the get-go."[13] However, ultimately, they all decided that it was in fact Mayfield's print.

Now the FBI ordered a "full-court press." Concerned that Mayfield was part of a "second wave" of terrorist attacks, they ordered twenty-four-hour surveillance.[14] The FBI was "one hundred percent positive" that this was his print.[15] All three examiners agreed. As the examiners did their work, they looked back and forth between Mayfield's print and the print from the bombing scene. As they looked back and forth, they changed which points they marked. One examiner changed five of his original seven points, which he had marked on the latent print, only after he looked at Mayfield's prints.[16] This was "reverse reasoning." The examiners changed their conclusions and found new similarities as they looked back and forth.

To be sure, Mayfield's lawyers hired their own fingerprint expert who looked at the print too. The defense expert has described how he began work on the case, comparing each of Mayfield's prints, one at a time, to the latent print from the bombing:

> So I started with the thumb, went to the index, went to the middle. No, no, no, no, no. Boom! I come up with one. Ah! Here's one with a couple of similarities, a couple of more, a couple of more. By the time I got to 15, I said, "This looks like an identification."[17]

Just like the two analysts knew that the first FBI analyst had found an identification, this defense expert also knew that the FBI had concluded it was Mayfield's print. In court, the defense expert told the judge: "I compared the latent prints to the known prints that were submitted on Brandon Mayfield, and I concluded that the latent print is the left index finger of Mr. Mayfield." Mayfield's own expert agreed with the FBI. Mayfield later recalled, "He actually confirmed what the other three examiners had said. And from that point on, I kind of felt like the train to a death penalty just pulled out of the station."[18]

The term that the FBI examiners used was "individualization." This meant that Mayfield, and not anyone else in the entire world, left the print. A conclusion of individualization, as the FBI put it at the time, was supported by "theories of biological uniqueness and permanence" as well as "more than one hundred years of operational experience." Fingerprints are unique, the experts would (and still do) say. After all, for over a century, fingerprint examiners have done their work well. Fingerprint examiners claimed to be infallible. The method had an error rate of "zero." Fingerprints are unique, after all. Everyone knows that fingerprints are unique. This means that no other person in the world could be the culprit.

At the first court hearing, Mayfield told the judge: "That's not my fingerprint, your honor." The judge rejected this defense. How could the fingerprint not be his, when four experts had agreed 100 percent? The judge ordered Mayfield arrested as a material witness to terrorism. Yet the

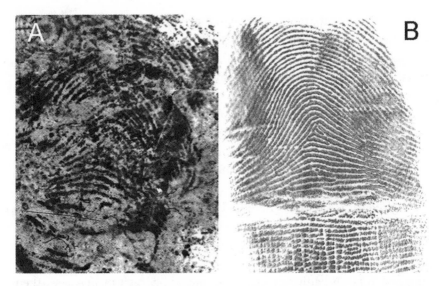

Latent print and Brandon Mayfield's print. Federal OIG report, https://oig.justice.gov /special/s0601/final.pdf.

fingerprint analysts were all wrong. Above is an image of Mayfield's finger-print to the right, and of the latent print from Madrid to the left.

Mayfield's print has some similarities in common with the Madrid print. But there are also specific differences between the two prints, which the experts all discounted. And consider how Mayfield first became a suspect. He was not detained near the crime scene or linked by a witness. Instead, his print was pulled from a database containing tens of millions of prints. Such databases are designed to locate prints that have as many similarities as possible, which makes the job of the expert far more challenging. The latent print from the bag of detonators was smudged and missing an awful lot of information. There may be over a hundred points in a pristine print, but the three FBI experts were impressed to find just fifteen.

Meanwhile, the Spanish authorities told the FBI that the FBI had it wrong—three weeks before Mayfield's arrest. The FBI responded that they had "absolute confidence." Indeed, the FBI agents were so sure that when the Spanish authorities responded, on April 13, 2004, that they believed the comparison was "negative," the agents flew to Madrid on April 21, with enlarged photographs, to present their work in person and try to convince the Spanish investigators to change their minds.

Mayfield had never been to Spain. The FBI began intensive surveillance and searches of his home, finding only that his daughter had written a middle school report on Spain. He was Muslim, which no doubt contributed to the FBI's intense suspicion. The FBI arrested Mayfield on May 6, and proceeded with a terrorism case until the Spanish authorities on May 19 informed the FBI they had connected the fingerprints to a known Algerian terrorist. The next day, on May 20, the FBI agreed to release Mayfield, and days later, charges were dropped.[19] The FBI eventually apologized. In 2006 Mayfield settled a civil rights case against the FBI for $1.9 million. The case would forever change forensic science in the United States and beyond. After all, these were experienced FBI analysts, examining fingerprints, which are supposed to be unique. If a fingerprint examination can be so badly botched in an incredibly high-profile case, then how easily can something else go wrong?

THE METHODS OF LATENT FINGERPRINT COMPARISON

You can quickly get a sense of what fingerprint examiners do from a description, but the work itself is challenging and tedious. It is not easy on the eyes. One must spend many hours classifying and examining prints. At first, one works on ten-print cards taken from suspects. Next, one graduates to examination of latent prints, or hidden prints from unknown persons found at crime scenes.

Fingerprints are formed before birth. These ridges cover not only our fingertips but also the entire underside of our fingers and hands and feet. These skin ridges are called friction skin. Our skin is usually covered with a thin film of perspiration or oil. When the finger or hand touches an item, a reproduction of those ridges is left by means of that perspiration or oil. That reproduction is called a latent print. How good the print is may depend on the type of surface. Some surfaces, such as metal or glass, can preserve a sharp image of a print. Other surfaces, like cloth, may preserve little to nothing. An ideal surface for preserving prints, like glass, can be wiped down; a print is only preserved if the object is undisturbed. The shape of the surface can distort the print. The way a person touches an object also affects how good the print is; as noted, people committing a crime do not normally try to leave a well-formed latent print. Further, while everyone has ridges on their fingers, some people tend not to leave clear prints. Some people have shallow ridges on their fingers, making it hard to leave prints. Scarring and wear can also change one's fingerprints. People who work with their hands a lot do not leave clear fingerprints.

In the first level of the analysis, the examiner classifies the overall shape of the print. The latent print from the Madrid case has what fingerprint examiners call an "arch," and the name is self-explanatory: the ridges form an arch shape. The other two shapes are a circular pattern called a "whorl," and a u-shaped "loop."

The second level focuses on smaller details called features or minutiae. The work that follows is subjective and based on experience. The examiner looks at the print and identifies these finer details, including places where ridges end, enclosures or islands occur, or other features. This examination process sometimes takes many hours, particularly if the print is highly incomplete. There are terms for many commonly observed details, like a "crossover" if ridges form an "x" shape, a delta if ridges come together in a "v," a ridge ending if a ridge comes to an end, and an "island" if there is a spot-shaped ridge surrounded by another ridge.

The third level of detail refers to even smaller features, such as ends of ridges and shapes created by the pores in the skin. It is not common for such details to be present in a latent print.

In the 1990s, fingerprint examiners developed new terminology for their work, calling it ACE-V, which stands for Analysis, Comparison, Evaluation, and Verification. This acronym simply means that examiners look at the prints carefully, compare them, reach a conclusion, and ask someone else to provide confirmation. It is not exactly a method; it is more like a set of very general steps. No fancy equipment is necessarily used either. In some labs, examiners still squint through a single ocular glass—think Mr. Peanut—while in others they take photos of the prints and look at them blown up on a computer screen.

During this process, the examiner first determines whether the latent print is suitable for comparison, based on whether there is adequate information in it. Many prints that police lift at crime scenes are not suitable for comparison. They are too smudged or distorted to be of any use. In a study that I worked on with colleagues, including several examiners at the Houston Forensic Science Center, we found that over half of the latent prints (56%) that the lab received were found to be "no value" or not suitable for comparison.[20]

If the print is of high-enough quality to work with, then the comparison process begins. There may be, in fact, a number of latent prints from a crime scene. In the Houston lab, for example, while most cases had just one print, the median case had four prints, the average was over eight prints, and a few outlier cases had as many as 150 latent prints. The latent prints may be compared to the prints of a suspect, if there is one.[21] The prints from a suspect will be pristine, ten-print cards.

If there is no suspect, the examiner conducts a search in a database, which will suggest a series of candidate prints. The examiner must still go through the list of possibilities carefully. To do this, the examiner traditionally makes a side-by-side comparison between the latent print and prints taken from a suspect. They look at them both using a magnifying glass, or today, more commonly, by looking at images on a computer screen. Next, the examiner evaluates the degree of similarity between the latent and the known prints, reaching one of three seemingly firm conclusions: that they are from the same source, from different sources, or that the comparison is wholly inconclusive. A good lab will have procedures for documenting this process. The examiner may mark each feature relied on, sometimes using a computer program. If one looks at prints side by side, one may tend to look for similarities and ignore differences; some labs now require the examiner to mark up the latent print first, and then the comparison print. Other labs do not require any type of marking or documentation.

If the examiner decides that the prints could have come from the same person, then the prints are passed to another examiner, to verify or reexamine that conclusion. In most labs another examiner conducts a verification only if an identification was found. The verifying examiner can see all of the results and any documentation by the first examiner. Few labs do this blind, where the verifier does a totally independent analysis and does not know what conclusion was reached by the first examiner.

UNTESTED ASSUMPTIONS

No one has carefully tested the basic assumptions that experts have relied upon for decades. First, are each person's fingerprints unique? You have probably long assumed that fingerprints are unique and that no two are alike. My colleague Gregory Mitchell and I surveyed two groups of over 1,200 adults in the United States, and we found that 95 percent believed fingerprints are unique—a higher percentage than those who thought DNA results were unique.[22] People think fingerprints are like snowflakes. In fact, now scientists have found that there are thirty-five basic shapes snowflakes may form and that snowflakes that form under similar conditions will form similar—and sometimes nearly identical—shapes.[23] Fingerprint examiners similarly assumed that all fingerprint patterns are completely different from each other, and not just that they are somewhat or mostly different from each other. Experts made the same strong assumption about bite marks, fibers, toolmarks, shoeprints, and a range of other types of forensics. We do not know if that strong assumption is true for fingerprints; it has never been tested. We do have good reasons, however, to suspect that, like for snowflakes, these other types of prints may sometimes look quite alike, at least at certain levels of detail.

Second, how often can one person's fingerprint look like another person's crime scene latent print? We do not know how often a smeared, partial latent fingerprint from a crime scene might look very much like someone else's print. It may depend on what level of detail one has in a print. We now know that errors can happen.

Third, how good are experts at making fingerprint comparisons? We need to know the error rates; after all, we are trusting experts to make decisions that can send people to prison or even death row. The U. S. Department of Justice standards explain that a fingerprint identification is "a statement of an examiner's belief." The National Academy of Sciences report emphasized fingerprint examiners rely on "a subjective assessment" that lacks adequate "statistical models." We do not know how common or rare it is to have particular features in a fingerprint. As a result, the NAS concluded that ACE-V "is not specific enough to qualify as a validated method."[24]

Fourth, we might assume that technology, like databases, will catch errors that fallible people make. However, in the Mayfield case, the technology contributed to his wrongful identification. In fact, modern databases may increase the challenges experts face because by design they search through millions of records to produce the best candidates: images that look as similar to each other as possible. Fortunately, as I will describe, research and technology can address these challenges, but only if we let better science come into the lab and the courtroom.

COMPARING EVERYTHING

Fingerprints leave very detailed information, if the print is a good one, but experts also examine far less promising evidence. Our shoes are mass-produced objects, and unless one has very unusual shoes—like the Bruno Magli Size Twelve Lorenzo shoeprint at issue in the trial of O. J. Simpson—one might share the same shoeprint as hundreds of thousands of others. Nevertheless, experts testify to "unique" patterns of wear on a person's shoes. Experts compare toolmarks, asking whether a firearm could have fired a particular shell casing, or whether a set of pliers could have cut a wire. Experts compare fibers, human hairs, and even animal hairs.

Experts also compare more obscure objects. A man was convicted of murder in Indiana, in two separate 1990s trials, based on a garbage bag comparison. The expert testified that irregularities in a roll of garbage bags can extend from one bag to the next, and that the bag used to wrap the victim shared "unique" similarities, showing that it was "connected to and a part of the bag" from the defendant's home.[25] Experts compare masking tape and duct tape. Experts compare cloth in clothing, studying lines on a plaid shirt or jeans in relation to clothes seen in a photo or video. In one case, an FBI "image analysis" expert claimed that even though it was a mass-produced shirt, only "1 in 650 billion shirts would randomly match so precisely," adding, "give or take a few billion."[26] Such pattern-comparison techniques are still in use and yet they lack adequate data. And for none of these techniques can the experts say what a conclusion based on them actually means. They cannot tell you how often such objects might coincidentally share similarities. They cannot tell you how likely it is that the evidence came from the source, and if they do, the numbers they offer, "give or take a few billion," are made up. Instead, these matchmakers just assert a personal opinion that evidence came from the same source.

FIREARMS

Of all the pattern-comparison techniques used, firearms comparisons are perhaps the most common, possibly even more so than fingerprint comparisons. Firearms violence is a major problem in the United States, with over 10,000 homicides involving firearms and almost 500,000 other crimes, such as robberies and assaults, committed using firearms.[27] Firearms comparisons are in great demand. Examiners seek to link crime scene evidence, such as spent shell casings or bullets, with a firearm. The assumption is that manufacturing processes used to cut, drill, and grind a gun leave markings on the barrel, breech face, and firing pin. When the firearm discharges, those components contact the ammunition and leave marks on it. Experts have assumed different firearms should leave different toolmarks on the ammunition, even if firearms are produced on the same production line. They believe these toolmarks allow them to definitively link spent ammunition to a single firearm.

For over a hundred years, firearms experts have testified in criminal trials.[28] Firearms experts traditionally testified in court by making "uniqueness" claims much like those made about fingerprints. Experts said that "no two firearms should produce the same microscopic features on bullets and cartridge cases such that they could be falsely identified as having been fired from the same firearm."[29] By the late 1990s, experts premised testimony on a "theory of identification" set out by a professional association, the Association of Firearms and Tool Mark Examiners (AFTE). AFTE instructs practitioners to use the phrase "source identification" to explain what they mean when they identify "sufficient agreement" when examining firearms.[30] At a general level, these firearms examiners examine markings that a firearm leaves on a discharged bullet of cartridge casing. The AFTE's so-called theory is circular. An identification occurs when the expert finds sufficient evidence defined as enough evidence to find an identification.

In recent years, scientists have called into question the validity and reliability of such testimony. In a 2008 report on ballistic imaging, the National Academy of Sciences concluded that definitive associations like "source identification" were not supported.[31] In its 2009 report, the NAS followed up and stated that categorical conclusions regarding firearms or toolmarks were not supported by research, and that, instead, more cautious claims should be made. The report stated that the "scientific knowledge base for tool mark and firearms analysis is fairly limited."[32] The AFTE theory of identification "is inadequate and does not explain how an expert can reach a given level of confidence in a conclusion." Judges have also raised concerns that this theory represents "unconstrained subjectivity masquerading as objectivity," it is "inherently vague" and "subjective," or "either tautological or wholly subjective."[33]

To this day, however, firearms examiners use terms like "source identification" in court—although, as I will describe in chapter 5, judges have begun to step in and require more cautious wording, such as that it is "more likely than not" that the ammunition came from the defendant's firearm, or that the firearm "cannot be excluded."[34] The Department of Justice announced guidelines in 2019: experts should use the term "source identification," which they define as "an examiner's conclusion that two toolmarks originated from the same source."[35] The guidelines sound much like the AFTE theory: examiners may call it an identification when they decide that it is one.

THE WAKE OF THE MAYFIELD ERROR

The Mayfield fingerprint error was a watershed event in the history of the FBI and in the modern history of forensic science. Imagine how many other people have been convicted where no independent scientists were examining the evidence. Fingerprint examiners long claimed an error rate of zero. A 1963 FBI report called "The Science of Fingerprints" began with an introductory letter by FBI director J. Edgar Hoover, singing the praises of the "science" of fingerprinting: "Of all the methods of identification, fingerprinting alone has proved to be both infallible and feasible."[36]

The three FBI examiners each gave a "100 percent positive identification." Yet the experts all got it wrong. In the investigation that followed, the FBI did make two changes. First, in cases with just a single latent fingerprint, the FBI said there should be a blind verification, which means a second expert looks at the prints and independently evaluates them. This was an important change, but many cases involve more than one latent fingerprint. Second, the FBI also changed the side-by-side comparison process, which can lead to circular reasoning. FBI examiners now examine the latent and suspect prints one at a time, rather than side by side.

The terminology used by fingerprint examiners has also changed in response to the Mayfield case. In 2017 the Department of Justice wrote up a model standard for fingerprint testimony, which states that examiners should not assert "100 percent level of certainty" or claim they have a zero-error rate. The examiner should not brag about the numbers of cases handled, or use terms like "reasonable scientific certainty." The term "individualization" should not be used. This move was embraced by many in the community, as part of a "constant evolution" to improve fingerprinting practices.[37] However, the standards still state that an examiner should testify that the prints originated from the same source. This is defined as an examiner's decision that the observed features have "sufficient correspondence." The fingerprint examiner can offer a conclusion of "source identification."[38] The approved term, "identification," still sounds an awful lot like "individualization," or a unique connection to a particular person. The examiner still claims that the prints "originated from the same source." Moreover, these are only federal standards. In state courts, fingerprint examiners still pronounce that a print definitely came from the defendant.

These differences in the words that fingerprint examiners use may not mean much—the most important word that an examiner says may be the word "fingerprint." Once jurors hear that the expert looked at fingerprints and found some kind of connection between them, the hundred-plus years of cultural association between fingerprints and unique individuality come into play. People do not know about all of the assumptions and subjectivity in the method. As one fingerprint examiner put it, "When we say, 'I am 100% certain of my conclusion,' we might mean that we have conducted a careful examination, reached the best conclusion possible with the data available, and that we would not have reported that conclusion unless we were confident that we had done our work well." Fingerprint examiner Heidi Eldridge asks: "But what does the jury hear? They hear, 'I'm an expert, and I'm telling you that this conclusion is fact and cannot possibly be wrong.'"[39]

PROBABILITIES

Forensic experts should reach conclusions using frequencies based on data. The expert should give us a number, rather than use words like "identification" that imply the evidence in fact came from a source. For DNA testing, conclusions are already presented as a population frequency, using statistics. The opposition to such approaches may be both cultural and strategic. In a survey of fingerprint examiners, Simon Cole, Valerie King, and Henry Swofford found that almost all of them currently report fingerprint conclusions in a categorical fashion, as an identification or not. Some admitted that they would prefer to offer probabilistic conclusions but are reluctant to do so. Over one-third agreed that it would be "scientifically more appropriate" to do so. One commented that "adding a numerical value to conclusions will give the jury more information." Almost 80 percent agreed that jurors might not understand probabilities, or feared that defense lawyers would take advantage of probabilities to sow reasonable doubt. Over 40 percent admitted they lacked training in probabilities so would not easily be able to testify about them. Almost half worried that a probabilistic conclusion "is too weak" when compared to a categorical "identification."[40]

We are not irrational or gullible people. If we are told the truth—that experts can be wrong—then our attitude changes. It is high time that jurors and lawyers and judges were all actually told, in every case, that experts are not foolproof. All evidence is probabilistic and nothing is 100 percent certain. We should be given frequencies. One aspect of that, which I discuss in the next chapter, is the need to be told about the error rates.

"I'll preach fingerprints till I die," said the supervising examiner in the Mayfield case. After making the most high-profile error in fingerprint history the examiner still maintained: "They're infallible. I still consider myself one of the best in the world."

4 Error Rates

Kenny Waters died in a tragic accident in September 2001, falling over a wall and onto the concrete below. Just six months earlier, DNA tests led to his release, after he served eighteen years in prison for a robbery and murder that he did not commit. His sister, Betty Anne Waters, shown with Kenny in photo, put herself through college and law school because she was determined to use a law degree to free her brother. She obtained a court order to preserve evidence from the scene and she wanted to test it. "If we didn't find the DNA—that was the holy grail—then we wanted the prints," she recalled, but "how do we find them?" In the major motion picture *Conviction,* Hilary Swank portrayed Betty Anne. Fortunately, she located a box of evidence in the courthouse that could still be DNA tested. However, she found no records of the crime scene fingerprints. It took Betty Anne twenty-nine years to solve the mystery of the missing fingerprints.

On the morning of May 21, 1980, a culprit stabbed a woman to death in Ayer, Massachusetts, and ransacked her home. After her daughter-in-law discovered the body, investigators found the kitchen faucet still running and bloodstains all over the house, as well as the murder weapon—a bloody paring knife. Police questioned Kenny Waters, who lived next door, but he explained that he had worked at the local diner until 8:30 a.m. the

Kenny and Betty Anne Waters.
Courtesy of Betty Anne Waters.

day she was killed and had been in court at 9 a.m. After the crime remained unsolved for two years, a cooperating witness surfaced, offering to testify for money. He told police that Waters's ex-girlfriend reported he confessed to her, which she initially denied, but then cooperated after police interrogated her and threatened to take away her children.[1] In 1983 the jury convicted Waters, who was sentenced to life without parole. At trial a forensic analyst spent most of the day dwelling on blood stains that were type O. Waters was type O. Many other stains did not match that type; for example, the blood on the paring knife was type B, consistent with the victim. Yet only at the very end of his testimony did the analyst admit that about 48 percent of people share the type O blood type. Moreover, hairs from the scene did not come either from the victim or from Waters.

At trial the police claimed that the fingerprints at the scene were not usable.[2] Years later, Betty Anne wondered, "Well, where are those fingerprints?" For seven years, she tried to track them down. In a civil rights suit, Innocence Project co-founder Barry Scheck represented Betty Anne, and requested all records in the case. The lawyers received testimony from the grand jury. A juror had asked whether there were any fingerprints, and the response was that the prints were so smeared that forensic analysts could not use them to include or exclude anybody. Yet a few police reports referred to prints excluding three other suspects. The reports did not say anything about Kenny, but indicated that there were latent fingerprints that could be compared to suspects. Betty Anne wanted those fingerprints.[3]

For the first time, when Barry Scheck questioned a police officer in the case, they learned what happened. This officer had processed the prints at the crime scene. Barry asked him, on the record in a deposition, what he did with the prints, and he said he had compared them and they eliminated Kenny. "I nearly fell off my chair," Betty Anne told me. The officer said that before Kenny's trial, he brought the prints home. Barry asked where the prints were. The officer said that after he retired and moved to Florida, he placed them in a rented storage unit. Betty Anne was determined to find them: "We're going to want to see that," she said. The next day the officer called back and said, "Oh, I don't think they're there," and declined to give them access. Never ones to give up, Barry and Betty Anne served a subpoena and, armed with a court order, they combed through the storage unit. Betty Anne recalled it was over a hundred degrees outside. The officer was sitting outside, insisting they would not find anything. They had to remove his furniture and belongings, but at the very back of the unit, they found a manila folder. Inside was a police report. It had a list of all of the family members, police, and suspects whose prints they had compared. Betty Anne recalled her "hands were shaking" as she read it; her "brother's name was there, not once, but twice." They had compared his fingerprints and eliminated him once, and then just to be sure, compared him again, and again eliminated him.

Betty Anne recalls that she came outside, and confronting the retired officer, said, "Why didn't you turn these over to the police or the defense or somebody?" He said, "Why? Kenny confessed." Betty Anne said, "He did not confess." She added, "He is innocent," and walked away.

"I want these fingerprints," Barry Scheck demanded in court after this revelation. The police report showed how police found two fingerprints in blood: one on a faucet and one on a lamp, which they believed were connected with the killer. Early on in the investigation, police eliminated both the victim and Kenny as the source. Scheck argued these prints were crucial evidence that the police had concealed. The judge agreed and ordered the government to turn over the evidence. Only then did the government produce the bloody latent fingerprint evidence. As Betty Anne put it,

"They knew he wasn't guilty. They knew from day one that Kenny was innocent." Not long afterward, the town of Ayer, Massachusetts, settled Waters' civil rights lawsuit for $3.4 million.[4]

This saga highlights how not only can errors remain hidden for years, but that more than one type of error can send an innocent person to prison. We do not just have to worry about a false hit, like in Brandon Mayfield's case, but also a false failure to exclude an innocent suspect, like Kenny Waters, as well as false claims that evidence is inconclusive or of "no value."

Indeed, Keith Harward was also convicted, in part, based on testimony that forensics were "inconclusive" and could not include or exclude him. While the key evidence of his guilt at trial, presented by the forensic dentists, focused on the bite mark evidence, the crime lab analyst had also tested fluids from a rape kit. The analyst testified that the results were inconclusive. Only after he sought DNA testing thirty years later, in 2015, did Harward's lawyers uncover the analyst's bench notes, which recorded secretions from a type O secretor. The victim was a type B secretor and Mr. Harward was a type A secretor. This meant that Harward should have been excluded from the rape kit evidence at the time of trial. When I saw the name of the lab analyst who testified in Harward's case, I was not surprised. The same lab analyst gave false testimony in the case of Troy Webb, another innocent man exonerated through post-conviction DNA testing in Virginia.[5] Following Harward's exoneration, the Virginia Department of Forensic Science announced an audit of the blood testing work of this analyst.[6] However, the lab does not have good records going back decades. We may never know how many others were convicted based on false lab reports calling evidence of innocence "inconclusive."

In this chapter I describe how error rates have been hidden from jurors, lawyers, judges, and the public. Experts have not just claimed to make an identification to a source to the exclusion of all others, as I described in the last chapter, but relatedly, they have claimed to be infallible. Whether it was a fingerprint, hair, bite mark, or other forensic pattern examiner, they claimed perfection. The error rates become even more concerning when one looks at the different types of errors an examiner can make: not just false positive, or mistaken, hits but also false negative, or mistaken, non-hits, as well as false conclusions that evidence is "inconclusive" or of no value to compare. There is not just one error rate, but several, and we need to bring all of these error rates into the open and into the courtroom.

INFALLIBLE EXPERTS

"The only man who never makes a mistake is the man who never does anything," as President Theodore Roosevelt famously put it. If you have watched a trial with forensic evidence, however, you may have heard from a person who claimed to be always right. Until recently, fingerprint examiners claimed mistakes could not happen. It was not just the FBI examiners in Brandon Mayfield's case who confidently claimed they were infallible. The FBI's manual on fingerprinting instructed that "of all the methods of identification, fingerprinting alone has proved to be . . . infallible."[7] There was no research to back this claim. No studies had been done on how rare or common it is for the latent prints to look similar or different. Moreover, errors had happened. Still, examiners continued to confidently testify that there was an error rate of "zero" for fingerprint comparisons. Mistakes were not possible: "there is no chance of error."[8] Only a careless or incompetent examiner could make a mistake, in special cases, and these were aberrations to be ignored.

When lawyers tried to challenge fingerprint evidence, the FBI was extremely aggressive in countering that the error rate was zero. In 1991 Byron Mitchell was tried and convicted of armed robbery in federal court in Philadelphia. After his conviction was reversed on appeal, his new lawyers focused on the fingerprint evidence. Two masked men with shotguns had stolen an armored vehicle. The government's theory was that Mitchell drove the getaway car, based on two latent prints from the outside of the driver's door and from the car's gear shift lever. Before the retrial in 1998, Mitchell's lawyers argued that the judge should not allow the fingerprint evidence to be introduced at trial, because fingerprint methods did not satisfy the rigorous requirements of evidence rules.[9] The FBI responded that "by following the scientific methodology" of fingerprint comparison, "the error rate remains zero."[10]

The FBI told the judge that it had conducted a new study. The FBI sent the prints from the defendant in the case, Mitchell, to thirty-four agencies.

In fact, nine of them (27%) did not identify any of the latent prints as Mitchell's. The FBI contacted these agencies and said they must have made a mistake, asking for a "do-over." This time, the FBI told them all to focus just on a blown-up image with "marked characteristics." The test "was rigged," as law professor Paul Giannelli later put it.[11] The judge still let the evidence in.

For decades, forensic analysts of different types testified they were 100 percent certain. As federal judge Harry T. Edwards put it, "The courts had been misled for a long time because we had been told, my colleagues and I, by some experts from the FBI that fingerprint comparisons involved essentially a zero error rate, without our ever understanding that's completely inaccurate."[12] For years, forensics professionals also made it hard to study error rates by refusing to participate in studies. Doing so might undermine their image of infallibility. When researchers did document high error rates, members of the field buried, discredited, or refused to publish the studies. Over time, outsider lawyers and researchers fought a battle to uncover crucial information about error rates.

BAD HAIR

By the late 1990s, more people were starting to ask questions about the reliability of forensic methods. The FBI began to reconsider hair comparisons, since analysts could now sometimes use a DNA test to verify whether the traditional visual comparison was correct or not. In 2002 the FBI went back and reviewed FBI lab cases subjected to both a microscopic comparison and to DNA analysis between 1996 and 2000. Hairs do not have nuclear DNA, but they do have mitochondria, the power-center of a cell. DNA in mitochondria is inherited from one's mother, so people who share the same matrilineal line share the same mitochondrial DNA profile. This type of testing, called mtDNA testing, can be used to show that hairs cannot come from a suspect, and they can include a suspect in a group of related individuals. In nine of eighty cases, or 11.25 percent, in which the FBI hair examiners concluded that the hairs could have come from the suspect, the DNA test showed the opposite. The FBI's response was not to cease using hair comparison evidence. Nor did they say that they would make sure that experts described error rates in court. Instead, the FBI just recommended both hair comparison and a DNA test should be done, where possible.[13] Compare the response in Canada: a judge led a public inquiry, which found that hair comparison evidence was "unlikely" to have enough value to "justify its reception at a criminal trial."[14] The Mounties, or the Royal Canadian Mounted Police Forensic Laboratory Services, stopped using hair comparisons.[15]

BITE MARKS

In the bite mark area, the American Board of Forensic Odontology, the professional association of forensic dentists, conducted a study to test its members. In the late 1990s, they gave dentists bite mark evidence of medium to good quality. The dentists were asked to compare four bite marks to seven sets of teeth, four of which made each of the marks. This is called a "closed set" study, since there was a correct answer for each of the four marks. Obviously, in a real case, one does not know if a suspect's teeth produced any of the evidence. In that study, of the sixty dentists who asked to take the study, only twenty-six filled it out, and those dentists were wrong in nearly half of their responses.[16] A 2002 study showed an almost 16 percent error rate, or about one in six, and a 2010 study similarly involved a one in six error rate.[17] A 2007 study had error rates as high as 15 percent.[18] None of these troubling findings blunted the force of the standard testimony dentists delivered in court, nor did dentists make a habit of describing these studies in reports or testimony.

ADMITTING ERROR

The experts' persistent and unsupported claims of zero error rates came to a head when the National Academy of Sciences issued its report in 2009. After years and years of insisting that fingerprint work was perfect, within days of the report publication, the International Association of Identification, a leading global organization for fingerprint examiners, finally decided to back off, slightly. The organization's president issued a letter stating: "It is suggested that members not assert 100% infallibility (zero error rate) when addressing the reliability of fingerprint comparisons." The president added: "Members are advised to avoid stating their conclusions in absolute terms."[19] The FBI backtracked, and their working group provided a new standard recommending use of the term "individualization," defined as "the likelihood the impression was made by another (different) source is so remote that it is considered as a practical impossibility." Basically, this FBI standard advised that an examiner could still say the fingerprint evidence came from a source, and that it is practically impossible (whatever that means) to make an error.

Two FBI fingerprint experts came to my classroom for a demonstration not long after the NAS report was published. A local federal judge presided over an informal moot court, where the law students had the chance to question the FBI analyst in a mock case. My students had never tried a case before, but they did a great job, considering their lack of trial experience. When they asked the FBI examiner whether she was sure of her findings, she responded that she was completely confident. She did admit errors could happen, but explained that she was aware of only the one error in the Mayfield case, and she emphasized that she had personally never made a mistake. The examiner admitted there was a theoretical possibility that error could occur, if an expert was sloppy or untrained, but she was adamant that there was no error rate in fingerprinting. None had been measured. The impressed judge, with apologies to my students, promptly ruled in favor of admitting the evidence.

FIRE-SCENE EVIDENCE

In arson investigations, examiners examine a crime scene to reconstruct what may have happened to decide whether a fire was deliberately set. When the instructors at the Federal Law Enforcement Training Center burned three similarly furnished rooms, and then tested fire examiners on whether they could identify in which part of the room a fire was started, they found high error rates. For fires that burned for 30 seconds, investigators selected the right quadrant of the room 84 percent of the time, but when fires burned for 180 seconds, they selected the right point of origin just 25 percent of the time, or no better than chance.[20] There had been little research on how one should measure the origin of a fire based on burn patterns. Indeed, the National Fire Academy's basic training changed in 2007, with a segment titled "Myths and Legends" intended to debunk many false methods used to interpret fire patterns.[21] Error rates may be finally changing the culture in the arson investigation world.

BLOOD PATTERN ANALYSIS

Blood pattern analysis (BPA) involves the examination of blood stains to try to reach conclusions about how a crime occurred. One of the early cases in the United States featuring BPA was the 1955 trial of Samuel Sheppard, in which a defense expert claimed to be able to approximate the speed at which blood fell in drops during a murder.[22] Despite use of BPA in court for decades, the method had never been scientifically vetted. The National Academy of Sciences report emphasized that given the "enormous" uncertainty inherent in interpreting bloodstain patterns, experts should testify about BPA with extreme caution.[23] Recently, one study found that out of 416 scenarios involving different types of blood patterns, BPA examiners wrongly identified the type in approximately 13.1 percent of the cases. The error rate increased to over 15 percent for cases involving impact and gunshot-produced spatter. Far more such work is needed to study error rates in that field.[24]

WHY NO RESEARCH?

Why has it taken so long for scientists to ask some of the most basic questions about forensic evidence, such as, "Is it even reliable?" The National Academy of Sciences report in 2009 put it diplomatically, stating that "some forensic science disciplines are supported by little rigorous systematic research to validate the discipline's basic premises and techniques." Yet there is "no evident reason why such research cannot be conducted."[25] There is no research, or very little research, on bite mark comparison evidence, fingerprint evidence, firearms evidence, hair comparison evidence, toolmark identifications, and a range of other types of forensic evidence. Law professor Paul Giannelli put it well when he asked: "Why no research?"[26]

One answer is that unlike DNA testing, these forensic methods did not develop in research labs, with scientists conducting rigorous studies. Instead, they developed in places like police stations. These pattern comparison techniques all involve a person, based on training or experience, looking at the evidence and making judgment calls. To study how good such a person is, one has to convince the person to participate in a study. What incentive do people have to participate in studies that might show how often they make errors? No one likes to be tested. However, researchers have started to conduct such studies, in response to new scientific scrutiny of forensics. The federal government increasingly funds basic research on reliability of forensic science, including through the National Institute of Justice (NIJ) and the National Institute for Standards and Technology (NIST).

WHAT ARE THE ERROR RATES?

When people are asked what they think are the error rates for various forensic techniques, they often give astronomically low numbers. Jay Koehler found that jurors estimated that the error rate for fingerprint comparison was 1 in 5.5 million, for bite mark comparison and hair comparison 1 in a million.[27] Are they right? For the most part, we do not know how often analysts incorrectly connect evidence (a false positive error). We do not know how often they miss a correct hit (a false negative report). We do not know how often they deem evidence inconclusive, when it is actually good evidence that can be valuably compared. Each of those types of errors matters.

Today, researchers have begun to measure these error rates, at least a little bit, for a few types of forensics. The results have come as a huge surprise to most people. The President's Council of Advisors on Science and Technology (PCAST) report from fall 2015 emphasized that experts must tell jurors about the error rates. What is a valid error-rate study? For a more objective method, like a drug test, you can test each step in the process by seeing whether it produces accurate results. However, for subjective techniques like fingerprinting, there are not clearly defined and objective steps. The person is the process: an examiner whose mind is a "black box" that reaches judgments based on experience. To test a "black box" examiner you can give such people evidence where the correct answer is known in advance. Ideally, the participants should not know that they are being tested. The samples, whether fingerprint, bite mark, or firearm evidence, should be of realistic difficulty.

Without information about error rates, the PCAST report notes that it is "scientifically meaningless" for a person to say evidence is a "match."[28] If we do not know how often they are wrong or right in reaching such judgments, then we have no way to know what their opinion is worth. For too many forensic techniques those error rate studies had never been done, or the studies that had been done were rigged. For bite mark and footwear comparisons, the scientists who wrote the PCAST report concluded that since no valid studies of error rates have been done, the techniques were not valid. For firearms comparisons, only a single black box study had been done, showing an error rate that could be as high as 1 in 46. This single study had not been published. The authors of the PCAST report concluded firearms comparisons, very commonly used in criminal cases, fall short and are not valid.[29]

FINGERPRINT ERROR RATES

The error rates are perhaps most shocking in fingerprinting, which examiners had claimed for decades was infallible. The PCAST report described how researchers had conducted two properly designed studies of the accuracy of latent fingerprint analysis. That alone is deeply disturbing. It was generous for the report to say that just two studies were enough to permit a technique to be used in court. While neither study is perfect, both found nontrivial error rates. One of the two studies was a larger-scale study supported by the FBI. The second was a smaller study by the Miami-Dade police department. The false positive rates could be as high as 1 in 306 in the FBI study and 1 in 18 in the Miami-Dade study. To be sure, the people participating in the FBI study knew that they were being tested. They knew that it was an important study for the field. They were likely very cautious in their work. Some of the errors that analysts made in these studies may have been clerical errors. Yet in the Miami study, for example, if one leaves out possible clerical errors, the error rate could still be as high as 1 in 73. Perhaps clerical errors should be included, though; they can have grave real-world consequences. We do not know whether the prints used in these studies were realistic or sufficiently challenging, either. We know that other fingerprint examiners may perform differently, based on their training and skill.

These findings still provide a wake-up call. It would shock jurors to hear of either a 1 in 18 or a 1 in 306 error rate. When a public defender in Joplin, Missouri, asked prospective jurors in a 2018 case about fingerprint evidence, they said things like, "I believe fingerprints are 100 percent accurate," and "fingerprints are everything when it comes to a crime scene," and "I mean, it's an identifier . . . We've been taught all our lives that fingerprint is what identifies us, and that it is unique." When asked whether they could consider evidence to the contrary, many responded they could not. One juror said: "I couldn't guarantee that I could put aside the belief that we're talking about, the unique nature of fingerprints . . . I can't."[30] However, I have found that educating jurors about such error rates does make them more reluctant to rely on the evidence. Examiners should admit that errors can occur and describe what we know from the research done so far. Unfortunately, that is not what examiners say in court; far from it.

FALSE NEGATIVES AND INCONCLUSIVES

There is more than one type of error. The reports and the studies have tended to focus only on false positive errors: falsely connecting evidence to the wrong source. Those errors are very serious in criminal cases: a false positive can cause a wrongful conviction. The analysts in Brandon Mayfield's case made false positive errors. However, there are also false negative errors: incorrectly failing to connect evidence that did in fact come from a source. False negative errors are extremely important too: they can cause the guilty to go free.

False negative errors may be far more common than false positives, and yet those error rates are often not studied or shared. The same FBI study on fingerprinting reported far higher rates of false negatives than false positives. That study reported how five examiners in the study made false positive errors, but that a massive *85 percent* of the 169 examiners made at least one false negative error. The study noted that examiners "operate in a culture where false positive errors are seen as more serious errors than false negatives."[31] If false negatives are a much greater problem in real labs, as they are in studies, it could mean that untold thousands of guilty culprits are not identified in real cases. We have no idea how often this happens.

Sometimes analysts also call the evidence "inconclusive" after they find it to be not of sufficient quality to reach a conclusion. They may call it "no value" evidence at the outset if it cannot be further analyzed. An inconclusive determination may be made only after the evidence is at first deemed suitable for comparison. In studies, it can be known in advance that all of the material is in fact of sufficient quality. An Ames Laboratory study of firearms errors found a false positive error rate of only 1.01 percent, but if one includes inconclusive errors, the error rate increased dramatically to 34.76 percent.[32] On one item in the FBI fingerprint study, the *majority* of the examiners found a print inconclusive. This too amounts to a huge error rate.

What if a child comes home and complains bitterly about failing a test, and insists instead that the teacher should have given a perfect score? After all, the child explains, none of the answers could possibly be wrong, because not one of the questions was answered. I would give a student 0 percent rather than 100 percent, if no question is answered. However, some experts maintain that on forensic studies, inconclusive errors should not be counted. The scientists who authored the PCAST report took that approach in part; they did not count inconclusive answers as errors, although they eliminated such answers entirely. Inconclusive errors may seem like safe choices, since they do not result in connecting evidence to the wrong person, but they really matter. After all, these were wrong answers to questions that had correct answers. In real cases, the same people who call evidence "inconclusive" in a study may make errors of other types, including false positives, when the experts do not know that they are being tested and do not decide "not to decide," as Itiel E. Dror and Glenn Langenburg put it.[33] Inconclusive errors should be studied far more carefully.

Analysts far more commonly decide evidence is of "no value" and decide not to conduct a comparison. When my colleagues and I examined fingerprint data from the Houston Forensic Science Center, we found the most common conclusion reached was to determine that prints were not of sufficient quality to compare.[34] Police officers often lift poor-quality prints. Seeing so many low-quality prints, however, can cause examiners to miss important information. It can be a serious error to conclude that evidence is of no value. In fact, the evidence might point to guilt, or the innocence of a suspect. A jury should hear what the chance is that evidence was incorrectly deemed to be of no value or inconclusive.

REPEATABLE AND REPRODUCIBLE

Not just accuracy in hit rates, but also repeatability and reproducibility, are hallmarks of sound science. Regarding repeatability, even if an examiner reaches a definitive answer in a case, we need to know how often the same examiner would reach the same answer if they did the work again. For many forensic methods, we do not know how consistent an examiner is. The authors of the FBI fingerprint study followed up by giving seventy-nine of the same examiners the same prints seven months later. In about 10 percent of cases, examiners changed the features and the number of features they marked. Some reached different conclusions; most changed their answers to "inconclusive." Some caught errors they made the first time, but 30 percent of false negative errors were repeated.[35] Regarding reproducibility, we know from studies like the FBI study that different examiners can and do reach different conclusions. Both repeatability and reproducibility must be measured for all forensic disciplines.

TELL JURORS THE ERROR RATES

People want to know how good forensic evidence really is. In studies of thousands of jury- eligible adults, I have found time and time again that error rates really matter. We need to tell people about these error rates. For example, law professor and psychologist Gregory Mitchell and I gave six hundred mock jurors eleven different fingerprint conclusions, with phrases like "individualized" and "reasonable degree of scientific certainty" and "made by the same individual" and "the defendant was the source." We found no differences in conviction votes among the jurors who heard each of the different conclusions.[36] Whether the expert used overstated or mild conclusion language did not matter. We followed up with a second study, where the fingerprint examiner admitted that there is a possibility of error: "recent studies have found that fingerprint examiners do sometimes make mistakes about the source of a fingerprint found at a crime scene." The expert admitted: "It is possible that the defendant was not the source of the print found at the scene of this robbery." After hearing that concession of fallibility, jurors gave markedly less weight to the evidence. Psychologist Jay Koehler similarly found that for shoeprint comparison testimony, jurors gave less weight to the evidence when they heard about an error rate.[37] However, telling jurors about error rates does not mean that they will refuse to convict. In a study that I worked on with psychologists Rebecca Grady and William Crozier, we gave the two upperbound fingerprint error rates from studies, 1 in 18 and 1 in 306, to many hundreds of people recruited online. These mock jurors gave less weight to the evidence when the judges disclosed error rate information to them. To be sure, most jurors would still convict, even after hearing about more concrete error rates. Moreover, for a novel (and untested) type of digital voice comparison, hearing the same error rate information did not affect jurors, perhaps because they were already skeptical of the evidence.[38]

A DEFENSE EXPERT

It can make a powerful difference in real cases, and not just in studies, for the jury to hear about error rates for evidence like fingerprint comparisons. In 2016, professor Simon Cole testified in a California trial, and although he studies science and technology, he does not claim to be a trained fingerprint examiner. Instead, he testifies about the methods and assumptions underlying fingerprint evidence. At trial, Cole described how when he began to study fingerprinting, he was surprised to find there were "no scientific studies that had measured the accuracy of how often fingerprint examiners are right and wrong when they reach conclusions."[39] In the years since, the scientific community has come to understand how important those fundamental questions are. At this trial Cole explained to the jury that he had been "arguing for a long time," including in a book examining the history of fingerprinting, that one can never made a definitive conclusion. Instead, "all these official reports and other scientists and scholars agree" now that one must measure error rates.

Cole told the jury that "the claim that you can determine . . . with absolute certainty that one single person is the source of a latent print isn't really a scientifically-supportable claim."[40] After all, "in any kind of scientific process there's some probability that you're right and there's some probability that you're wrong." He added, "It may be small, the probability that you're wrong, but it's always still there and should be acknowledged in reporting your findings." Yet when the prosecutor asked him, "Would you agree that you have no opinion about the fingerprints in this particular case?" Cole agreed.[41] His testimony was about the technique of fingerprinting, not the reliability of the work done in the case. He had not examined the prints in the case.

After the trial concluded and the jurors deliberated, the jury acquitted the defendant.

STATISTICS AND FINGERPRINTS

"Why has nothing changed in the past 30 years. Why do we still not have a tool?" asked Henry Swofford, a young, statistically savvy chief of the U. S. Army Criminal Investigation Laboratory's fingerprint branch, who made it his mission to make fingerprint work more quantitative.[42] Swofford was willing to do something that no crime lab has done: replace old-fashioned "match" testimony with a big data solution.

What if methods like fingerprinting were done objectively, or even by a computer? "It is a hard problem to solve," says statistician Karen Kafadar.[43] In February 2018 something remarkable occurred in a case involving fingerprint evidence at a military trial at the Fort Huachuca military base in Arizona. The examiner said the prints had "corresponding ridge detail," but then went further, stating the probability of observing this amount of correspondence is greater when impressions are made by the same source. There was nothing unusual about saying that. Next, the fingerprint examiner did something radical: the analyst did not declare an "identification." Instead, the examiner gave the jury a number, reflecting the probability of seeing a degree of correspondence.[44] In other words, the strength of the fingerprint comparison was presented to the jury as a matter of degrees, not as an absolute. After over a hundred years of fingerprinting, this examiner used numbers rather than words like "identification." It was a long time in coming. The examiner used a new software program created by Swofford. Swofford worked with Kafadar and other statisticians, publishing a peer-reviewed validation study. Swofford aimed to revolutionize fingerprinting—and maybe all of forensics. Rather than claim 100 percent certainty, the Army crime lab issued a new policy requiring all examiners to use software to provide a probability. Others proposed ways of using statistical modeling for fingerprinting, but no lab had previously used it in practice, much less as a standard policy. That is why that military trial in Arizona was such a special event.

This software does not conduct a fingerprint comparison. A human examiner marks the fingerprint and concludes that it is a "hit." The program can only offer information about the strength of the hit. In addition, the program does not tell you how common or rare any particular combinations of features on a fingerprint might be. The software relies on degrees of correspondence within a database of two thousand prints known to match, and a database of two thousand prints known not to match. It is a start, though, and the program is not a black box: Swofford made it available for free and online. Swofford hopes this program will encourage other vendors, like the companies that market fingerprint database software, to improve on it. "I want to strengthen the foundations of our science," he explains.[45]

JURORS AND STATISTICS

One objection to bringing more data into forensics might be that it is too complicated for jurors to understand. Most people do not have a deep understanding of probabilities or statistics. One does not need any statistics training to serve on a jury, however: jurors are supposed to represent the entire community.

We already present DNA results to jurors using probabilities, and there is evidence that jurors can misunderstand the evidence. An analyst will tell the jury how many people in the population could randomly be expected to have the same combination of genetic markers. Studies have found that when jurors are told that a DNA result could be shared by one in hundreds of millions or billions of people, their eyes glaze over. After hearing such large numbers, people just assume the DNA came from the defendant.[46] That is a serious mistake, and it is one that lawyers have sometimes encouraged. For example, in an Ohio case, the prosecutor asked: "Are you saying that the probability that the DNA that was found in the question samples came from anyone else . . . is one in 7,000,000?" The analyst answered, "Yes, approximately."[47] Professors William Thompson and Edward Schumann termed this the "prosecutor's fallacy," because prosecutors have had a tendency to argue that evidence shows that the defendant was in fact the source.[48] DNA evidence cannot show the probability that the evidence came from a source. It can only show how rare or common a set of genetic characteristics are in the population.

For fingerprint evidence, I wondered whether jurors could understand statistical conclusions using Swofford's software. Law professor Gregory Mitchell, psychologist Nicholas Scurich, and I found people can and do distinguish between strong and weak conclusions presented using that software. Rather than an all-or-nothing fingerprint conclusion, statistics give us a more nuanced picture. No other labs have so far adopted such methods. At a conference I organized in spring 2018, the lawyer for a major crime lab stood up after Swofford described his approach. He asked: "Do you mean, even if there is a really good match, you still give the jury a number?" Swofford responded, yes, that is precisely the point. The lab lawyer shook his head, incredulous, and sat down.

ERROR RATES IN COURT

The solution is simple: if the error rates are unknown and untested, which is true for many forensic techniques, then the evidence should not be allowed in court. If error rates are known and they are significant, then the forensics should not be allowed. If error rates are known and not too high, then the expert should disclose them in court, and we can judge the evidence more reasonably.

Most forensic examiners still do not provide this type of information when they testify. In early 2019 the U. S. Department of Justice explained that there was no need to require experts to say anything about error rates. Why? Ted Hunt, a former Kansas City prosecutor and senior advisor to the DOJ on forensic policy, explained that an examiner makes a "source identification," based on skill and experience.[49] The examiner does not base the decision on statistics but rather on training and competence. Hunt claimed the "current consensus of scientific thought" does not require an expert to admit anything about error. Besides, there are many steps to a forensic process, and each step can go wrong. In a way, Hunt was right. The studies do not capture all of the ways that errors happen in real cases, with examiners of varying skill, evidence of varying quality, and in cases that vary in their difficulty. Error rates are probably far higher than the few existing studies would suggest. In the next chapter, I turn to the hunt to unpack additional ways that forensic errors happen in real cases.

5 Overstatement

The tragedy that gave rise to perhaps the biggest scandal in American forensics began at the Watergate complex in Washington, DC, almost exactly nine years after the bungled break-in at the Democratic National Committee headquarters ordered by President Richard Nixon. On June 22, 1981, leaving work at the Watergate, a twenty-one-year-old student at Georgetown University never returned home. Coworkers formed a search party and found her body on Rock Creek. She had five bullet wounds in her head, her purse lay nearby with its contents untouched, and police found evidence of a rape. The police had no leads—but found a single hair on the body that did not appear to belong to the victim. The murder remained unsolved for months, until an informant called and claimed a $50 tip for offering a name: Donald Eugene Gates. The informant collected $1,300 from the police Crime Solvers account for recounting that while he and Gates were drinking and "a little high," Gates opened up and told him that a couple of days earlier he had gone on "a hell of a caper." He tried to rob a "pretty white girl" but, when she resisted, he raped her. Then "after it dawned on him what he had done, he shot her" and left her "cut and dry" in the park. In return, the prosecutors dropped a string of shoplifting and larceny cases the informant faced.[1] Gates had been arrested for

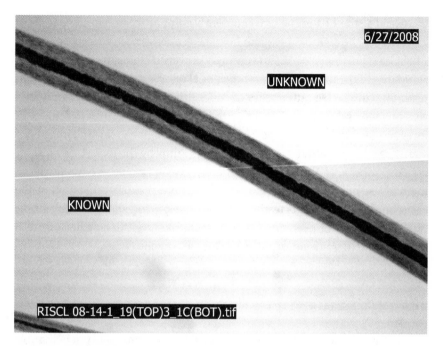

6/27/2008

UNKNOWN

KNOWN

RISCL 08-14-1_19(TOP)3_1C(BOT).tif

Example of trace hair under microscope.

failing to appear in court—and police required him to give a sample of his hair when he was booked. Based on the informant testimony and a hair comparison, Gates was convicted of murder.

Fast-forward twenty-five years after this sensational murder investigation, and Gates still maintained that he was innocent, that the forensics were all wrong, and that he needed legal help. Sandra Levick worked at the Public Defender Service in Washington, DC, when Gates's case reached her desk. Sandra no longer did regular criminal trials. As the chief lawyer for the four-person Special Litigation Division, Levick worked on the X-files of a public defender's office—unusual cases raising systemic issues, like challenges to broad practices, and technical issues relating to forensic science. Levick began to focus on the single crime scene hair (see photo).

Levick's personal crash-course in microscopic hair comparison would unravel a national scandal: the Watergate of American forensics. In this chapter I will describe how the self-proclaimed best forensics examiners in the world at the FBI crime lab confidently compared hairs in thousands of cases across the country. I explain how these microscopic hair comparisons work; how unsupported their seemingly powerful claims were, even by the standards of the time; and how the scandal of overstatement in courtroom testimony unraveled, after years of concealment, only because tough lawyers pushed and pushed. I describe three broad types of overstatement in forensic conclusions: unsupported conclusion language; false claims about statistics and probabilities; and improper claims by the expert about their own experience. In the ensuing FBI audit, lawyers would eventually document abuse of courtroom testimony on a grand scale, in almost all of the cases in which FBI agents testified. For decades, no one had paid any attention to a culture of overstated and unscientific forensic conclusions, at a terrible cost, to innocent people like Donald Eugene Gates.

THE BEST IN THE WORLD

One unsavory informant's story about a "caper" was probably not believable enough to convict someone of murder, so at Gates's trial, the prosecutors brought in a scientist from the most eminent crime lab in the country—perhaps the entire world. FBI special agent Michael Malone told the jury that it was "highly unlikely" that the hair found on the victim could have come from anyone other than Gates. Malone had worked in the Hair and Fibers Unit at the FBI crime lab beginning in 1974.[2] The FBI crime lab carries great weight. FBI director J. Edgar Hoover founded the FBI crime lab in 1932, and in its early days it consisted of a single room.[3] The FBI Technical Crime Laboratory began to train agents to examine latent fingerprints, handwriting, and ballistic evidence. The lab garnered early fame when analysts performed high-profile work in the Charles Lindbergh kidnapping case. In time, the FBI lab became the largest crime lab in the country and the center of innovation and training on forensics in the United States. The FBI facility in Quantico, Virginia, is one of the largest and most prestigious crime labs in the world, with about five hundred agents working full time. The FBI prides itself on setting the standard for forensic practice.

In his own telling, even among the big-league players at the FBI lab, Malone was a star. Malone described his extensive experience with hair evidence. "The whole time I was in the lab I got nothing but exceptional and superior ratings," Malone told reporters in 2001. "This is going to sound like bragging, but we were the best in the world for hairs."[4] Malone had a biology degree and taught high school science for two years. He joined the FBI not as a scientist but as a field investigator. After four years of that work, in 1974 he joined the lab as a hair and fiber analyst. His title, Special Agent, refers to an investigative agent, as opposed to a scientist.[5]

UNDER A MICROSCOPE

The fictional detective Sherlock Holmes put it this way: "It has long been an axiom of mine that the little things are infinitely the most important."[6] Detective fiction may have helped to inspire the birth of crime labs like the FBI lab, an early pioneer in using microscopes to study the little things, like hairs, that might connect to a culprit. Unless a person wears a cafeteria-style hairnet or is bald, it is hard to avoid shedding hairs. Human and animal hairs easily stick to objects and can be transferred to and from clothing. Not only can a culprit leave hairs behind on clothing or furniture, but a culprit can pick up hairs from a victim or from a pet without realizing it. Hairs are also resilient. They grow from skin cells that become filled with filaments of a waterproof protein called keratin, which makes up our hair, nails, and covers our skin.

A hair comparison is very much like what it sounds. The simple version of the process is as follows: an expert looks at hairs carefully and then compares them under a microscope. First, the analyst looks at the crime scene hairs with the naked eye. The analyst looks for features like the color and form of the hair shaft—is it straight, wavy, curved, or kinky? And how thick is the hair shaft—is it fine or medium or coarse? We can tell with the naked eye whether hairs are curly or straight, dark or reddish or light, long or short, or dyed or cut in distinctive ways.

Next, the hairs are mounted on slides to view under a microscope. The examiner tries to identify what part of the body the crime scene hairs might have come from. A suspect then gives hair samples from the relevant area of their body. Police do not give an arrestee a choice in the matter. Ideally, if head hairs are being compared, then police take fifty head hairs from the suspect's scalp. If pubic hairs are being compared, then ideally twenty-five hairs are taken by pulling and combing. Examiners pluck such a large set of hairs because the hairs on our body are so different from each other. Even within, say, our head hair, there is an enormous amount of variation. From the crime scene, however, examiners may not have many hairs to compare this large group of samples to; they may have no more than a single hair.

Under the microscope, the examiner is looking first for "major characteristics." These can include the color (white, black, blonde, brown, red, etc.), and how the hair pigment is distributed; it can be streaked, or clumped, or patchy. The examiner looks at whether the hair is dyed, bleached, or permed. The hollow interior of a hair, called the medulla, can be translucent or fragmented, or continuous along the shaft. The examiner looks at the form of the hair (arced, crimped, curly, straight, wavy).

The examiner also looks for secondary characteristics. Here the terminology gets obscure. The examiner looks at whether the "cuticular margin," or the outmost part of the hair shaft, is cracked, looped, smooth, or serrated. The examiner looks at the size of the pigment (coarse, fine, or medium). The examiner looks at the tip of the hair, and whether it is cut, frayed, split, or tapered. The examiner measures the diameter of the hair shaft. The examiner may note the cross-sectional shape of hair: the shape of the shaft when cut at a right angle. The examiner may note the "cortical fusi" or small spaces between cells in a hair shaft. There is no one measurement the examiner is focusing on. There is no set number of characteristics they must find. The examiner is just generally looking at the group of hairs from the suspect and then the crime scene hair or hairs to make a comparison.

Because of the potential importance of hair evidence, the FBI, as the standard setter in forensics, gathered together top scientists from around the world in 1984 to discuss methods and to produce a handbook on hair evidence. The big question: Is it possible to tell whether hairs came from a particular individual? The scientists gathered by the FBI concluded that the answer is no. Microscopic hair examination is "[n]ot positive evidence."[7] The FBI field manual from the late 1970s said the same thing: hair comparison is "not a positive means of identification."[8] We do not know how common or rare it is to have similarities in microscopic features of hair. There was and is no standard for finding sets of hairs similar. No one can say for sure.[9] A hair comparison might narrow the pool of people since it might definitely exclude a person, but to include a person, one cannot say whether a million or a thousand or a hundred other people might also have hairs that look similar. There are no databases. In fact, the FBI admitted that even the most qualified examiners may disagree about whether hairs could come from the same source. The 1985 International Symposium on Forensic Hair Comparisons that the FBI convened adopted these as standards for the field. Examiners can say that hairs are "consistent," but nothing more. Hair evidence is "could-be evidence," as one top examiner has put it.[10] One leading forensic science handbook put it well: to exclude suspects, "hair is a rather good form of evidence." After all, "If the evidence hair is blond, straight, and 12 inches long, it may be emphatically eliminated as having originated from a person whose exemplar hair is black, curly, and two inches long." As evidence of guilt, however, "hair is a miserable form of evidence."[11]

HAIR ON THE STAND

On the stand at Donald Eugene Gates's trial, Special Agent Malone exuded confidence, as he overstated the evidence in several ways. First, he described his years of work. He had conducted about ten thousand hair examinations over eight years, but only twice had he seen hairs from different people that he could not tell apart. This implied that his own personal error rate was extremely low. He went further. It was "highly likely" that the hairs came from Gates. There was no support for that statement, either. Finally, he concluded the hairs were "microscopically indistinguishable."[12] This overstated testimony illustrates three ways forensic experts have overstated conclusions to mislead jurors: false probability conclusions, flawed statistics, and misleading claims based on experience.

The Gates case involved a claim that the hairs were "microscopically indistinguishable." This type of conclusion language is as common as it is unsupported. Indeed, Sandra Levick soon found other hair cases in Washington, DC, in which FBI agents overstated conclusions. Santae Tribble was convicted of murder in Washington, DC, in 1980 based on a hair comparison. The agent testified that the crime scene hairs "matched in all microscopic characteristics with the head hair samples submitted to me from Santae Tribble." The term "match" could imply that the hair in fact came from Tribble and could not have come from anyone else.

In cases of innocent people, other experts reached such categorical conclusions, using a variety of terms such as "identification," "individualized," or "match." This type of overstatement was, years later, singled out by the FBI as a "type one" error, in which the expert inappropriately claims that evidence can be associated with a specific individual to the exclusion of all others.[13] The expert should instead admit that hair comparisons cannot be used to make a positive identification.

The culture in many forensic disciplines was that if the evidence was good enough, you were required to "call it." Expressing any doubt at all, much less admitting that one cannot ever make a positive identification, was frowned upon. As a forensic analyst friend told me, supervisors might tell examiners who seemed hesitant: "You are supposed to be an *expert*. Stick to your guns. Make an identification." In many disciplines, written guidelines called for aggressive conclusions in testimony. Training encouraged analysts to focus on their credentials, the general methods they follow, and a bare conclusion of an identification. Most of the time, defense lawyers would not question or follow up, so no more need be said. Traditional expert testimony by someone like Malone could be summed up, as my forensic analyst friend puts it, like this: "I am a serious expert. I follow scientific methods. I ID'ed him. The end."

FAULTY STATISTICS AND PROBABILITIES

Forensic experts have exaggerated conclusions by making up statistics out of whole cloth. In Timothy Durham's case, an analyst at the Tulsa Police Laboratory testified that the particular reddish-yellow hue of his hair and the crime scene hair were only found in "about 5 percent of the population." That number was pulled out of the air. When an expert presents a DNA test result to the jury, well-grounded statistics can be used, because DNA is based on population data. In disciplines like hair or fingerprint comparisons, there is no such data and there are no statistics. However, in case after case, I have read analysts offering made-up statistics that were not based on any underlying data. When Peter Neufeld and I studied trial transcripts of persons later exonerated by DNA evidence, microscopic hair comparison analysis played a role in 65 of the 137 trials that we examined.[14] Sometimes, the experts instead offered the jury a probability using words, not numbers. The expert says, as the agent did in the Gates case, that it is "highly unlikely" that the evidence came from anyone else. Unfortunately, in many of the cases of innocent people who were later exonerated by DNA, the analysts similarly made up probabilities, saying that it was "very likely" from the same source or that the features were "rare." The science does not permit an expert to say whether ten, a hundred, or a million other people might have the same characteristics. The FBI would later call this type of overstatement a "type two" error.

OVERSTATING EXPERIENCE

In the Gates case, Malone provided the jurors with a third type of overstatement by pontificating about his ten thousand hair examinations over eight years. If he had been more up front with the jurors, he would have admitted that the hairs he was given in the lab should have been easy to tell apart, because he knew they in fact came from different people. In sexual assault cases, the analyst often knows in advance that the hairs came from a female victim and a male suspect. The FBI would later call such experience-based claims "type three" errors. Today, the Department of Justice has forbidden experts in federal cases from using years of experience or numbers of cases to bolster their expertise.

At the time, however, such claims were troublingly common. For example, in the well-known case of the Exonerated Five, wrongly convicted of the 1989 attack on a jogger in Central Park, a detective from the New York City Police Department told the jury that he had "in fact looked at thousands of standards and haven't seen two that matched exactly."[15] FBI agents similarly testified regularly in court that their experience showed how reliable their work was. In Santae Tribble's case, the FBI agent explained that "[o]nly on very rare occasions" had he ever seen that the hairs of two different people had the same microscopic characteristics. In a case in Illinois, an FBI special agent claimed that he compared evidence samples to his own hair "in excess of 25,000 hair examinations, and I have yet to find either a head hair or a pubic hair that matches my own."[16] In Tennessee, a special agent testified in a capital case that "there is only one chance out of 4,500 or 5,000 that the unknown hair came from a different individual."[17] In Indiana, an FBI agent testified he had failed to distinguish between different people only once in 1,500 cases.[18] The agent said that "it was possible, though extremely rare, for someone else to have hair that would be indistinguishable from that of the defendant."[19]

Nor did judges step in to put a stop to such overstated testimony. In fact, while judges are supposed to exclude testimony that is wholly unreliable, as I will describe in chapter 8, they typically did not view questioning the conclusion of an expert on the stand as part of their job. Their job was to decide whether the expert was using a reliable method, not whether the expert was overstating findings or making unscientific assertions on the stand.

UNETHICAL

Not only is some expert testimony overstated and unscientific, it should also be considered unethical. It is troubling that no single ethical code applies to all practicing forensic analysts in the United States. However, professional groups have set out ethical codes that shed light on problematic testimony such as the kinds discussed here, including the American Board of Criminalists (ABC) and the American Academy of Forensic Sciences (AAFS). As a general matter, these codes ask analysts to conduct an independent evaluation of evidence and offer truthful and nonmisleading testimony in court. The ABC Code of Ethics asks that all analysts render opinions "only to the extent justified" by the evidence, and present their testimony "in a clear, straightforward manner." The AAFS Code forbids a member from "materially misrepresenting" the "data or scientific principles upon which an expert opinion or conclusion is based." The AAFS Guidelines add: "Unlike attorneys, forensic scientists are not adversaries. They take an oath in court to tell the whole truth. They should make every effort to uphold that oath."[20] If only such rules were enforced against the experts that testified in so many innocent people's cases.

GATES IS CONVICTED

After hearing the overstated hair evidence, the jury sentenced Donald Eugene Gates to twenty years to life for armed rape, murder, and carrying a pistol without a license. He tried to get a DNA test in 1988, but the technology was new and the results were inconclusive. Over twenty years later, Sandra Levick filed a request for DNA, and battled in court for two years, as prosecutors argued about the procedures to be followed, and emphasized there was no reason for quick action. "I just don't think you can ignore the fact that he comes before the Court as a person who was convicted with all of the evidence before the Court," and this evidence, after all, included "a microscopically indistinguishable pubic hair."[21] The DNA tests went forward, and in 2009 the results cleared Gates. On December 15, 2009, Gates was released after twenty-eight years in prison. He walked out with nothing but $75 and a bus ticket. Levick began to ask new questions about how reliable hair evidence really was.

THE WHISTLEBLOWER AND THE INSPECTOR

In the mid-1990s a whistleblower named Frederic Whitehurst at the FBI complained of errors and overstatement at the lab. An investigation began in 1995, "after reports that sloppy work by examiners at the FBI lab was producing unreliable forensic evidence in court trials."[22] Whitehurst said colleagues engaged in perjury and even fabrication of evidence, including in some of the highest-profile cases, like the World Trade Center bombing and an attempted assassination of former president George H. W. Bush. Whitehurst eventually sent over two hundred letters to the Office of the Inspector General of the Department of Justice, led by Michael Bromwich. In response, Bromwich conducted an inquiry into the allegations. In April 1997 the inspector general released a massive 517-page report, which did not agree with some of the "hyperbole" in Whitehurst's allegations but found "significant problems" in both cases and practices at the lab.

Meanwhile, Sandra Levick wanted to know how many other people had been convicted based on problematic FBI hair testimony. When Donald Gates walked out of prison, exonerated by DNA testing, the response by the government was that the mistaken hair analysis was a one-off. Levick's motion, asking that the judge vacate Gates's conviction, included a bombshell: his case may not have been an isolated example at all. In the 1990s, Bromwich's report had identified Malone as one of seven FBI agents under investigation.[23] The report found Malone "falsely testified" before a judicial committee investigating bribery by a judge, including by claiming to have conducted a forensic test that he did not personally conduct and which was "outside his expertise."[24] Turning to Malone's testimony about hair, the investigation team found 96 percent of Malone's cases were "problematic." His lab notes were "in pencil and not dated." He made statements that "had no scientific basis." Yet Malone continued to work at the FBI as a contractor, even after he retired in 1999.[25]

How did the FBI lab assure quality in its forensics work during this time? Before 1992 there was "no formal quality assurance plan" for the FBI lab. Instead, agents largely had on-the-job training.[26] By the mid-1990s the lab pushed for accreditation and other types of controls on the quality of casework. Based on the systematic problems identified, however, in the 1997 report and a follow-up 1998 report, the FBI made changes.[27] And the Department of Justice set up a task force to review cases that might have been affected by these problems. It was a nine-year effort, and it ended in 2004.

An independent scientist visiting the FBI lab at Quantico, in December 2003, reviewed Gates's case as part of the task force. The scientist spent forty-five minutes examining the case. It took seven and a half months for the scientists to get to the case, and this was many years after the inquiry had begun.[28] The report noted: "The [lab report] results are not adequately documented in the [bench] notes." In addition, the "notes are not dated and are in pencil instead of ink. Abbreviations are used that are hard to interpret."[29] The ready conclusion was that the analysis was not adequately documented and there was no evidence that appropriate work was done.

Gates had never been told of this as he languished in prison. Indeed, Levick first learned about this only after working on Gates's case for years. Moreover, in 2002 the DOJ raised questions about whether others were "as sloppy as Malone," but while the issue "ha[d] been raised with the FBI" it had not been "resolved to date." When Levick asked for an inquiry, the federal prosecutors responded by arguing that this was an isolated problem and that the agent in the case may have been a bad apple, but there was no problem with the barrel. There was "no legal and scientific basis for conducting such a 'massive' audit." The prosecutors added that it is just a "misconception" that hair evidence is "pseudo-science."[30] The DC Superior Court judge in Gates's case, Fred Ugast, was shocked that this could happen. Judge Ugast asked for a full investigation, not just into Malone's cases but into other cases in DC that might have been affected.

SANTAE TRIBBLE

Sandra Levick soon learned that the problem extended far beyond one FBI agent and one innocent man. In the cases of Santae Tribble and Kirk Odom, different FBI agents testified, but in a similarly overstated manner. A Diamond Cab driver, returning home at 3 a.m. after a taxi-driving shift, was robbed and shot on his own doorstep by a man wearing a stocking mask. His wife saw the murder from inside her house. Police used a tracking dog to search the neighborhood, and the dog found the stocking a block away. In the stocking they found thirteen hairs. One hair, the FBI analyst concluded, belonged to Tribble.

At a three-day trial, Tribble maintained his innocence. He was seventeen years old, and said he and his girlfriend and brother were all at a birthday party that night and were fast asleep by 3 a.m. Tribble was paroled in 2003, still maintaining his innocence, after twenty-three years in prison. Nine years later, DNA tests exonerated him. A different hair analyst, an experienced expert who spent fifteen years at the FBI lab and was now with the DC police, reexamined the hairs. He found one was from a Caucasian person and the others included head and limb hairs. Then a private lab did DNA tests. In fact, the hairs belonged to three other people—and a dog. "Such is the true state of hair microscopy," Levick said, that "two FBI-trained analysts . . . could not even distinguish human hairs from canine hairs."

KIRK ODOM

Kirk Odom had yet another FBI agent testify at his trial in spring 1981. Odom was accused of breaking into a woman's house and raping her. Odom remembered well what he had been doing that night: he was at home, with his mother, waiting for his sister to return from the hospital with a newborn baby. At trial the jury didn't believe the alibi.[31] He was nineteen and sentenced to twenty to sixty-six years.

The FBI agent told the jury that the hair was "microscopically like" Odom's. He had performed thousands of examinations of hair evidence, and almost always could distinguish between hair samples. On appeal, the government said, "it is a very rare phenomenon; only eight or ten times in the past ten years, while performing thousands of analyses," that an FBI agent could not "distinguish even microscopically between two or three known samples."

Odom kept writing letters proclaiming his innocence. In 2010 Odom had completed his sentence and was working doing HVAC repair, while still on lifetime parole as a convicted sex offender, and he sought an exoneration. Levick decided to seek a DNA testing. She located the victim's bedsheets, robe, and the hair, all of which fortunately was still preserved. In 2012 DNA tests by two laboratories, one selected by the defense and one by the prosecutors, concluded that the hair could not have come from Odom.

IN THE DARK

Dozens of boxes and over ten thousand pages of documents collected by Michael Bromwich and his investigators made their way to Spencer Hsu, a journalist at the *Washington Post*. Hsu found that less than half of the time, prosecutors had told the defense about the flaws in the hair evidence. In 2002 the DOJ sent out letters to prosecutors in cases with flawed hair testimony, but Donald Gates's lawyer had never heard anything about that. The DOJ had identified sixty-four people on death row whose cases had flawed hair testimony. The task force never notified the authorities in the cases—so, executions proceeded. Texas officials executed

Benjamin Boyle after the 1997 report, but before the task force got to his case. The hair testimony in his case was "scientifically unsupportable," "overstated," and it played a crucial role in his conviction.[32] Other death row inmates were executed or died of natural causes in prison. The project languished for over eight years and case reviews either did not occur, or when they did, the prosecutors rarely disclosed errors to the defense.

Michael Bromwich later said: "It is deeply troubling that after going through so much time and trouble to identify problematic conduct by FBI forensic analysts the DOJ Task Force apparently failed to follow through and ensure that defense counsel was notified in every single case." The DOJ itself later reviewed the task force efforts and said that there were "serious deficiencies."[33]

Fortunately, the lawyers at the Public Defender Service did not give up. "December 18, 2010 will mark the one-year anniversary of Mr. Gates' exoneration. That date should not pass without action by this Court." Sandra Levick asked for a full audit of all cases involving FBI hair comparisons, at least in federal cases and in serious crimes. After the two additional DNA exonerations, the U. S. attorney and the FBI agreed to review not just the work of the examiners in those particular cases but also the work of all convictions based on hair analysis. Meanwhile, the prosecutors retested the evidence from the Rock Creek murder that sent Gates to prison. In 2012 they obtained a hit on the true culprit: a janitor who worked in the Watergate complex and who had died years earlier. The government also agreed to provide free DNA testing and waive any procedural barriers to re-litigating cases in post-conviction proceedings. These steps set an important template for future responses to mass forensics errors.

TESTIMONIAL OVERSTATEMENT

The FBI finally agreed to conduct a massive audit of its old cases with hair testimony, one of the largest in history. The FBI also opened its doors to outside collaborators: the Innocence Project and the National Association of Criminal Defense Lawyers. In March 2015, after the FBI analyzed five hundred cases, it announced that "at least 90 percent" of trial transcripts contained erroneous statements. The FBI noted that defendants in at least 35 of the cases had received the death penalty, and errors were identified in 33 of those cases. Nine had already been executed and five died of other causes on death row. The FBI also announced that 26 of 28 agents either gave testimony or submitted lab reports with erroneous statements.

In response to the FBI and DOJ audit, many other states, including Florida, Massachusetts, New York, North Carolina, Texas, and Virginia, among others, began to review cases that involved hair analysis. Many more states need to do the same. The FBI also expanded its review beyond cases in which trial testimony was given to cases where there was a guilty plea. Yet finding records in old cases is a challenge. In Virginia, the Department of Forensic Services asked for help in locating any old cases with testimony about hair evidence. The lab had no way of identifying old cases; it had no database of its analysts' work going back that far. By combing legal rulings and news reports and contacting public defenders and criminal lawyers' groups, my colleagues and I found just twelve trial records with hair evidence. Several had erroneous testimony. The lab sent out letters to lawyers in those cases, notifying them of this finding. But there were likely hundreds if not thousands of cases in the 1980s and 1990s that had similar testimony.

In the end, the FBI reviewed 2,900 cases. The FBI team concluded that 96 percent of those cases had flawed hair testimony, including 33 of 35 death penalty cases. They called it testimonial overstatement. That was an understatement. The FBI still emphasized: "It's important to note that microscopic hair comparison analysis is a valid scientific technique still conducted by the FBI Laboratory."[34] It continues to be conducted by the FBI and other laboratories, hopefully mostly as a preliminary exam before conducting a DNA test. But a mitochondrial DNA test is not always possible. And similar comparisons are done on fibers, like from cloth or carpet, which are not human or animal hair, and cannot be DNA tested.

The FBI also asked an outside risk management company to do a root cause analysis of what went wrong at the FBI. Their report emphasized that the FBI hair and fibers experts should have known that their testimony was not supported by science. The company found that FBI lab supervisors did not take any leadership role in addressing testimony errors. They did not document standards that were already in place for hair testimony, either, and they did not ensure that examiners were trained or prepared for how to appropriately testify. The firm uncovered internal FBI memos that cautioned against using terms like "completely indistinguishable" and "perfectly matched," but which reviewed unscientific testimony and found that there was "no obvious error or misrepresentation." Prosecutors sometimes prompted the unscientific testimony, and put improper words in the examiners' mouths. This review of the testimony, however, found that the vast majority of this testimony came from the FBI examiners themselves, with only about 10 percent consisting of prosecutors asking prompting questions, such as by asking the examiner to say whether the hairs were a "match" or "exactly the same." This was mostly an FBI problem. In general, examiners were basically told to use their "best judgment" when they testified in court. Moreover, these examiners believed they were the "world's leading organization" in hair analysis.[35]

In response to these problems, in 2016 the Department of Justice also announced that it would conduct a "stress test" to assess reliability of forensic work at the FBI crime lab. The focus would be on how well scientific evidence was being communicated in court, given the findings of the hair audit that the evidence "wasn't always properly communicated to juries" in the past. That stress test never occurred.

NO STANDARDS FOR TESTIMONY

Perhaps still more troubling is that testimony by examiners at the hair and fiber unit at the FBI was entirely typical, and for decades there generally have been no standards for what forensic examiners should say in court. In response to these errors, the Department of Justice has slowly released rules for testimony. In 2017 the DOJ released model standards for testimony about fingerprints. They addressed all three types of overstatement discussed in the FBI review of hair cases. They rejected statements of "100% level of certainty" or claims of a zero percent error rate. The examiner should not tout the number of cases they have handled as a way to show they are accurate, or use terms like "reasonable scientific certainty." The term "individualization" should not be used.[36] That said, the term "source identification" was used. The DOJ adopted standards for several other disciplines in the years since, which similarly address some of the most egregious overstatements, yet still did not change basic practices. In 2019 the FBI announced results of the follow-up investigation into hair testimony cases. The overstated testimony of people like Malone was not due to "malicious intent," but rather a lack of standards for testimony. With a new system of review of testimony and new standards in place, the FBI audit ended.[37]

Statisticians have a much better approach toward courtroom testimony. The American Statistical Association (ASA) has set out guidelines for forensic evidence. They put it simply: all statements and opinions should "accurately convey the strengths and limitations of forensic findings." That principle can guide all forensic reporting. The ASA emphasizes that in order to make any statements regarding a probability, there "must be data from a relevant population." Without such data, any statistical statements, whether using numbers or words, lack empirical support. Forensic examiners often make claims based on their own "subjective sense of how probable the evidence is." In such situations, the ASA strongly counsels against suggesting that evidence came from the same source. There is always some degree of uncertainty in measurement and the possibility that evidence may have come from a different source. Such uncertainty must be measured and disclosed. Any claim that an expert makes should be set out in "a comprehensive report by the forensic scientist," which "should report the limitations and uncertainty associated with measurements, and the inferences that could be drawn from them." For forensic methods that lack statistical support, the ASA recommends acknowledging the lack of a statistical or empirical basis in reports, and then clearly describing what comparisons were made and what steps were followed.[38]

Those standards are a breath of fresh air. Whether it is a fingerprint comparison or a hair comparison, the examiner should admit that studies have not been conducted permitting one to state how likely it is that the evidence in fact came from the source. The examiner should make clear that there is no way of knowing how certain such a conclusion can be, without well-founded research on the question. The examiner can then explain the comparison process and what features were found to be similar. If there is evidence of what the error rates are for such comparisons, then those error rates must be disclosed too.

COMPENSATION

"It feels like the God of the King James Bible is real, and he answered my prayers," said Donald Gates as he left the courtroom in the federal court in Washington, DC. He had brought a civil rights case seeking meaningful compensation. The jurors in Gates's civil rights case had found the DC police liable for his wrongful conviction, including by making up his supposed confession to the police informant.[39] Peter Neufeld, co-founder of the Innocence Project, represented Gates as part of the team, and argued that the police "brazenly lie[d] under oath" in the case. After the jury verdict, the city settled, and Gates received $16.65 million in damages for his twenty-seven years in prison.[40]

The DC government paid $39 million in combined compensation to Gates, Tribble, and Odom. According to the written opinion of DC Superior Court Judge John M. Mott, Tribble's "journey of injustice subjected [him] to all the horror, degradation, and threats to personal security and privacy inherent in prison life, each heightened by his youth, actual innocence, and life sentence." Judge Mott continued: "Mr. Tribble's ordeal did not merely deprive him of his liberty in a constitutional sense— it ruined his life, leaving him broken in body and spirit and, quite literally, dying."[41] "Ms. Levick has been like an angel," Tribble added, "and I thank God for DNA."

6 Qualifications

"Maybe I'm a dinosaur. I lost confidence in myself, and I feel I let my co-workers down," explained a firearms examiner at the Metropolitan crime lab in Washington, DC. In 2016, he failed a proficiency test, a routine test that many labs give to analysts annually. A test designed for a firearms examiner might include, for example, three cartridge cases test-fired from a suspect's weapon, and four expended cartridge cases from a crime scene.[1] Perhaps two of the cartridges from the crime scene were in fact fired from the suspect's weapon, while two others were fired by a different weapon. The people taking the test must examine each of the items, mark their answers, and report their results to the test provider. There is no time limit to take the test, there are no proctors, and people can discuss or share their work with colleagues. These proficiency tests are not designed to be very challenging. After he failed the test, the concerned supervisors responded by reviewing a sample of his recent case work, and they readily uncovered a serious error in a real case: he had incorrectly linked shell casings to a weapon. The lab supervisors expanded their audit to include 120 cases he had handled that year, and they found a second error. In response, the analyst retired from the lab, saying: "I was wrong, I don't want to embarrass the unit."[2] Yet it was not his fault alone; a different colleague had reviewed his work in each case, so a total of three examiners made mistakes. In fall 2019 the Department of Justice asked the lab to turn over years of firearms files for a wider audit.[3] How many other errors might be caught if labs gave analysts more challenging proficiency tests, or if audits of casework were routine? In this chapter I discuss the fundamental need for rigorous proficiency testing, so that we know how good a forensic analyst actually is.

A "QUALIFIED" EXAMINER

"Is that a subjective standard?" asked the North Carolina trial judge, wondering how the examiner decided shotgun shells could be deemed an "identification." The defendant, charged with murder in a deadly shooting, sought to challenge the examiner who had linked shell casings from the crime scene to his weapon. The prosecution had asked the judge for permission to allow an examiner from the local police department to testify as an expert. The witness answered the judge's question: "It is subjective. It is based upon the training and experience of the examiner."[4] The examiner then explained how she found "sufficient agreement" between several shell casings found at the scene and those fired from the defendant's firearm. She looked at whether the cartridges could have come from a .45 caliber weapon. She then looked, under a microscope, at "little scratches" on the surface of each cartridge. She had no notes documenting which scratches supported her conclusion. She went on to say that she was "proficient" in "seeing the amount of agreement" in toolmarks based upon "experience and knowledge and training." The judge asked, "Is there a percentage assigned to that"? The examiner explained, no, there is not.

The judge used scare quotes in open court, emphasizing that she was a "quote, qualified, closed quote, firearms and toolmark examiner." The examiner had a bachelor's degree in anthropology, uncompleted master's work, and had worked as a forensic technician for the local police for three years. During the first year, she took a course from a for-profit company. At the end of that year, she took a proficiency test from a company called Collaborative Testing Services. After taking that test, she was deemed qualified by the police.[5] She then became a "provisional" member of a professional group, the Association of Firearm and Toolmark Examiners, but did not have enough training to take their exams; they require five years of fieldwork before becoming a member. The judge noted that the local police did not have protocols or standardized procedures for the examination of firearm toolmarks.

The judge decided that "the subjective nature of this science, her lack of experience and absence of knowledge as to what methodology or protocols she used is especially troubling to the court." The judge observed that it was not possible to tell whether she had reliably applied methods and that the examiner was not qualified to be an expert. The judge ordered that "all testimony" of this examiner "regarding her examination of the subject shell casings be excluded."[6]

WHAT IS EXPERTISE?

These cases raise a larger question: What is expertise? A person should only be considered an expert if they are in fact very good at forensics work. Expertise can be proven objectively, through rigorous tests. Instead, our judges often rely on whether a person has testified in the past, or the person's years of experience, or the person's credentials, often flimsy ones, since in the past there have not been good certificate or degree programs for many forensics. Training, degrees, and certificate programs can be improved. Even more important, though, is that we rigorously test our experts. We have national testing rules for clinical laboratories that handle tests that screen for medical conditions. Other countries have required that forensic labs test their analysts. If we allow forensic experts to provide evidence in court, then we should require them to provide evidence that they are in fact experts.

We rely on experts every day in almost everything that we do. The vehicles we drive, the food we eat, and the water we drink—all must comply with safety standards set and evaluated by scientific experts. What makes someone an expert? One would hope that being an expert would mean being objectively good at a task. Yet sometimes we rely on people who give us advice or make decisions based on their experience and training, and not on sound scientific standards. We may not know how good these people really are at their jobs. This can have quite grave consequences.

Take, for example, the airport screeners that work for the Transportation Safety Administration (TSA). Although sophisticated machines display colorful images of our luggage making its way through conveyer belts, humans must view those screens for hours on end and interpret patterns to assess whether a shape is a threatening object, or just a child's toy or an electric toothbrush. The TSA does not just hire people who say that they have experience detecting weapons on screens. The stakes are too high. That is why the TSA conducts blind tests. They test TSA screeners by placing real weapons and explosives inside luggage. The screeners are not told they are being tested—unlike the firearms and fingerprint lab examiners who are told about each test. In one such TSA effort, the screeners failed 67 of 70 tests, and those shocking findings resulted in wholesale reassignment of supervisors and new airport procedures.[7]

What about the forensic evidence that we use in our criminal courts? While experts assert that they are largely infallible and describe their impressive credentials to the jury, we often do not know how good they actually are at their work. The FBI analysts who traveled the country testifying about hair comparisons were self-proclaimed experts. They said that they were the best in the world, based on their training and their experience conducting thousands of examinations. It is only natural that credentials impress jurors at a trial. Pamela Fish at the Chicago Police Laboratory had impressive credentials too. Fish had bachelor's and master's degrees in biology before she was hired, and completed, while at the lab, a PhD in biology from the Illinois Institute of Technology. Fish was promoted to head the biochemistry unit. Yet when a man named John Willis was exonerated after seven years in prison by DNA tests, in a case in which she misreported blood typing evidence, a subsequent audit found Fish made errors in nine cases and failed to report evidence of innocence. Only after three additional DNA exonerations in her cases did the state decline to renew her contract.[8]

It is also only natural that a person who has studied, trained, and worked for thousands of hours would personally feel like an expert. However, anyone can get complacent about one's abilities, if one's skill is never actually tested. Doctors make judgments based on experience in thousands of cases, and if a patient returns with worse symptoms, then a doctor knows a mistake may have occurred. An athlete is tested in competitions and knows whether hours of training provided a competitive edge.

In forensics, however, there is no patient who returns to the office and a win or loss in court may have nothing to do with the quality of the forensics. No one may detect an error because, if the examiner reports a "hit," there is great pressure for defendants to plead guilty, even if they are innocent. The forensics may never get tested by anyone else.

It is also not surprising that forensic experts tout their years of experience and the number of cases that they have worked on. That may be the main credential they have to offer. Many labs traditionally hired a police officer or a recent university graduate, with very little experience in forensics work. There are now far more degree programs in forensic science, but traditionally a person learned the work on-the-job, from the old-timers, and without any background in scientific fundamentals.[9]

PROFICIENCY TESTING

The scientific definition of expertise does not rely on experience or credentials. Instead, it relies on objective evidence that an expert is good at what they say they are doing. Proficiency testing is a way to test reliability of a particular self-proclaimed expert to find out if they are as good as they say they are. International scientific organizations define proficiency testing as "an evaluation of participant performance against pre-established criteria by means of interlaboratory comparisons."[10] What is unusual about the forensics we use in criminal cases is that we accept self-proclaimed expertise in the courts without demanding any testing. That is why the problem of unreliable testimony raises a more fundamental problem, common to bite marks, fingerprinting, hair, and any technique that involves some amount of subjectivity, as most do to some extent. If the expert relies on experience to reach a conclusion, then how good is any given individual expert?

A judge cannot hire a courtroom translator based on the person telling the judge that they speak both English and a foreign language fluently. Judges require that a person pass proficiency tests showing that they have true expertise in English and the relevant foreign languages, as well as an understanding of legal terminology. Often courts require candidates to pass both written and oral exams in order to work as courtroom translators.[11] Clinical laboratories that test medical samples are subjected to a detailed set of regulations, under the Clinical Laboratories Improvement Act (CLIA), requiring the lab analysts to be regularly proficiency tested under realistic conditions.[12]

The Office of the Inspector General audits DNA laboratories to assess how well they upload DNA profiles into the federal CODIS databank system, including by selecting fifty or more DNA profiles at random to review. They found that 11 of 18 labs audited violated federal requirements. They found error rates of 8 percent or more in the DNA profiles entered. These errors included entering prohibited persons, such as crime victims, into the database.[13] Or take a blind study by the Centers for Disease Control of labs that did drug testing in the mid-1980s—they found astounding error rates ranging from 11 to 94 percent or even 19 to 100 percent.[14] Such testing, which is required in medical laboratories, is not done for the forensic disciplines in a meaningful way.

In 1974 a federal grant to the Forensic Sciences Foundation (FSF) funded administration of twenty-one proficiency tests at crime laboratories around the country. The disheartening results uncovered "serious problems" in several forensics disciplines. Yet, in 1979, forensic practitioners voted against a proposal to create a system of peer review through training, certification, and proficiency testing for all types of forensics. The FSF continued its work through the early 1990s, when it was folded into the Collaborative Testing Services (CTS), a company that sells and conducts proficiency tests and measures. CTS has become a leading proficiency test provider and nine hundred laboratories in more than eighty countries participate in CTS testing.

All accredited crime laboratories are required to have annual proficiency tests, but it is widely agreed that these tests are extremely elementary. In hearings conducted by the National Commission on Forensic Science, the president of CTS explained "that he has been under commercial pressure to make proficiency tests easier."[15] Comments from test-takers (which to its credit, CTS publishes) also suggest these tests are not particularly difficult, but that it depends on who you ask. Comments on the CTS's 1999 test include: "Quite easy!" and "The test was a poor gauge of proficiency. All the comparisons were very easy," although another said, "Good, fair realistic test. Very similar to real case work." For a 2015 test, one person commented, "This test was not as good as last year's test. Some of the photographs were not clear . . ." and another wrote, "This test seemed less difficult than previous tests taken."

These proficiency tests are not blind: the lab analysts know they are being tested. There are no proctors or supervised testing conditions. People can take as long as they want to take the test. They can share their work with others in the lab or work in groups. Even in the DNA testing area, where the National Academy of Sciences recommended blind testing, there have been "virtually no blind proficiency tests" used to estimate error rates, despite an influential NAS report stating that "laboratory error rates must be continually estimated in blind proficiency testing."[16] The passage rates also tell you something about how challenging a test is. One disturbing truth about these proficiency tests is how often people do make errors on them, despite their ease. Gregory Mitchell and I collected results on thirty-nine different CTS proficiency tests on fingerprint comparisons from 1995 to 2016. We found widely varying error rates, with false positive rates ranging from 1 to 23 percent. Overall, the tests had on average a 7 percent false positive rate and 7 percent false negative rate during the time period.[17]

In a 1995 CTS test, 22 percent of the participants made at least one error and the reaction in the latent fingerprint community ranged from "shock to disbelief," paired with "consternation."[18] Some suspected that, as a result, CTS made its tests consistently easier. However, in the very next year, 38 of the 147 laboratories (19.89%) "correctly identified less than six of the [nine] latent prints." As a result, CTS recommended that those labs "review the experience levels of their examiners and provide additional training," as well as consider conducting more "internal proficiency testing." More recent testing cycles also report high error rates.

A recent study of people taking fingerprint proficiency tests, by my colleagues Daniel Murrie, Sharon Kelley, and Brett Gardner, involved adding several questions to a test that CTS sent out to fingerprint examiners in spring 2019. The test included twelve latent prints and four sets of known prints belonging to four different people. The examiners were asked to compare the prints and report their findings for each of the twelve latent prints. They asked the people tested how many cases they testify on in each year, how long they took to take the test, and how challenging each of the sample prints were. Most of these examiners were quite experienced; they had an average of almost twelve years of experience. Most indicated that they had completed hundreds of hours of training on latent print exams. Most said that they testify on five or fewer occasions each year. Almost all of them said that they completed their work on the proficiency test individually, but two-thirds did say that they had their test responses verified by another examiner before submitting the answers. They said they took an average of 9.5 hours to complete the test. The examiners mostly answered that the prints were not challenging, although they also said they were realistic of casework. In general, people described the prints as of high quality. The examiners who made at least one error on that test, 6.6 percent (13 of 200 examiners), mostly were examiners who had less experience and less training. Those examiners similarly thought the test was easy, and yet they made mistakes.[19]

It is essential that jurors know about the error rate for a particular expert. Greg Mitchell and I also studied how jurors consider information about the proficiency of an individual expert. We gave thousands of people participating in our experiment information about a simple crime that hinged on the reliability of a fingerprint comparison and then we provided information about how the expert did on their last set of proficiency tests. We described a fictional rigorous test, with a hundred individual tests and a score out of 100. Not surprisingly, jurors reacted very consistently to this information and gave less weight to the fingerprint evidence the less accurately the expert performed on the proficiency tests.[20]

FALSE CREDENTIALS

It may take work to design and insist upon real proficiency tests, but it also takes work to verify credentials, which is something lawyers and judges have not always done well. Take the head of the Maryland State Police firearms unit, who for years repeatedly lied about his credentials, falsely claiming he had a degree from Rochester Institute of Technology in photo science, or in aerospace engineering, or in mechanical engineering from the University of Maryland. When lawyers in a case asked, he gave them a fraudulent transcript purporting to be from the University of Maryland. When this came to light, he tragically committed suicide, after suddenly retiring. The prosecutor in Baltimore commented, "Whatever the investigation turns up concerning his resume, we believe he built his expertise well after that happened," but also announced a review of his old cases, as defense lawyers planned challenges.[21] A notorious example is forensic examiner Fred Zain, who performed poorly in the basic FBI serology course in 1977, but this was not included in his personnel file, and not long afterward, he was promoted to supervisor of serology division at the West Virginia State Police Crime Laboratory. The West Virginia courts would later reopen all of the cases that he worked on and review the work of his entire division, resulting in nine convictions reversed, including innocent people exonerated by DNA tests, and over 180 cases reviewed for errors.[22]

There have been troubling exposes of online forensics certificate programs, and other professional associations in forensics that require annual payments but no meaningful quality control. A graduate student in investigative reporting, as part of a *Frontline* documentary, paid $660, took an essentially open-book exam, and within two hours was notified that she would be mailed a diploma as a Certified Forensic Consultant. This certification might actually impress some judges and jurors, but it did not require any rigorous testing or skill. As Judge Harry Edwards put it, many of these forensics certifiers are not "real certification programs" that give "serious tests" and will not revoke a license if a person fails. Unfortunately, there is no authorized, scientific organization that regulates who can be an expert in a discipline.[23] In more recent years, the American Academy for Forensic Science, a leading national professional group, has reviewed and accredited certification programs, which is a positive step.[24]

There are no formal qualifications at all for some forensics jobs. In most states, people elect the county coroner, who makes forensic determinations about the cause of a person's death. In some states, there are few rules about who can be elected as coroner. Those people have often been morticians, people who run funeral homes, while some are paramedics or nurses. "Typical qualifications for election as a coroner include being a registered voter, attaining a minimum age requirement ranging from 18 to 25 years, being free of felony convictions, and completing a training program, which can be of varying length," as a National Academy of Sciences report noted. In other states, a medical examiner is not elected, and must be qualified and appointed. However, in some places, the person must be a board-certified forensic pathologist but not necessarily a physician. It is hard to find doctors to do the job.

Credentials can be earned on the job, and continuing education is important. After all, science and technology continue to change and improve. Forensic science education programs are typically not accredited and may be informal. There also needs to be training on the legal system, ethics, and quality control, among many other topics. As the National Academy of Sciences report noted, however, there has long been "no sustainable source" of funding, at either the state or federal level, for graduate education or research in forensic science.[25] Labs may be looking for more forensic scientists with scientific degrees, but for training in forensic science applications, few degree programs existed. That has started to change, with new degree programs around the country, increased federal funding, and more interest in forensic science jobs. Indeed, there may be something of a *CSI* effect in which more students are excited to look into careers in forensic science due to media depictions.

Other credentials may be quite accurately claimed, but it is hard to say whether they are meaningful. For example, how much training and proficiency must a dentist have before coming into court as a forensic odontologist? Dental training, after all, does not teach people how to compare bite marks from crime scenes. The American Board of Forensic Odontology (ABFO), the group created for and by forensic dentists, provides a certification, which largely consists of paying membership fees and attending annual ABFO events. At the 2017 meeting where Keith Harward spoke about his wrongful convictions, the dentists' group, the ABFO, voted to make it easier to remain a certified member. Members must attend annual workshops and take an online test every five years. With twenty-five multiple-choice questions, open-book, no time limit, and no limit to the number of times a dentist can take the test, this is far from a rigorous measure of proficiency, but it is also not so different than what many crime labs require.[26]

NATIONAL REGULATION OF QUALITY

After World War II, medical laboratories conducted an experiment to assess the level of agreement across medical laboratories within

Pennsylvania. They found a shocking number of errors. Lives were at stake if diseases, for example, were not correctly identified. Soon, a consortium of medical laboratories began circulating specimen samples to determine their accuracy: proficiency tests.[27] In 1967 federal legislation was passed to ensure that medical labs conducted accurate tests, the Clinical Laboratory Improvement Act (CLIA).[28] Then, in the mid-1980s, reporters at the *Wall Street Journal* wrote about misdiagnosed cancer and lax standards at labs conducting cytology tests of Pap smears. Their Pulitzer Prize–winning series included such headlines as "Lax Laboratories," "Physician's Carelessness with Pap Tests," and "Risk Factor: Inaccuracy in Testing Cholesterol." The reporters documented "large numbers of false negative results," of failure to detect cancerous cells, which resulted in "unnecessary suffering and even death in women who did not receive prompt treatment for cervical cancer."[29]

The swift response by lawmakers to these clinical lab failures was completely different from the indifferent response to crime lab failures. In 1988 Congress passed a tougher federal law extending regulation to basically all clinical laboratories, whether public or not. The law required that proficiency testing reflect "to the extent practicable . . . normal working conditions" to make tests realistic. The law also permitted the agency to conduct "announced and unannounced on-site proficiency testing of such individuals." After all, the lawmakers concluded, "regular proficiency testing was vital evidence of a laboratory's competence." While not perfect, in part because it does not insist on blind testing, the law contains comprehensive regulation of quality control at clinical laboratories. In the area of cytology, or cancer screening for abnormal cells, analysts who do not receive scores of at least 90 percent must be retested. If an analyst fails a second test, they must receive remedial training and have all of their casework reexamined. If an analyst fails a third test, the analyst may not resume work absent remedial training and retesting. All labs must permit random samples to be validated through inspections, and the federal agency can monitor and supervise on-site any labs not found to be fully compliant.

We need similarly serious federal legislation and quality controls imposed on crime labs. To be sure, in recent years, more labs have obtained accreditation, which involves having a professional scientific group periodically evaluate whether a forensic crime laboratory meets scientific standards. Some states have required that their labs be accredited.[30] Accreditation is a good step to ensure minimal standards are being met, at least in the procedures and management systems adopted in a laboratory. However, accreditation does not ensure that valid methods are used. Nor does accreditation ensure that reliable and consistent casework is being done, since it typically involves review of procedures and protocols but not casework. Accreditation is not sufficient to ensure that adequate quality controls and standards are followed in a crime laboratory. Neither is certification. As a related form of quality assurance, individual forensic practitioners can and should also be certified in all categories of testing in which they perform examinations, provided a certification examination is available. Such certifications should be provided by accrediting or professional organizations, based on rigorous standards and including regular and rigorous tests of their proficiency. Professionals should not, in contrast, be permitted to evaluate evidence simply based on their experience, without an independent certification. Still, today certifications are not very demanding and do not ensure that the evidence is accurately tested.

REGULATION IN OTHER COUNTRIES

Some other countries that lack resources for large crime laboratories like those in the United States have still managed to establish far more rigorous systems for quality control in forensics. In Germany an organization called GEDNAP conducts proficiency testing of all DNA laboratories. The group, founded by the German Society for Legal Medicine, is independent of the laboratories themselves. It is run through the central involvement of research scientists; the tests are designed by a laboratory at the University of Munster. The program has expanded to include over 220 laboratories from 38 countries, with two tests per year, permitting an international framework for quality control. The testing is not blind for the laboratories; the participants know that they are being tested. However, GEDNAP does review samples blind by anonymizing test submissions.

In the U. K., laboratories are required by the United Kingdom Accreditation Service to "define the level and frequency of participation" in proficiency testing and each laboratory must "be prepared to justify their policy and approach" in appropriate proficiency testing. A lab plan for proficiency testing must be "regularly reviewed" in response to changes in the lab. In Ontario, Canada, the Centre of Forensic Sciences (CFS) supplements the required proficiency tests with an in-house program of blind proficiency testing managed by the CFS Quality Assurance unit. Police and fire investigation agencies submit dummy cases that are used to test the lab analysts. Each of these models suggests far more can be done in the United States to regulate proficiency and assure the quality of work performed by forensic laboratories and their analysts.

REFORMS

This discussion of the need for objective testing of forensic experts should not be taken to suggest that education does not help. As a law professor who teaches graduate students, I would be the first to say that education conveys necessary skills. One long-standing problem in forensics has been that many practitioners came from a law enforcement background and did not have a grounding in science. Increasingly, however, applicants to crime laboratories have forensic science degrees, advanced degrees, and a background in science. Statistics is increasingly understood as relevant to forensics work, since practitioners must understand concepts underlying claims of probability and error rates. This is progress but it is not enough. Certifications should be nationally regulated to include regular proficiency testing, and disqualification and retraining in response to errors. For example, the American Bar Association has called for "demanding written examinations, proficiency testing, continuing education, recertification procedures, an ethical code, and effective disciplinary procedures" for all forensic analysts.[31] As I will describe in chapter 11, only one lab in the United States, the Houston Forensic Science Center, is conducting large-scale blind proficiency testing, but there has been progress, and more labs are beginning to follow that example.

As one federal judge put it, after an expert testified "he achieved a 100% passage rate on the proficiency tests that he took and that all of his peers *always* passed their proficiency tests," proficiency testing "in such a 'Lake Wobegon' environment is not meaningful."[32] Judges should require that real proficiency tests be done if someone is to serve as an expert. Blind proficiency testing should be required and it should be demanding. This is not impractical or prohibitively expensive to do. Unfortunately, very little of this testing is currently done in criminal cases where the stakes involve nothing less than life and liberty. No person should be called an expert unless they can demonstrate, based on rigorous testing, that they do reliable work. If forensic analysts are permitted to provide evidence in court, then we should require them to first provide objective evidence that they are in fact experts.

7 Hidden Bias

"Ah, back to France!" commented a judge, chef Raymond Oliver of Le Grand Vefour in Paris, tasting a white wine. People can be swayed by the presentation of food and drink, the brand, the price, the surroundings, and of course, the company, but this was a blind taste test. In the 1976 Judgment of Paris, red and white California wines were pitted against the most prestigious French wines. The panel of judges included leading experts. Chef Oliver was considered among the greatest of French chefs and a champion of traditional cuisine. The white wine Chef Oliver savored, however, was neither French nor traditional—it was a Chardonnay from California's Napa Valley. The winning red and white wines were California wines. One mortified judge wanted her scorecard back, so no one would know that she had given top ratings to California wines. In the years since, the test encouraged a global rise in great wines across the United States and throughout the world.[1]

The blindfolded figure of justice weighing the scales conveys an image of impartial judging central to our justice system. Statues depicting blind justice grace the facades of our courthouses and preside over our courtrooms. We may all be personally biased, but we expect blind justice in our criminal courts. Yet the people who investigate crimes and test forensic evidence cannot literally be blind to the evidence: their job involves looking at the evidence to analyze it. If forensic experts are not blind, and nevertheless must make judgment calls, then it is inevitable that they can be biased by what they see and hear and then make mistakes. Indeed, forensic experts, most of whom work for the police, will tend to be biased in favor of finding a hit that can convict a suspect. This should not be surprising. Take it from Nobel Prize–winning economists Daniel Kahneman and Amos Tversky, who pioneered the study of the behavioral short-cuts that people use every day. They wrote in 1973 that confirmation bias is likely to play an important role in the criminal justice system. Beliefs in the likelihood "of the guilt of the suspect" can impact people, even highly trained experts.[2]

We expect scientists to run tests more like the Judgment of Paris. While they do not literally cover their eyes while they work, scientists keep out information that might bias results. They include controls and placebos, among a range of measures to deal with bias. Scientists retain data and make it available to others, which makes it possible for other researchers to attempt to replicate the findings.

Unfortunately, in forensic science, testing is rarely blind. The examiner knows which evidence is from the crime scene and which is from a defendant. Traditionally, the forensic analyst would talk to police about the other evidence in the case, and hear all sorts of biasing information about the defendant as well. In this chapter I describe how a group of researchers, mostly in psychology, brought cognitive bias in forensics to light. In the span of a decade, cognitive bias went from being almost totally unheard of in forensics to common knowledge in the lab. We can especially thank Itiel Dror for helping to bring about this sea change. I describe Dror's early experiments, the sources for bias in crime lab settings, and the different types of bias. Cognitive bias is particularly concerning because forensic analysts usually work for law enforcement, use subjective standards, and do not have to document their work. The solution is blinding: lab procedures that remove biasing information from the work of forensics. Methods to improve documentation and make forensic work more objective can also help. As humans, we are all biased, but we do not all hold the life and liberty of the accused in our hands.

THE JUDGMENT OF LONDON

Psychologist Itiel Dror was the first to convene the equivalent of the Judgment of Paris in forensic science, and by doing so illustrated just how grave the consequences of bias can be when forensic comparisons are conducted. Dror researches at University College London, and his collaborator, David Charlton, was a true believer in the infallibility of fingerprint work. Charlton supervised a lab in the U. K. and edited the Fingerprint Society's magazine, *Fingerprint Whorld*. Dror convinced him to help test examiners, just to see if they might be vulnerable to biasing information.[3] Charlton told Dror that the test was a waste of time, since cognitive bias did not play a role in fingerprint work. Nevertheless, Dror persisted in convincing him to try.

In their study, five highly experienced fingerprint examiners reviewed prints in the course of their ordinary work. This was an experiment, however, and as Dror put it, "what I did was, as we say in England, a bit tricky." What the examiners did not know was that Dror and colleagues actually had given these five experienced examiners the same prints that each of the five had looked at five years before in a real-life case and which each had previously found to be from the same source. Other experts had separately looked at those prints and agreed that they were from the same source. Yet Dror and colleagues did not tell them that. Instead, they informed the five examiners that these were the pair of prints from the Madrid bombing case, the infamous fingerprint case where three senior FBI examiners all got it wrong. Everyone in the fingerprint world had heard about the Mayfield error. Having been given this powerfully biasing information, four of these five examiners now reached a different conclusion than the one they had made before. Only one persisted in reporting that the prints came from the same source. Three changed their minds and concluded that these were "definite non-match" prints, while the fourth called the evidence "inconclusive."[4]

When Dror told Charlton the news that four of the five examiners changed their findings, the revelation hit him hard: "I felt like I shot my profession in the foot." Dror was not surprised at all. All people can be influenced by biasing information, no matter how expert they are. These were not experts bent on convicting the innocent: these were ordinary examiners doing their job. As Dror notes, "We're talking about dedicated, hard-working, honest, competent forensic examiners."[5] Nor is the problem unique to fingerprinting. Indeed, the findings that bias can impact experienced and competent forensic experts has been replicated, time and again, by a host of researchers, for a range of forensic techniques.

This does not mean that fingerprint experts get it wrong 80 percent of the time when they are given biasing information. Yet experts often receive biasing information, and it need not be such powerfully biasing information to affect their work. Indeed, despite his shock at the results, David Charlton teamed up with Dror in a second study in 2006, examining the work of practicing forensic examiners. This time they gave six latent print examiners prints that they had previously examined, but added biasing statements reflecting information that would quite typically be passed onto experts in a criminal investigation, like that the suspect confessed to the crime. This time, two-thirds of the examiners changed at least one of their conclusions.[6]

REAL-LIFE BIAS

"My name is Peter Stout, and I am biased," the president of the Houston Forensic Science Center (HSFC) likes to say. People associate bias with discrimination, but what scientists have shown is that we constantly make unconscious judgments. Most of these judgments are innocuous and helpful. We always process information based on our expectations, our experience, and our perspective. Doing so can help us take efficient short-cuts, but it can also blind us to errors. Forensic scientists need to acknowledge that bias is pervasive, human, and it can be minimized if proper procedures are in place. Awareness, by itself, or willpower is not effective; labs need to create firewalls against bias.

Forensic experts commonly receive all sorts of biasing information. Touring a local crime lab in 2019, the deputy director repeatedly told my students and me that the job is to compare prints to the "bad guys." The attitude was not surprising; the entire lab was overseen by the district attorney's office: they all worked for the prosecutors. Most small crime labs report to the chief of police and are incorporated as part of a local sheriff's office or police department. The National Academy of Sciences report warned that a "lack of independence" in crime labs can damage the objectivity of forensic science. Yet very few labs in the United States are independent.

Forensic analysts often take phone calls from the investigating detectives or prosecutors. In Scotland, Shirley McKie had her fingerprints erroneously matched to a crime scene in a high-profile case. A government report, investigating what went wrong, described how police gave the forensic analysts instructions about which evidence to test, which not to test, and what the test results should be. One analyst commented how police make you feel like "just a useless lab rat" when you call in a negative result, and the officer says, "No, it has got to be him."[7] The analyst may be told a preliminary match is to a person of interest. Police may tell the analyst more: that the suspect confessed or has been identified by eyewitnesses, and they should review the evidence quickly. The colleagues who review their work are usually not blind either. They may know the first analyst made a match and they just confirm it. Analysts may be told about a suspect's race, criminal record, and other evidence in the case. Even the forms that police use to submit requests for forensic testing include biasing information. For example, a suspect's name or the neighborhood where a crime took place may convey information about race.

People may assume only the more subjective evidence that involves visual comparisons might fall prey to cognitive biases. Yet even DNA testing can involve subjective and biased interpretation. Itiel Dror and Greg Hampikian have studied how contextual information can even affect DNA results (to some analysts they gave information about a sexual assault case showing how the prosecution hinged on the DNA result, and to others they shared nothing about the details of the crime).[8] Studies have now been done in a wide range of forensic disciplines. A 2012 study of arson investigators found that when fire investigators were given information suggesting that the fire was or was not an accident, they skewed their conclusions.[9] Another study by Dror and colleagues examined forensic anthropologists studying human remains. Biasing information caused them to get basic information wrong, like the gender and age of the skeleton.[10]

CONFIRMATION BIAS

People have a natural tendency to look for evidence to support what they already know or expect to be true. This effect also works across different types of evidence. For example, psychologist Saul Kassin and colleagues conducted a study in which being told a suspect confessed caused people to be more likely to find a forensic match.[11] One solution is to ask experts to do their work blind to such extraneous information. They can look at the fingerprints, or toolmarks, or firearms evidence, without being told extra facts about the case or the criminal suspect—things they do not need when conducting their forensic work. Take the case of LaFonso Rollins, an innocent man who had falsely confessed, and who could have been cleared by DNA tests, which were available at the time of his conviction. A crime lab analyst asked supervisors if he could conduct the DNA test, but they responded that since Rollins had confessed, no DNA test should be conducted. Rollins served ten years in prison before DNA tests exonerated him.[12]

ADVERSARIAL BIAS

We all face a bias in favor of the team we work on. Lawyers know experts can be biased by the side that pays their fees; that is why lawyers "shop" for experts who support their side. Still, people are often surprised that forensic experts can be biased. Crime lab analysts are not typically highly paid hired guns but rather salaried government employees. Psychologist Daniel Murrie and colleagues have shown in a series of studies how there is a strong "allegiance effect" among forensic psychologists.[13] They gave over a hundred practicing doctoral-level forensic psychologists four different case files for a consultation, using standard risk-assessment scoring instruments. These doctors were told that the evaluation was commissioned on behalf of a "special prosecution unit" or by a "public defender service." They were all given the same exact four case files, from actual cases, with extensive records that they would typically rely upon, including police, court, and mental health data. The doctors who were told they were hired by the prosecution gave higher risk scores, while those hired by the defense gave lower scores. Everyone was biased by the side that retained them.

Law professor and psychologist Greg Mitchell and I conducted a "battle of the experts" experiment to see what would happen if mock jurors heard from a defense expert, and not just a prosecution fingerprint expert. These jurors watched a video of a fingerprint expert for the prosecution and found it very compelling: most would convict a defendant just based on that short video. However, when they saw a video of a defense expert, everything changed. Just having a defense expert re-explain how fingerprint methods work had a real impact on conviction rates. Further, if the defense expert reached a different conclusion, such as that the evidence was inconclusive, jurors were extremely unlikely to convict the defendant. The defense expert completely neutralized the prosecution fingerprint evidence. We wondered if one actor might have been a more convincing expert (after all, one had recently played the role of Sherlock Holmes in a university theater production). We had our two actors switch roles. We found it did not matter which actor the jurors saw as the prosecution or the defense expert.[14] Yet in real criminal cases, there usually is no battle of the experts. Judges often refuse requests from indigent defendants for funds to hire their own expert. The one-sided presentation of forensic science amplifies bias and it is manifestly unfair.

CONTEXT BIAS

Have you ever thought that a dog looked like its owner or that a couple looked more alike the more often you saw them together? This can be the result of an innocuous type of bias. There is a human tendency to find similarities when looking at objects side by side. Such circular reasoning may have been a problem in the Mayfield case.[15] In Scotland, after the high-profile error in the McKie case, the investigation described this as "flip-flopping," as a person may unconsciously focus on similarities, not differences, when looking between fingerprints.[16] That is why in forensic science, it is important to first just look at the crime scene evidence and observe it and document it in detail, before seeing the suspect reference materials, let alone before making any comparison. Only then can one see if those same details are present in the evidence from a suspect. Rather than a back-and-forth or circular process, the comparison can be done using a linear process. This procedure is called Linear Sequential Unmasking (LSU), which only now has started to be adopted by labs.[17] In Mayfield's case the FBI concluded that the examiners changed their assessments as they looked at Mayfield's print and the Madrid print. The FBI adopted the LSU approach after the Mayfield case.[18]

Technology can introduce new forms of bias as well. For example, the way the algorithms present possible prints can bias examiners. Itiel Dror and colleagues have studied how when the true match is farther down in the list of candidates, the examiner is less likely to pick it. They expect that the best matches should appear first, or they may become tired as they trudge through each of the possibilities and make more mistakes due to fatigue.[19]

The context can bias a forensic analyst's conclusions in myriad ways. My colleagues Brett Gardner, Sharon Kelley, Daniel Murrie, and Kellyn Blaisdell studied the forms that 148 crime laboratories across the United States use for police to submit evidence to them. They found that many labs request all sorts of information that is irrelevant to the task of fingerprint comparison. One in six labs requested information with a very high potential for bias.[20] Many ask for the victim and the suspect's gender and race, which are not needed for comparing fingerprints. Others asked police to state whether the suspect was a "serious violent felon," or a "flight risk," or to write down, "What are you trying to establish with the evidence?" One solution is to limit the extraneous information an examiner receives. The National Commission on Forensic Science explained in 2015 that "forensic science service providers should rely solely on task-relevant information when performing forensic analyses."[21] Another solution is to separate roles, so the person collecting information is not the same person who analyzes the data in the lab.

BIAS AND AMBIGUITY

A "bias blind spot" also stands out in the research on bias.[22] People are not aware of their own bias. When Daniel Murrie and colleagues asked, forensic experts responded that they could not possibly be biased. Those who worked at hospitals thought that independent psychiatrists might be biased; those who were independent pointed to the psychiatrists who worked at hospitals. No one thought that they themselves could be biased.

In general, the more subjective and open to interpretation the evidence is, the more experts are subject to the influence of contextual bias.[23] An example is the area of blood pattern analysis. Blood stains and patterns are very difficult to interpret. The NAS report stresses that blood pattern interpretation is "in many cases" "difficult or impossible" due to the complexities of overlapping patterns.[24] Furthermore, the report noted that "the opinions of bloodstain analysts are more subjective than scientific." A recent study found that experts made errors in approximately 13.1 percent of the cases. The researchers also found that as stains and spatters became harder to interpret, experts would grasp for contextual information to give them leads. In those cases, the examiners were more easily biased, and 23 percent made errors.[25]

Another area in which experts reach very different conclusions is in the forensic medical evaluation of infant deaths due to head trauma, commonly called "shaken baby syndrome" or SBS. Studies have given doctors casefiles and asked them to reach a judgment as to whether a death was caused by SBS, and found that experts reached opposite conclusions based on the side that asked them to examine the file.[26] Perhaps the most high-profile example was the battle of the experts in the Louise Woodward trial, the "nanny case." The team of prosecution experts concluded that SBS was the cause of death, while the defense presented experts who testified the infant had received a skull fracture weeks earlier, and that a "slight jar" could have caused the fatal injury. Woodward was convicted, but the sentence was reduced to involuntary manslaughter and time served.[27] More recent convictions have been overturned due to new research calling into question the bases for reaching judgments that a baby died due to violent shaking, as opposed to other medical cases. A Canadian inquiry into wrongful convictions based on SBS findings in Ontario found "the real possibility of past error."[28] We do not know how many people were wrongly convicted, but there have thousands of SBS convictions in the United States and many more around the world.[29] These findings highlight a central concern for forensic evidence generally: the more ambiguous the evidence, and the more room for subjective decision making, the more room there is for bias to cause an erroneous conclusion.

The forensic cognitive bias studies, however, point the way to some solutions. The brief, objective, and highly structured risk assessment measure that Daniel Murrie and colleagues used in their experiments produced less-biased results. Doctors using a more open-ended assessment were more easily biased. One way to reduce the problem of cognitive bias, then, is to develop more objective tasks.

DOCUMENTATION

Yet another problem with traditional forensic work is that it is not easy for anyone else to assess the reliability of the particular work done in a case. Traditionally, experts would simply just say they reached a conclusion. They would not document the steps they took to reach that conclusion. There is far more room for bias if one does not have to document one's work. This was the issue in a fingerprint case in North Carolina, in which I became involved, bringing together a group of well-known scholars to write a brief.[30] In the case of Juan McPhaul, the appeals judges had said that it was an error to admit the testimony of a fingerprint analyst, and not because of error rates in the discipline or the analyst's own proficiency. Instead, the problem was with the reliability of the work the analyst did in McPhaul's case.[31] McPhaul had been convicted of armed robbery. The Fayetteville Police Department fingerprint examiner testified that fingerprints found on certain pieces of evidence—a car, two Domino's pizza boxes, and a Domino's chicken wing box—belonged to McPhaul. The examiner told the jury that the print on the Domino's chicken wing box was "[t]he right middle finger of Juan Foronte McPhaul," as were the prints on a Domino's pizza box. Not only did the examiner use very strong language, with nothing to qualify it and no acknowledgment of error rates or potential biases of any kind, but the analyst could not say how she reached this conclusion. The expert was unable to say what features of the prints were compared, what process was followed (the examiner did not even describe the general ACE-V steps to be followed), or the duration of the examination. Both the defense lawyer and the judge repeatedly asked how the comparison was conducted and the examiner simply would not say. She could not say what points were found on the prints. She had no documentation of the process. The judge kept pushing her to explain. The examiner said she proceeded by "going back and forth" until satisfied. Based on this undocumented and loose process, the examiner said that "the impressions made belonged to Mr. McPhaul." Ultimately, the North Carolina appellate judges agreed it was an error to admit this testimony, but upheld McPhaul's conviction due to other evidence of his guilt. The case illustrates how important it is that work be documented so that we know what the expert actually did.

VERIFICATION

Not only may police officers and others outside the lab influence the forensic examiners, but forensic examiners may influence each other. After all, many techniques, like fingerprint comparison, include a verification step where a supervisor or colleague reviews the work. The verifier can change the outcome: they can decide, for example, that a print that excludes the suspect should be deemed as inconclusive. I once received an anonymous note from a whistleblowing analyst at a leading crime lab complaining that supervisors were doing just that: changing a finding that the evidence excluded a suspect into a finding that was inconclusive.

For a picture of what everyday casework is like inside a crime lab, take the data gathered with colleagues at the University of Virginia and staff at the Houston Forensic Science Center. We examined two years of data from the lab's fingerprinting unit: over 2,500 cases and 12,000 latent prints.[32] We obtained the data after-the-fact; no one in the lab knew that their work would later be examined. We found that 56 percent of the latent prints from the crime scene were found to be of no value, and not of high-enough quality to compare, and no further work was done. Of the rest, 26 percent were found to match a suspect, and 13 percent were exclusions. We found that 7 percent of the time, the verifier disagreed with the examiner who did the initial work. In some of those cases, 3 percent or eighty-two cases, the disagreement could not be quickly resolved, and there was a "consultation," where they talked through their disagreement.

In a really small number of cases, just eight in two years, they used a con-flict resolution process because they could not work it out. We wondered whether the more experienced or senior fingerprint examiner would win out, and we found no such pattern. The examiner and the verifier won out equally often. It may be that some are pushier or more convincing, regard-less of their role or experience. These data illustrate, though, how foren-sics work is an interpersonal project. Multiple people can work on a case and they can disagree about fundamental conclusions.

One key improvement is to make the review blind. The reviewer should not review only cases in which there was an identification. After all, it is also important that no value or inconclusive evidence be checked. A reviewer who does not redo the analysis, but just looks it over, will tend to confirm what the first expert already found. That is what happened when the multiple examiners reviewed the prints in the Brandon Mayfield case. In response, the FBI instituted a system of "blind verification." Under the new procedure, an independent examiner, who does not know what results the first examiner reached, must examine a fingerprint in a case with a single latent print. All forensics work should use such blind procedures.

BLIND RESEARCH

Similar problems of bias plague the scant research done on forensics. None of the error-rate studies that the PCAST report talked about, not even the leading fingerprint studies done by the FBI, were blind. I have talked to people who participated in the studies: they knew well that they were being tested, and they knew that this was a study with high stakes for their field. People who know they are being tested behave differently: this is called the Hawthorne effect. We may all be wary of studies that are done by groups with an obvious agenda, like a company that wants to show that its new product is the best. In forensics, the studies have tended to come from professional groups of forensic scientists, or crime labs, like the FBI. That is what has made studies like Itiel Dror's so remarkable: they get at how forensic scientists behave when they do not know they are being tested.

BLIND JUSTICE

Blind lady justice may not be the right mythological image for what good scientists do. Better personae might be the relations of the three dreadful snake-haired Gorgons of Greek mythology, who turned anyone who saw them into stone. Their three less well-known sisters, the Graea (or the gray witches), shared one eye between them. The mythic hero Perseus seized their eye, and refused to return it until they told him how to safely approach the most fearsome Gorgon, Medusa. The idea of sharing an eye between people sounds grotesque, but it captures how a proper scientific method alternates between seeing and blinding.

In the past, crime labs, which are not scientific research labs, did not try to examine these problems. For decades, examiners comparing bite marks, fingerprints, fiber, and toolmarks all proceeded on the assumption that their experience and good judgment were enough. Law professor Michael Risinger forcefully argued that it was a problematic omission for the National Academy of Sciences in its 2009 report not to mention selectively blinding or masking forensics work. The report highlighted the need to further study the role of cognitive bias in forensics but offered no recommendations for how to address the problem.[33] It did not discuss processes that limit or eliminate biasing information, or blind verification.

The mounting number of studies initially by Itiel Dror, and now replicated by many other researchers, have brought cognitive bias into the mainstream discussion on forensic science. Today, labs and government groups are finally taking notice. In the U.K., detailed government guidance, from the Forensic Science Regulator, recommends the use of debiasing techniques for forensic labs, emphasizing that the "most powerful means of safeguarding against the introduction of contextual bias" is to be sure that the forensic practitioner "only has the information about the case that is relevant to the analysis."[34] In the U.S., the National Institute of Standards and Technology (NIST) has begun to issue reports on how systematic factors, like poor training and poor procedures, can contribute to bias, but that processes can be improved to remove biasing information from forensic experts' work.[35]

In 2018 Itiel Dror was invited to give the plenary keynote presentation at the annual meeting of the American Academy of Forensic Science, about the science of cognitive bias. Dror highlighted one of the themes of the NIST reports, which was that human error is inevitable. There needs to be a culture of openness about errors. Forensic analysts should feel free to come forward and discuss concerns rather than feel like they must conceal mistakes.[36] Dror regularly circles the globe, giving talks and trainings at leading forensic laboratories. It is not enough, though, to be more open to hearing about the problem of cognitive bias. Few labs are instituting measures to prevent against bias. All labs must adopt blinding and other procedures to combat bias, because, simply put, we are all biased.

8 The Gatekeepers

A qualified examiner straps a device to your body to measure your blood pressure, your pulse, the rate of your breathing, and the sweat on your skin. The examiner then asks simple questions, before reaching the key questions, like "Did you use drugs at work?" or "Did you fire the gun?" William Moulton Marston, who had both law and psychology degrees from Harvard, developed the technique, beginning in 1915, and he frequently sought to testify in court.[1]

Imagine what would happen if judges closely scrutinized the forensic evidence used in criminal cases. We would not be as worried about reliability in the lab, because judges would only allow the most reliable evidence into the courtroom. That world does exist, where judges have long agreed that Marston's lie detector, the polygraph, cannot typically be allowed in court. In one of the earliest cases on standards for allowing scientific evidence in court, *Frye v. United States*, the judges of the prestigious U.S. Court of Appeals in Washington, DC, ruled in 1923 that new scientific methods, like the polygraph, could only be allowed in court based on "general acceptance" in the scientific community.[2] The defendant's lawyer offered to conduct a test in the courtroom, in front of the jury, to show that the defendant was telling the truth. The judges, however, ruled that this new method was not proven and lacked "scientific recognition." Polygraph advocates have claimed accurate rates of 90 percent, but a 2003 National Academy of Sciences report, examining fifty-seven studies done on polygraph work, found no evidence of validity. The report described "no serious effort in the U. S. government to develop the scientific basis" for detection of deception using "any technique," including the polygraph, despite criticisms of the underlying science that "have been raised prominently for decades."[3] To be sure, the government continues to heavily rely on the polygraph, including in national security settings, despite these scientists' criticism.

Nevertheless, virtually all U. S. courts have agreed polygraph evidence cannot be used, except in unusual situations, such as when both sides agree to use it. Why were courts so concerned about the polygraph, and not techniques like bite mark comparison? One explanation is precedent: judges are strongly bound to follow previous judicial rulings. Another reason may be special discomfort with lie detection: it implicates Fifth Amendment self-incrimination rights and it appears to probe into a person's mind. Judges have argued the evidence has an aura of infallibility, it interferes with the role of the jury, and it is not reliable. The U. S. Supreme Court ruled that military courts could ban polygraph tests, with Justice Clarence Thomas stating studies have found polygraph tests "little better than could be obtained by the toss of a coin." Yet reliability concerns extend to many other types of forensics. Justice Thomas added that unlike "fingerprints, ballistics, or DNA," polygraph does something different: an opinion "about whether the witness was telling the truth," which is the role of the jury ultimately to determine.[4] There is yet another potential explanation: the defense often seeks to use polygraph evidence to argue that the defendant was telling the truth when claiming innocence, and judges may tend to lean toward the prosecution.

FINGERPRINT FLIP-FLOP

Perhaps the most remarkable case study of judicial reluctance to scrutinize forensics is the case of Carlos Ivan Llera-Plaza, who faced the death penalty in Philadelphia, along with two others. He was accused of operating a drug gang linked to four murders. His lawyers sought to exclude the

FBI fingerprint examiners from the trial. Judges had let experts describe fingerprint matches for a hundred years, but federal law had recently changed. Regular witnesses can only describe what they saw or heard themselves. Judges let expert witnesses do far more than that: an expert can offer the jury opinions and conclusions about the evidence, with the gravitas of a person designated as an expert. Judges serve as the gatekeepers who decide whether a person can properly testify as an expert. In the past, following the *Frye* test, the courts had allowed people to serve as experts only if their method was "generally accepted" in the scientific community. Those standards were considered loose. After all, the community of astrologers may all themselves agree that what they do is valid and accepted among their group.

The law changed in 1993, when the U. S. Supreme Court decided the case of *Daubert v. Merrell Dow Pharmaceuticals Inc.*[5] (As federal judge Jed Rakoff has pointed out, "There's a very real debate over whether it should be pronounced 'Dow-bert' or 'Daw-bert.' Mr. Daubert is on record as saying both.")[6] The case was about expert evidence concerning Bendectin, a drug used to combat morning sickness that consisted of an antihistamine and vitamin B. Experts claimed evidence that it caused birth defects. The studies were later shown to be based on false data, but in the meantime, the drug makers took a useful medicine off the market and spent millions in defense costs. The justices in the *Daubert* case held that to be allowed in court, an expert must do more than use a method that is "generally accepted," under the test set out in the *Frye* case, decided in 1923. This was 1993, and judges now understood far more about the proper role of science in the courts.

For an expert to take the stand, the method used must be scientifically valid and reliable. It must be based on "more than subjective belief or unsupported speculation."[7] First, the method should include conclusions that can be tested. Second, the method should be subjected to peer review in scholarly publications. Third, the method should have some known error rate. Fourth, there should be standards maintained in the discipline. Fifth, there should be general acceptance of the method in the scientific community. These factors changed the emphasis from whether a technique had been accepted for a long time, to whether today it stands up to rigorous scientific testing.

Lawyers assumed that judges would scrutinize forensics as never before. After all, many forensic techniques had no solid research base. Innocence Project co-founder Barry Scheck, who watched the oral arguments in the case, commented that "*Daubert* calls upon courts to undertake a much more sophisticated and informed analysis of scientific evidence."[8] Law professor Randolph Jonakait put it more bluntly, stating that after *Daubert*, "much of forensic science is in serious trouble."[9] Forensic analysts scrambled to create new forensic science journals. The FBI created "scientific working groups" of forensic analysts to write standards for their fields. Lawyers watched eagerly to see what would happen when judges put forensics to the *Daubert* test.

In some early cases, judges did step in as gatekeepers. In a handwriting comparison case, a federal judge ruled that the day-to-day work of document examiners was not supported by scientific research, and did not satisfy *Daubert* (but the judge then let it in, calling it "technical" evidence which was not scientific and did not need to be sound science).[10] Another judge said that the hair comparison evidence in Ronald Williamson's case was unreliable and did not meet "any of the requirements" of *Daubert*. The appellate court reversed, finding that the error in admitting the evidence did not rise to the level of a constitutional violation. Williamson was later exonerated by post-conviction DNA evidence; John Grisham wrote his nonfiction book *The Innocent Man* about the case.[11] Meanwhile, the U. S. Supreme Court in 1999 ruled in *Kumho Tire Co., Ltd. v. Carmichael* that the *Daubert* rule applies to all expert evidence, whether it is called technical or scientific.[12] In 2000 the Court approved an updated version of the federal rule of evidence, Rule 702, that deals with expert evidence, to reflect these requirements that experts use reliable methods and reliably apply them to their work. States soon began adopting the federal approach.

The first big test came in Llera-Plaza's case, in the Philadelphia courtroom of federal judge Louis Pollak. Pollak was no shrinking violet. He had been a prominent civil rights lawyer and the dean of both Yale and the University of Pennsylvania law schools before becoming a judge. Judge Pollak reviewed the evidence and concluded that when examiners compare latent prints, they used no set standards, there had been no peer-reviewed scientific research on fingerprinting, and the method's rate of error is "in limbo." Judge Pollak shook the forensics world by issuing an opinion in January 2002, concluding that fingerprint evidence was "hard to square" with the demands of *Daubert,* which requires judges to assure validity and reliability of evidence before admitting it at trial. These FBI experts could not testify to their "opinion" that any prints came from the defendants.[13] The judge emphasized "fingerprint identification techniques have not been tested in a manner that could be properly characterized as scientific." Judge Pollak also highlighted how fingerprint examiners were not rigorously tested for their proficiency; it was hard to say how good they were at their work. "Accordingly," the judge said, "expert witnesses will not be permitted to . . . present 'evaluation' testimony as to their 'opinion' . . . that a particular latent print is in fact the print of a particular person."[14]

Two months after this powerful ruling, Judge Pollak reversed course. "In short, I have changed my mind," the judge said.[15] What changed? The prosecutors and the FBI had gone on the warpath. The Department of Justice had said "prosecutorial effectiveness . . . would be seriously compromised" if their ability to use fingerprints was affected. The judge agreed to hold hearings. In his courtroom in 2002, the FBI's fingerprint examiners described how they had performed "spectacularly well" on proficiency tests conducted since 1995,[16] making errors on fewer than 1 percent of the test items.[17] Judge Pollak was impressed with evidence that fingerprinting, with more oversight, had been found reliable in the U. K. However, according to one of the defense's experts, an esteemed examiner formerly employed by Scotland Yard, if he gave his experts tests like those used by the FBI "they'd fall about laughing."[18] Judge Pollak did say he still had real concerns about the reliability of fingerprint examiners. Nevertheless, there was no evidence that error rates were "unacceptably high." After all, fingerprint evidence had been used in court for almost one hundred years, and during that time, no FBI identification had ever been proved wrong.

While this claim of infallibility no longer holds after the Brandon Mayfield case, to this day, judges have not seriously questioned fingerprint evidence. In the federal courts, one court after another found the evidence admissible, even after revelations that FBI procedures were subpar. Eleven appellate rulings occurred after both *Daubert* and the revisions in 2000 to Rule 702, yet most of those judges never even discussed the reliability requirements of those rules. Several judges discussed error rates in a roundabout way, noting that whatever the error rate is, it must be low.

Other judges have said that since the error rate must be low, a trial judge does not even have to hold a hearing. After all, fingerprint evidence has long been "generally accepted" in our courts.[19] Even worse, judges have barred defense lawyers from questioning fingerprint examiners about known errors in fingerprint cases, like in Mayfield's case.[20]

SILENT JUDGES

"It is revolting to have no better reason for a rule of law than that so it was laid down in the time of Henry IV," wrote Justice Oliver Wendell Holmes in 1897. He added, "It is still more revolting if the grounds upon which it was laid down have vanished long since, and the rule simply persists from blind imitation of the past."[21] Justice Holmes, who sought to bring more facts and science into legal thinking, would have been highly revolted by the role that "blind imitation" of prior rulings, called precedent by judges, plays in forensic science. The weight of the past, preventing judges from considering new evidence that forensics are unreliable, powerfully explains why judges did not step in to insist that all science be used accurately in court. Judges have failed to step in when new scientific reports have called forensics into question. Judges have failed to step in when the law changed, particularly after the U.S. Supreme Court's decision in *Daubert*. Judges may have been comfortable, in cases like *Daubert*, with cutting back on evidence used by plaintiffs' lawyers suing major corporations, but judges remain highly reluctant to limit the evidence used by prosecutors in criminal cases. As Innocence Project co-founder Peter Neufeld put it, *Daubert* has been largely "irrelevant" in criminal cases.[22] A closer look at state courts shows just how dire the situation is.

STATE JUDGES

The modern *Daubert* test is sometimes described as a reliability test, and most states now follow it, including Florida. Yet in November 2015, a criminal court in Florida admitted bite mark evidence. The judge, a former prosecutor and public defender, simply recounted the expert's credentials, described the methodology, and concluded that the bite mark testimony was the product of reliable principles. By 2015 the unreliability of bite mark evidence was well known. There had been a large number of DNA exonerations. The "limited studies" were, according to the court, irrelevant—including a study finding error rates as high as 63 percent. The judge said bite mark evidence "is a comparison-based science and . . . the lack of such studies or databases is not an accurate indicator of its reliability." The judge did say, though, that the testimony will be limited to a conclusion "that Defendant cannot be excluded as the biter." The judge emphasized that "bite mark identification or analysis has been accepted in Florida courts as early as 1984, and has been found to be generally accepted in the relevant scientific community in other jurisdictions."[23] The reasoning was typical "grandfathering" reasoning, as professor Simon Cole has put it, analogizing this to racially discriminatory rules allowing people in the post–Civil War South to vote only if their (white) grandfathers could vote.[24] If it was good evidence in the past, it is good evidence now: it is precedent.

Consider how judges have ruled on hair comparison evidence. Federal judge Jed Rakoff has noted two cases from Kentucky as illustrative. Judge Rakoff pointed out that in 1999, after the state adopted a *Daubert* standard, a trial judge said that no hearing or discussion was even necessary before admitting hair comparison evidence. The case went up to the Supreme Court of Kentucky, which agreed: "Evidence of hair analysis by microscopic comparison has been admissible in this commonwealth for many years." Those justices admitted they "have never specifically addressed the scientific reliability of this method of hair analysis," but in an amazing bit of reasoning, they concluded "we must assume that it" was sound, "for otherwise, the evidence would never have been admitted in the first place."[25] Judge Rakoff summarized, "Forgive me, I love the state of Kentucky, it's a beautiful state, but this is junk." One might assume—given the dozens of DNA exonerations in cases involving hair comparison, the FBI audit, and the statements in the National Academy of Sciences report—that this ruling would not stand the test of time. In 2013 a defense lawyer in Kentucky tried to bring a new *Daubert* challenge to hair evidence.[26] In *Meskimen v. Commonwealth*, the Kentucky Supreme Court said that a judge did not have to even hold a hearing on the issue. Why?

Because such evidence "has been admissible in the state of Kentucky for many years."[27]

We see the same "pass the buck" reasoning in every area of forensics. In the fingerprint area, courts continually repeat the mantra that the evidence has been used for a hundred years. Judge Pollak emphasized that through use in casework, fingerprinting "been tested empirically over a period of 100 years."[28] He may have been repeating how an FBI agent put it in another court, stating: "The 100 years of fingerprint employment has been empirical studies."[29] In real cases, an analyst does not know whether the conclusion was right or wrong. Some judges are convinced that other judges are somehow "testing" the evidence. One federal judge claimed that fingerprint examiners "have been tested in adversarial proceedings with the highest possible stakes—liberty and sometimes life."[30] In 2003 an FBI agent could only gloat, "We're winning 41 times out of 41," when fingerprint evidence is challenged in court, and "I think that says something."[31] It does say something.

It can be even worse in states that still rely on the old *Frye* general acceptance rule, and not on *Daubert*. A judge in Pennsylvania would not allow a hearing to discuss the reliability of bite mark evidence. The judge admitted that, putting it mildly, "the use of bite mark evidence is beginning to face challenges," but decided that it was still "generally accepted in the relevant scientific community," presumably meaning by the forensic dentists themselves.[32]

ADOPTING THE FEDERAL RULE

Judges are supposed to apply a reliability test, but in practice they do not. Rule 702 states that an expert may testify if that testimony is "the product of reliable principles and methods," which are "reliably applied" to the facts of a case. Or as the advisory committee that wrote the rule put it, judges must "exclude unreliable expert testimony." Few criminal cases result in appeals. When they do, judges often avoid discussing scientific issues, by finding the error "harmless" due to other evidence of guilt in the case. Even when appellate judges do address expert evidence head-on, they defer to the discretion of a trial judge. The U. S. Supreme Court has emphasized "abuse of discretion" review of a judge's decision regarding expert evidence, meaning the trial judge must have done something truly arbitrary or irrational to result in reversal on appeal.[33] Further, judges still say that evidence should be presumed reliable because it has been used for decades.

In many states, judges have walled off entire techniques from meaningful review. What judges have said is that they can take "judicial notice" of the reliability of a technique because it has been used for a long time. They can consider its reliability a fact. One example is a Kentucky Supreme Court opinion, stating that based on "overwhelming acceptance of hair comparison evidence over fifty years," the judges would take "judicial notice that this particular technique is deemed scientifically reliable."[34]

Innocence Project lawyer Chris Fabricant and I assembled an archive of all state criminal appeal rulings that in some minimal fashion discussed the reliability rule for experts. We found over 800 cases that mention the term reliability, but only 229 cases that actually said something about whether the evidence was reliable. The judges almost always agreed that the forensic evidence was properly admitted. They often cited to prior rulings, stating that it was already established that a type of evidence could be used. For example, an Arizona appellate court emphasized that "our supreme court has sustained convictions based solely on expert testimony about fingerprint or palm print evidence because the evidence is sufficiently reliable."[35]

Even if those old cases were decided by judges who did not have a modern reliability rule, those old cases were still used. Other cases cite to the qualifications of the particular expert. Very few state judges cite to scientific reports, like the 2009 National Academy of Sciences report. In the handful of cases that do acknowledge a concern with reliability, judges failed to act. These rulings were one-sided. Judges rarely ruled in favor of the defense, and there were over twice as many prosecution victories.[36] Judges are constrained by prior rulings and precedent from higher courts. But even when they are not constrained, they prefer to follow the lead of other judges rather than make an original ruling. In short, the supposed reliability test adopted in Rule 702 is rarely applied to assess reliability. Chris Fabricant and I concluded that the reliability test is in practice a myth.

JUDICIAL PSYCHOLOGY AND INCENTIVES

Judge Jed Rakoff began a talk at a conference that I organized of statisticians, crime lab leaders, and law professors, explaining the problem as follows: "I should tell you at the outset that most judges know beans about science." He admitted, "I was an English major, most of my colleagues were either history majors or political science majors." He recalled, "I took something that was popularly called 'Physics for Poets.' The poetry was great." Yet the fact that judges (and lawyers generally) are often largely scientifically illiterate (I certainly did not take any real science courses in college) is not a good enough excuse. Judge Rakoff pointed out that issues of science and technology are inescapable in modern courtrooms. Litigation over complex topics from patents, to toxic chemicals, to algorithms used in sentencing, all implicate science. Judges, just like lawyers, can quickly become expert in complex and technical subjects, and one way that lawyers can do that is by hiring top experts to explain those subjects to us. We may not have taken chemistry, but we can hire the best chemists to explain the methods to us, step by step, and then do the same in the courtroom. Moreover, while some forensic techniques, like DNA, are highly technical, others, like fingerprinting, are "not rocket science," as the judge put it.[37]

So why have judges stayed on the sidelines? Judge Rakoff suggested one reason, "to be frank, is the pro-prosecution bias" of so many judges. Most judges come from a prosecution background. Their bias may not be conscious; Judge Rakoff noted, "I was a federal prosecutor, I'm very familiar with how you become used to certain kinds of testimony."[38] If you have yourself relied on firearms or fingerprints experts many times as a lawyer, you are likely to be comfortable with others using it. Moreover, judges often do not hear from both sides. Forensic experts who work at crime labs testify frequently in court and can be polished, smooth, and confident: but they only testify for the prosecution. Particularly in state court, the defense will struggle to get funding to hire an expert and likely cannot retain anyone who currently works in a crime lab, since everyone in those labs works for law enforcement. Finally, the "dead weight" of precedent keeps experts in court, even if the science changes, and even, as happened after *Daubert*, when the law changes.

In one case, a Maryland judge did exclude fingerprint evidence. The judge noted that the FBI analyst in the case had claimed "no error rate" for fingerprinting and "100 percent certainty." However, the judge's opinion had to be withdrawn, and not because the judge took it back. State prosecutors dropped the charges and federal prosecutors refiled the case in federal court, where the defendant faced a much harsher sentence—and the federal judge let the evidence in.[39] That experience sent a grim warning that defendants who might consider challenging fingerprint evidence might face federal charges.

LIMITING THE TESTIMONY

Some judges let forensic evidence pass through their gate, but with limits. In a case on firearms evidence, federal judge Nancy Gertner ruled: "Because of the subjective nature of the matching analysis, a firearms examiner must be qualified through training, experience, and/or proficiency testing to provide expert testimony." The quality assurance manager at the Massachusetts State Crime Lab testified that in 2005 none of the 255 test-takers answered incorrectly. The judge noted: "One could read these results to mean that . . . the test was somewhat elementary." Yet the judge ultimately found the expert evidence admissible, while barring testimony expressing complete certainty regarding the conclusion of a match.[40] Another judge in Maryland followed suit.[41] Judges in the District of Columbia barred firearms experts from testifying with a "reasonable degree of scientific certainty."[42] Most recently, a judge in DC went further and ruled that the most an expert can say is that the defendant's firearm "cannot be excluded." That limit may be effective in court. Psychologists Nicholas Scurich and William Crozier, Jr., and I surveyed 1,400 people in a mock jury study, and we found it made no difference to conviction votes when firearms experts used terms like "reasonable degree of scientific certainty" versus "more likely than not" versus a "source identification." However, testimony that goes no further than the defendant's firearm "cannot be excluded" did reduce conviction votes.[43] Perhaps only stronger limits on testimony will be effective in the courtroom.

DISCOVERY

Federal judge Jed Rakoff resigned, exiting the National Commission of Forensic Science for shirking its duty. The commission had said that it would not address the topic of discovery, meaning documents and information that must be shared in a criminal case. Discovery, or the documents and evidence that the sides exchange before a case goes to trial, can be very extensive in civil cases, where the person sues for money. In a civil case, experts must provide detailed reports that include all of the research that they relied upon. Next, the lawyers for both sides can question the expert, before trial, during lengthy depositions. Those depositions can be grueling, and after the deposition, both sides have a detailed picture of what the expert will say and what the conclusions are based on. In criminal cases, nothing like that occurs. Often forensic reports are a page or two in length. There are no depositions; if the defense is lucky, maybe the analyst will answer basic questions on the phone. As the authoritative notes to the federal rules put it, "it is difficult to test expert testimony at trial without advance notice and preparation."[44] After Judge Rakoff resigned, emphasizing that it was essential that pretrial discovery on forensics be tackled by the commission, the group reconsidered and Judge Rakoff resumed his place on that body. The commission ultimately recommended, quite forcefully, that prosecutors turn over all forensic evidence–related documentation.[45]

Yet prosecutors often do not do so, including because they may not themselves have any. I recently gave a presentation to over a hundred prosecutors, and asked whether any of them had seen anything other than the two-page report that their lab generates, such as underlying notes or documentation. None had seen anything other than a two-page report. Meanwhile, judges have traditionally done nothing about this problem. As law professor Paul Giannelli has documented, many judges have concluded that a lab only needs to share a result in the form of a certification stating the forensic conclusions rather than the underlying notes detailing the analysis.[46] Many judges do not require that defense lawyers be given underlying bench notes or records.[47] In many DNA exonerees cases, only years later it came to light that forensic reports documented their innocence. Concealed forensics may never come to light.

The law is part of the problem. Many states require very little discovery in criminal cases. On tours of crime labs, the staff has proudly told my students and me that they are scientists, and they share findings with all sides. When we ask whether that means they share their underlying notes with the defense, they awkwardly admit, "Well, we do that only if the defense gets a court order." Federal law is not much better. Judge Nancy Gertner issued a standing order directing lawyers on both sides to identify and provide disclosures concerning forensic evidence in criminal cases.[48] Such rules should be routine, as should broad disclosure and discovery of complete files concerning forensic analysis, including bench notes and lab reports, but other judges have not followed suit. More commonly, judges actively prevent any meaningful discovery into potential problems with forensic analysis. To take just one example, when appellate judges in South Carolina held that a trial judge should have ordered the prosecutor to turn over proficiency tests of DNA experts, the state supreme court reversed.[49] Systemic deficiencies could be averted by best practices requiring full-file discovery of forensic evidence and not just the bare result.[50]

This concern with discovery also highlights how, more generally, both defense lawyers and prosecutors have also failed to carefully scrutinize forensics. Lawyers often lack scientific training, and in criminal cases, they also lack resources. A battle of the experts can ensue in civil cases, where millions of dollars are at stake, and both sides hire top experts to explain technical questions to the jury. In criminal cases, however, forensics are often entirely one-sided. Judges typically deny defense requests to obtain their own forensic experts. Prosecutors do not hear any other views either; they must depend on their local crime lab. An independent expert can make a powerful difference and judges should routinely provide them.

THE U. S. SUPREME COURT

More than twenty-five years after *Daubert*, the ruling appears largely ineffective in our criminal courts. Why hasn't the U. S. Supreme Court stepped in? The importance of forensic and DNA evidence is not lost on the Court; Chief Justice John Roberts wrote that DNA has "the potential to significantly improve both the criminal justice system and police investigative practices ... to exonerate the wrongly convicted and to identify the guilty."[51] Yet our constitutional criminal procedure rules provide very little guidance concerning the appropriate use of forensic evidence.[52]

One fairly hollow protection comes from the Sixth Amendment's Confrontation Clause, which gives the defense the right to question a prosecution witness at trial. The Supreme Court, in a series of rulings, required that the defense be offered the right to question crime lab analysts. It is not enough to just show the jury a report, which in that case was a certificate displaying drug testing results. Justice Antonin Scalia wrote a majority opinion in *Melendez-Diaz v. Massachusetts*, arguing that the ability to cross-examine a lab analyst serves important reliability goals. Justice Scalia highlighted: "Forensic evidence is not uniquely immune from the risk of manipulation." He added, "A forensic analyst responding to a request from a law enforcement official may feel pressure—or have an incentive—to alter the evidence in a manner favorable to the prosecution."[53] Justice Scalia cited to the 2009 National Academy of Sciences report on forensics and also to an article that I wrote with Peter Neufeld documenting the role forensics played in the wrongful convictions of people later exonerated by DNA testing.

That ruling has impacted a host of forensic techniques. Take the case of Donald Bullcoming, arrested for driving while intoxicated, after rear-ending another pickup truck. The central evidence against him was a lab report stating his blood alcohol level was above the legal limit. The prosecution did not call the analyst who actually tested his blood sample; he was placed on unpaid leave for an undisclosed reason. The Court, in an opinion by Justice Ruth Bader Ginsburg, ruled that the defense must have an opportunity to cross-examine the analyst who did the testing. In contrast, in a third ruling, *Williams v. Illinois*, the Court said that where the DNA analyst did perform a DNA test, but also told the jury about a second test done by another lab, there was no constitutional problem.[54] In response to these rulings, labs can designate a forensic analyst, experienced at testifying in court, to take the lead in a case. After all, labs may have a number of people working as technicians and analysts in a single case.[55] As a result, this constitutional right has limited practical benefits. Further, few cases go to trial, and even at a trial, the most vigorous cross-examination may not uncover underlying flaws in the forensics. If the defense does not have access to the underlying records of the analysis, then they may not know what questions to ask.[56]

RETHINKING JUDGES AS GATEKEEPERS

Judges could more forcefully intervene by ordering full discovery for forensics. Both sides should have all of the information before an expert is allowed to take the stand.[57] Judges can more often appoint independent experts in criminal cases, or at least allow the defense to hire an expert. When cases do go to trial, judges can ensure that information about proficiency and error rates is disclosed to the jury. They can limit testimony to bar exaggerated claims of infallible and categorical conclusions. They can also bar forensics of unknown reliability. Judges can reverse convictions based on false or overstated evidence. The DC Circuit Court of Appeals did that, not because of a new forensic result, but because by the FBI's own admission, the hair testimony presented had been false.[58]

One judge whose views of forensics have dramatically changed is Judge Harry Edwards, who chaired the National Academy of Sciences committee. Having spent so much time learning from scientists about each of the forensic disciplines and producing the landmark report, Judge Edwards said, "I, and many of my colleagues, assumed that the forensic disciplines were based on solid scientific methodology, were valid and reliable."[59] However, Judge Edwards has also been candid that he has had little luck in convincing his colleagues to more carefully examine forensic evidence; his efforts have largely fallen on deaf ears. Judges have all of the tools that they need to get science right in their courtrooms. Particularly now that we know so much more about error rates in forensics, it is time for judges to serve as far more forceful gatekeepers.

PART III Failed Labs

9 Failed Quality Control

"She knew her chemistry," an officer at the lab recalled. Lab analyst Sonja Farak was always "meticulous in her note-taking and in her work." Later, reviewing her notes, the officer said, "I rarely found a mistake or an error in any of her work."[1] The senior chemist agreed: she was "a trusted employee" and "did a great job."[2] Yet in January 2013, the state police conducted an inventory and realized that four drug samples of cocaine and oxycodone were missing. The police searched her desk and found the missing samples; searching her car, they found lab materials and drugs. That night, police arrested Farak. Forensic analysts colloquially refer to the work of controlled substances testing as "doing drugs." They normally do not mean to be taken literally, but in this case, Farak had been almost continuously altering samples, stealing, and using drugs at the lab for nine years. She found "positive side effects" of methamphetamine: it was an "energy boost." "I felt amazing," she later said, "I felt more alert . . . it gave me the pep I was looking for."[3] Soon she turned to other drugs. A judge later concluded that by 2010, "Farak performed all of her lab work while she was under the influence of narcotics."[4]

Unlike the lab analyst, Nicole had been clean and sober for years. She worked for a group that provides services to addicts near Springfield,

Massachusetts. She was an active member of Alcoholics Anonymous, the mother of a four-year-old boy, and pregnant with a girl. Yet, she wrote, "my experiences with the criminal justice system have haunted my family and me."[5] She had a criminal record for drug possession. This made it very difficult to pursue jobs in medicine: "On numerous occasions, I have had to talk about my criminal history when trying to rent a home." She was applying for financial aid in community college, and worried she would be denied aid. "In each of these situations, and more, I feel embarrassed and judged by how other people react to my criminal history." She had been charged multiple times with drug possession. The state never notified her that the drug tests were potentially tainted by Farak's misconduct. Nicole never would have pleaded guilty to possession of drugs if she had known about it.

Tens of thousands of people just like Nicole were convicted based on evidence from these corrupt lab analysts. Perhaps the largest-scale reversal of criminal convictions in American history occurred due to rampant errors in what turned out to extend to not just one but two major Massachusetts drug testing labs. It took years for police to uncover the lab misconduct, and judges took action after still additional years passed, where prosecutors were not quick to disclose what had happened or to share records with the defense. For example, Nicole was not even told about this fraud until September 2017.[6] So far, judges have reversed forty thousand cases, but judges may eventually reverse far more cases—perhaps tens of thousands more if judges examine the cases handled by other lab staff.

QUALITY CONTROL

While I was working on this book, I spent most of a day in the emergency room of the Duke University Hospital. Eating lunch at a faculty meeting, I looked at my biodegradable fork, and realized that a piece of one of the plastic tines was missing. I had swallowed it. Since it felt like something might be stuck in my throat, I spent hours in the ER corridor waiting for the results (fortunately, the tine had gone down). Hospitals have backlogs just like crime labs do, but at this hospital, they used triage. My problem was embarrassing, but fortunately not threatening, and the doctors were right to keep me waiting for a few hours, while they saw other patients with more urgent needs. Each step of the procedure was rechecked and documented. The doctor who reviewed a scan of my throat worked independently and separate from the doctor who ran the camera down my nostril and into my throat. The doctor saved a video of the camerawork, in case anyone later needed to reexamine the diagnosis. Moreover, if they both missed something, and I felt more pain or developed a fever, they told me to call my doctor right away and come back.

As leading genetic scientist Eric Lander has pointed out, a brief experience at a hospital involves far more quality control than a test that lands a person in prison. Lander put it this way: "At present, forensic science is virtually unregulated—with the paradoxical result that clinical laboratories must meet higher standards to be allowed to diagnose strep throat than forensic labs must meet to put a defendant on death row."[7] Lander made that observation in 1989. Thirty years later, crime labs remain virtually unregulated. In this chapter, I will discuss the scope of these quality control scandals and why the problem is not just unreliable methods or the work of individual examiners but the systems that labs put into place. A rash of lab scandals resulted from poor quality control. I describe how crime labs have grown with federal funding but very little concern for quality. I describe how accreditation largely does not test quality. Nor are there good procedures to reopen thousands of cases when scandals occur, like the one in Massachusetts. The crime lab system needs quality control rules, like those that a clinical laboratory must follow.

LAB SCANDALS

The large-scale fraud at the Massachusetts lab was of record size but no aberration. I have documented over 130 crime lab scandals, involving errors or audits of multiple cases, at labs across the country. Law professor Sandra Guerra Thompson carefully documented a laundry list of such systems failures in her important 2015 book *Cops in Labcoats,* as has the National Association of Criminal Defense Lawyers (NACDL).[8] There are so many recurring forensic scandals that I found dozens and dozens of more recent events—hardly a month goes by that I do not find more labs to add to the list. It is not just small labs like in Massachusetts; it is also large urban labs in Chicago, Detroit, New York City, Oklahoma City, and San Francisco, as well as the FBI lab.[9] Entire labs have been closed, including the Detroit and Houston crime labs.[10] The San Francisco lab's drug analysis unit was closed after an analyst, a twenty-seven-year veteran, was caught stealing cocaine; prosecutors dismissed a thousand cases and thousands more had to be reviewed. Prosecutors had known "at the highest levels" that she was not a good witness, calling her "increasingly UNDEPENDABLE for testimony," but she remained on the job.[11]

All types of forensic disciplines have been affected. In Lubbock, Texas, a medical examiner was prosecuted and convicted for falsifying autopsies. West Virginia lab supervisor Fred Zain not only may have lied and falsified results in hundreds of cases in the state, but he supervised the lab and consulted on cases in twenty other states. West Virginia paid $6.5 million to innocent people that Zain had essentially convicted.[12] Audits uncovered errors in DNA work, drug testing, firearms, hair comparison, and handwriting units, among others. These instances cannot easily be dismissed as just a few bad apples, because so many of these bad apples exist. These known lab scandals only represent the tip of the iceberg, and indeed, these are the positive situations in which the problem at least does come to light. Whether they involve massive errors, fraud, or backlogged cases that are not tested at all, the errors usually surface after years of totally undetected misconduct. Lab supervisors never even suspected that there was something wrong with Farak's work until she was accidentally caught. Any reviews apparently consisted only in reviewing her paperwork. They did not actually retest any of the evidence. Who normally tests the evidence to check for quality control problems? At most labs, no one does. Aside from easy annual reviews, many labs do not have routine quality control checks of the actual casework. The few that do often do not report quality issues to the public. That is why at every stage of the process, lab work can and does go wrong.

ASSEMBLY-LINE CRIME LABS

Supreme Court Justice Louis Brandeis famously wrote that states can be laboratories for experimentation in law and policy: "It is one of the happy incidents of the federal system that a single courageous State may, if its citizens choose, serve as a laboratory; and try novel social and economic experiments without risk to the rest of the country."[13] Disappointingly, the actual laboratories that states run have not been a home for experimentation. In response to these problems, some labs and some entire states have developed new approaches toward oversight.

Crime labs have come a long way since the 1930s, when FBI director J. Edgar Hoover established one of the first American crime labs at the FBI, setting up a small shop in a single room.[14] At that time, Los Angeles and Chicago had crime labs, as did a few other cities, in response to gangsters operating in the wake of Prohibition. Police officers operated these labs, and they were small, handling hundreds of cases a year and not the tens of thousands that a modern lab may process.[15] The FBI Technical Crime Laboratory, as it was called, began to train agents to examine fingerprints, handwriting, and ballistics. They garnered early fame when analysts performed high-profile work in the Charles Lindbergh kidnapping case. In time, the FBI lab became the largest in the country and the center of innovation and training on forensics in the United States. However, many individual police departments set up their own crime labs, often with FBI assistance. By the 1960s every state had crime labs, although many were set up rapidly and with poor equipment, staffing, and standards.[16] Small "cop shops" contained in police departments were run by police officers assigned to do forensics work. Today, more labs have people trained in forensic science. There are police crime labs, regional crime labs, crime labs that cover entire states, as well as private crime laboratories.

We know far too little about the work that crime labs do. The only global data that we have comes from researchers at the federal Bureau of Justice Statistics, who conduct surveys of crime laboratories. There are problems with their data, including because it is self-reported data from labs themselves, but over time they have documented a steady increase in lab size and funding. Today, there are over four hundred publicly funded crime labs. In 2002 there were 11,000 full-time personnel at crime labs; by 2009 there were about 13,000, and in 2014 there were 14,300 lab employees.[17] This personnel expansion was, unsurprisingly, also accompanied by larger crime lab budgets. Crime labs had to expand their footprint due to the drug war, with its demands for high-volume drug testing. More recently, the opioid crisis has placed great burdens on society, on the criminal system, and on crime labs. Labs have been tasked with handling and testing potentially incredibly powerful and toxic synthetic opioid substances, even in miniscule doses. New synthetic substances have labels that may not appear phony at a casual glance. As one doctor put it, "What happens when fentanyl changes on a weekly or month basis?" What happens is that fatal overdoses have surged, as have demands on labs to identify these drugs. "As soon as you identify one, another one is coming," commented an analyst at the Georgia Bureau of Investigation. "They're coming fast and furious."[18] This has slowed the turnaround time for drug testing, increasing costs, and created new risks for lab staff. The Bureau of Justice Statistics is working on an updated survey, but their 2014 data does not reflect the impact of opioids on labs.

Roughly the other half of the work of crime labs relates to identifying culprits and assessing how crimes occurred, according to these federal surveys. That work includes DNA testing, but despite the prominence of DNA testing, relatively few cases involve biological material that can be DNA tested. Still, modern DNA testing also called for increased budgets, since it requires expensive testing equipment. The bulk of requests police make, when they ask crime labs to link evidence to suspects, does not involve DNA but rather traditional forensic methods—such as latent fingerprints, firearms, and toolmarks. As the high-profile dispute in 2016 between the federal government and Apple over unlocking a smartphone indicated, digital forensics is an increasingly prominent type of analysis.[19]

The budgets of these publicly funded labs have grown too. In 2014 they totaled $1.7 billion.[20] How are these labs funded, exactly? In some states, any criminal defendant is charged a fixed crime lab fee, say $50 or $60. A defendant may be charged a larger fee, $600 in my home state of North Carolina, if a forensic test is actually done in the case. That money may go directly to the crime lab, or it may just go to the state's general operating budget, but it supports increased lab funding.[21] The surge in DNA databanks also helped to push the growth of crime labs. Although relatively few cases use DNA to solve crimes, massive numbers of people arrested and convicted of crimes have their DNA entered in new DNA databanks, which required more equipment and staff, largely funded by federal grants. Congress and federal agencies have awarded hundreds of millions of dollars in grants to eliminate backlogs, purchase new equipment, and expand DNA testing to add more information to federal DNA databanks. In the 2004 Justice for All Act, Congress sought to reduce backlogs in DNA testing, with a half billion dollars provided under a section of the law called the Debbie Smith Act, named after a Virginia woman who waited six years for DNA testing in her sexual assault case. Best known is the Paul Coverdell Forensic Science Improvement Grants Program to reduce backlogs. Yet this federal funding has not been effective; backlogs have only grown.

BACKLOGS

Catherine, a single mother in Los Angeles, was sexually assaulted repeatedly by a stranger who broke into her house in the middle of the night. The police brought her to the Santa Monica–UCLA Medical Center's Rape Treatment Center, where a nurse scanned her body for any possible hairs, debris, or fibers, or any semen or saliva from the assailant. Physical injuries were photographed, and samples were collected, from fingernail scrapings, hair combings, urine, saliva, and blood. A nurse collected this evidence in labeled containers and placed it in a larger envelope or box: a sexual assault or "rape kit." The detective suspected that this was a serial rapist, so he personally drove the kit to the state lab, where they said it could take eight months to process it. The kit "sat for months," and when it was eventually tested, a "cold hit" identified the offender in a DNA databank. During the months they waited, the rapist had assaulted two other victims, including a child. Her case was one of at least 12,600 untested rape kits that largely languished in police storage. Most were never sent to a lab for DNA testing. Some cases remained untested for more than ten years, past the ten-year statute of limitations to prosecute a person for rape in California. In 2009, after a Human Rights Watch report and public protests, Los Angeles County police and sheriffs began to work to address these backlogs. That review also uncovered that despite almost $5 million in federal funds for backlog elimination, much of it remained unspent.[22]

Touring a local crime lab with my law students, the deputy director told us: "You have to love this work. If you didn't, you'd become an alcoholic."

The work can be incredibly tedious. For hours on end, analysts must study detailed patterns in fingerprints or drug test results or DNA results, note their findings, prepare reports, and then do it again and again. The repetition can be numbing. Even more all-consuming is the pressure to move quickly. Our host at a local lab compared the case-flow to the famous *I Love Lucy* episode where Lucille Ball works for a day in a chocolate factory and cannot keep up with the assembly line. "I think we're fighting a losing game," she tells her friend Ethel, as the chocolate moves faster than they can wrap it properly. They resort to stuffing their mouths, shirts, and hats with unwrapped bonbons. Similarly, police continue to submit requests to test new evidence, day in and day out, and the resulting workloads at any crime lab can be crushing. The longer a lab takes to test drugs, the longer an innocent person might remain in jail facing faulty charges. The longer a lab takes to test DNA, the longer a guilty person might continue to commit new crimes. Backlogs at some labs can delay casework by many months. Scandals have resulted when it has come to light that labs were not only backlogged, but simply not testing the evidence.[23] Innocent people have been convicted, where lab analysts failed to test evidence that could have cleared them at trial. As a result of backlogs, the ski mask worn by a robber was not tested before the trial of a man named Cody Davis. Four months after his trial and conviction, the lab finally tested the mask. The DNA results cleared Davis, who was then exonerated.[24]

When the federal government gives large grants specifically to reduce lab backlogs, the result can be more backlogs. The incentives are misplaced, since the labs that eliminate backlogs can no longer qualify for the grants. In fact, the federal data shows that backlogs have grown as the federal funding increased. Labs have tested more and more DNA evidence to add to the federal databases, using federal funds. Not only the federal government but also states have passed new laws requiring that DNA be collected from all people arrested and convicted of a growing list of crimes. In addition, the federal money is mostly for DNA, a small part of lab casework. Disciplines like toxicology, controlled substances testing, and fingerprint comparisons are the "workhorses" of the modern crime lab, as Peter Stout puts it, but they are not supported by these grants. Tellingly, federal funds may not be used for research to improve forensic science; most can only be used to reduce backlogs, add more people's information to government databases, and implement new technologies and processes.[25] As a result, few crime labs do any research; in 2014 only 0.5 percent had any resources for research.[26] Newer, faster, bigger, and cheaper is the mantra, but not better and more accurate.

INSIDE CRIME LABS

If you have never been on a tour of a crime lab, you should consider it. Crime writer Michael Connelly described how his first tour of the Los Angeles area Forensic Science Center changed his view of crime-solving: "This is the place where cases are truly made, truly solved."[27] The inside of a crime lab looks nothing like what you see on *CSI*. Despite the growth in crime labs, half of all crime labs have less than twenty-four employees. One quarter have nine or fewer employees. The inside of the Houston lab is nothing like the inside of the Virginia Department of Forensic Science, the U. S. military lab, or a small local police lab. Some labs only give you a virtual tour, walking you down hallways to peer into lab windows; due to fear of contamination, you cannot walk up to the equipment or see people doing analysis. Others let you get into the thick of their crime-solving work and look over the shoulders of analysts as they peer at bullet casings and drug paraphernalia.

"And did you reach a conclusion regarding that comparison?" the prosecutor asked the Chicago Police Department (CPD) examiner. "I did." The prosecutor followed up: "What was your conclusion?" The examiner said: it was an "identification."[28] In response, the judge in Chicago, Illinois, concluded there was not enough evidence to convict. The judge was "bothered" by the fact that the only evidence was a single print and could not understand why the analyst examined "only one lift" of a fingerprint, but not the other five from the crime scene. The examiner did not seem particularly qualified. She had a bachelor's degree in architecture and design and became an examiner "by virtue of 240 hours of classroom training and a one year . . . shadowing process." She was not certified. The lab had "no accreditation, no auditing system, no quality review, no error check process, no written professional development," and it had no standard operating procedures. The least-regulated labs in the country are local, unaccredited police labs, where untrained people or beat cops may be assigned to forensic work. One of the largest such outfits is the CPD lab, but there are many hundreds of "cop shop" labs. As fingerprint examiner Glenn Langenburg puts it, "we have no way of knowing how good the CPD is at what they're doing. They're not following standards."[29]

MASS ERROR IN DRUG TESTING

The scandal that led to the reversal of forty-thousand-plus cases in Massachusetts began in 2012, when police arrested another lab analyst, not Farak, but a chemist named Annie Dookhan, who had worked since 2004 at a second Massachusetts state crime lab in Jamaica Plain. This was the largest lab that tested drugs seized in the state. Dookhan had been caught forging a co-worker's initials. She promptly admitted to the state police: "I screwed up bigtime." One of her co-workers said that "it was almost like Dookhan wanted to get caught." Yet for more than eight years, she did not, and in fact, her colleagues had called her "superwoman." She was testing more than twice as many cases as the second most productive person in the lab. She explained, "I am not a workaholic, but it is just in my nature to assist in any way possible." She tripled her productivity using the technique of not actually doing the tests. She had been "dry labbing" for years: it is enough of a phenomenon in forensics that there is a term for pretending to do a test and not actually doing it. Dookhan was also regularly contaminating samples, mixing drugs to match her fake reports, and falsifying reports.[30] She even testified that a piece of a cashew tested as crack cocaine.

You might assume that drug testing would be difficult to get wrong, since it is based on principles of chemistry. The follow-up tests used by chemists who work at crime labs use far more accurate than field tests. They typically run samples through two devices: a gas chromatograph and a mass spectrometer. The gas chromatograph separates mixtures into components, while the mass spectrometer breaks down which substances were detected. These results are compared to a sample of a known controlled substance, called a reference standard. The technique is in part automated and well validated. As the National Academy of Sciences put it: "the analysis of controlled substances is a mature forensic science discipline and one of the areas with a strong scientific underpinning." There is "broad agreement nationwide about best practices."[31]

That said, just like with any technique, there is room for human interpretation and error. Drugs that police seize are often not pure. Even if the base structure of cocaine is always the same, the cocaine sold on the street can be cut with all sorts of other substances. Synthetic drugs can be a cocktail of legal and illegal substances. When the material is tested, the results may not line up and there will be results that do not look quite like the pristine lab standard for the substance. There is then a question of judgment regarding how many differences from a reference sample can support a conclusion regarding the drug type. Sampling can be a major issue too. Although sometimes only trace amounts in a syringe or vial are tested, there can be major drug hauls where hundreds or thousands of packages of drugs are seized. It can take weeks just to test a sample.

Meanwhile, a typical report sent from the lab to the lawyers may say little about what was done in the lab, making it hard to tell whether the testing was done well or not. It may state something like, "Received: Item 1—a sealed plastic bag containing 25.6 g of green-brown plant material." The report will then state the conclusion: "Results: The green-brown plant material in item 1 was identified as marijuana." The report has very few words in it and it is conclusory. Scientists have an ethical responsibility to help nonscientists understand their conclusions and yet forensic reports are often short and incomprehensible.

One study done on the readability of typical forensic reports found that the conclusions were written at a difficult level, suitable for people with an education in science.[32] That is why it is crucial that examiners "prepare reports and testify using clear and straightforward terminology, clearly distinguishing data from interpretations, opinions, and conclusions and disclosing known limitations that are necessary to understand the significance of the findings."[33] Without detailed and understandable documentation, lawyers and judges may have no way of knowing whether quality controls were followed or interpretations were correct. They have no way to detect even the most flagrant misconduct.

THE RESPONSE

When Dookhan's dry-labbing misconduct came to light, state lawmakers held hearings and resolved that this type of crime lab disaster could never happen again. And then it did. They learned how Sonja Farak was stealing drugs and working while high or drunk almost all of the time when she was on the job at a lab in Amherst, Massachusetts. The lab shared space in a building with the University of Massachusetts, and it tested suspected illegal drugs for the entire western half of the state. The lab was not accredited and had a small staff.

The lab was a disaster. They had no written protocols for testing. Samples were left unsealed. Chemists did not run "blank" tests to clean the equipment between each test. Instead, they ran them whenever they wanted, often after five, ten, or a dozen tests. This could mean that residue or "carry over" from one test would contaminate the results of other tests that followed. They did not use samples of drugs that came from pharmaceutical companies; instead, they made their own standards. Farak received "no continuing education, proficiency testing, or real supervision." The supervisor of the lab testified at hearings that he never reviewed her work.[34] None of the others in the lab had noticed a thing. None asked Farak about discrepancies in the evidence.

By 2005 Farak was stealing standards used to compare methamphetamine "every morning," and over the next few years she began to consume meth "several times per day."[35] She had only "a few days or a week of sobriety" during the four years that followed. By 2009 she had run through the lab's entire methamphetamine standard supply, so she turned to amphetamine and phentermine, which she said made her more alert and focused. She turned to drugs seized by police to feed her habit. Then she turned to the lab's cocaine standards.

This was just still the beginning. In 2010 a clinician who Farak began to see took notes: "She admits to stealing drugs from the . . . lab. . . . She has episodes of spacing out for hours at home, and admits to worrying about what others are thinking about her at-work." And "when abusing stimulants, she has had perceptual disturbances in the past, including paranoia and auditory hallucinations." Still, no one noticed anything wrong at the lab. In 2011 "she began to smoke rocks of crack cocaine." She had used up lab standards of methamphetamine, amphetamine, and ketamine, while the cocaine standards were mostly gone. She was using crack cocaine "during work hours in the lab." She used LSD that police had submitted for testing, and was so "very impaired" that she could not drive or do any testing work that day. In her lab notebook, she indicated she prepared and signed certificates on a variety of drug samples that day.[36] By 2012 Farak was smoking crack "ten to twelve times a day," including "at the lab, at home, and while driving." Still, no one at work had noticed. Then she began taking other chemists' samples. Farak would steal drugs after they had been analyzed, or before they had been weighed. Farak altered recorded weights of evidence so people would not notice the discrepancies.

Police were not seizing as much crack cocaine by 2012, so Farak began to manufacture it herself in the lab. After hours in the lab, she took seized powder cocaine, dissolved it in water, added baking soda, and heated the mixture, drying it to create crack.[37] She did this several times, when there was enough cocaine to "make a quantity worth [her] time."[38] She testified in a criminal trial in January 2013, and took a lunch break in her car, where she had a "pretty fair amount of crack," and ate lunch, and "got pretty high." No one suspected her of being under the influence when she testified. Even at the end, Farak tried to do her work diligently because she wanted to feed her habit: "I also thought that it would draw less attention if I also tested everything correctly."[39]

In January 2013, the state attorney general prosecuted Farak for drug theft and tampering. Defendants asked for relief and to have their cases dismissed. Prosecutors opposed their motions. A judge said that, based on the evidence, she was only stealing and tampering with cocaine for about six months, in the second half of 2012. Defendants continued to appeal. In November 2013 Dookhan pleaded guilty to obstruction of justice, perjury, and evidence tampering; she was paroled in April 2016. In January 2014 Farak pleaded guilty. Defendants only slowly learned that the attorney general had withheld hundreds of pages of evidence suggesting that the misconduct began before 2012.[40] Nor, to this day, has the work by other lab staff at these scandal-plagued labs been audited or reopened.

This entire saga raises the question: What is the rule about what a lab must do when errors come to light? The Massachusetts labs and courts seemed to be making it up as they went along. In fact, when problems

come to light, even the leading standards from international organizations fall far short. The International Organization for Standardization
(ISO) is a worldwide federation of standard-setting groups, and it devel-
ops detailed requirements for quality controls, including in laboratories.
When there are complaints, or errors occur, or there is nonconforming
work, the ISO requires that a lab must "take action to control and correct"
the problem or "address the consequences," and do so "as applicable."[41]
That language does not create clear responsibilities. When people may be
in prison due to past errors or "nonconforming" work, then labs should
have ethical obligations to do far more. They must notify all of the people
potentially harmed and notify the courts. Then they should review and
correct any potential errors.

ACCREDITATION

There is a deep need for standard rules and procedures at labs. As the
National Academy of Sciences summarized, "Forensic science facilities
exhibit wide variability in capacity, oversight, staffing, certification, and
accreditation across federal and state jurisdictions."[42] Accreditation
involves having a professional scientific body periodically evaluate
whether a laboratory meets scientific standards. The National Commission
on Forensic Science, convened by the Department of Justice, strongly recommended that all forensic science service providers become accredited,
since doing so can promote compliance with industry best practices, promote standardization, and improve the quality of services provided.[43]
Very few labs are required by state law to be accredited.[44] However, more
labs do voluntarily seek out accreditation, and a growing number are
accredited. Nearly nine in ten (88%) of the nation's 409 publicly funded
forensic crime laboratories were accredited by a professional science
organization in 2014.[45]

Yet accreditation is no substitute for quality control. Greg Taylor can
tell you why: he was wrongly convicted in North Carolina and spent seventeen years in prison for a crime he did not commit, because a lab analyst
concealed favorable blood testing results. A key piece of evidence at
Taylor's trial was testimony by a crime lab analyst, who had processed the

scene where the victim's body had been found. Coincidentally, Taylor's truck was stuck in the mud fifty yards away. The analyst conducted a presumptive test for blood on the truck, which the analyst admitted was just "an initial test," to determine if a stain is human blood. The supervising analyst explained that this is "very specific for blood, in that that's what it reacts to." The stains, on the fender, under the passenger wheel, and on the undercarriage of the truck, tested positive using this presumptive field test. However, subsequent testing in the lab showed that it was not human blood. Those test results were not shared with the defense or the jury. Nor is it uncommon for those presumptive tests to incorrectly suggest that a stain is blood; one common substance that can do so is rust, which might be expected in the undercarriage of an old truck.[46]

In North Carolina, the State Bureau of Investigation, or SBI lab, had long been accredited, and yet its analysts concealed evidence in Taylor's case and many more. Investigators, at the state attorney general's request, conducted an audit and found 230 cases where similar evidence had been concealed, by eight different analysts over sixteen years. There was a widespread practice at the lab of disclosing only the preliminary "presumptive" test results of blood, but not later lab tests that are more accurate. Indeed, one of the analysts in Taylor's case defended his work, saying that his report was incomplete but "technically true," and anyway, how he wrote reports was dictated by his superiors. Why didn't the accrediting body at the time, called ASCLD-LAB, catch these deep problems? For one, ASCLD-LAB was headed by two former top agents at the SBI. More fundamentally, the accreditor largely did a paper review of the policies and procedures at the lab. Every year the accreditor would pay a site visit and review five cases from each lab analyst. However, the analysts could "cherry-pick" which cases they reviewed. As one ASCLD-LAB auditor put it, "any lab across the country can dress it up and make it look as pretty as it wants."[47]

Today ASCL-LAB has been folded into the work of a larger organization, ANSI-ASQ National Accreditation Board (ANAB), that follows the standards that come from the ISO.[48] Those ISO standards require that labs have procedures for monitoring validity of results and that labs must use proficiency testing or tests to compare results between labs, but the ISO language is not clear and asks that labs do quality control testing "where available and appropriate." The ISO rules say that "appropriate action shall be taken" if incorrect results are detected.[49] These quality controls lack real clarity or teeth.

MASS DISASTER

The judges in Massachusetts had to unwind a mass forensics disaster. Almost everyone had pleaded guilty after they were told that the crime lab had determined the various seized substances were drugs. While some may have been guilty, some may not have been. Since none of the samples were properly tested, there was no way to know for sure. The highest court in the state, the Supreme Judicial Council, ruled in 2015 that no one convicted based on Dookhan's testimony could be charged with a more serious offense, and each person could renegotiate any plea deals. The Court declined, however, to implement a "global remedy."[50] That changed. The lower court judge asked to be told how many cases were affected, and learned that there were over twenty thousand such cases. In 2017 the Supreme Judicial Council reconsidered and said that there should be a global remedy: all cases should be reversed. A dissenting judge said that this decision was "too little and too late."[51] In the response to the Farak revelations, the top court ruled in 2018 that the state must dismiss all of the cases that Farak worked on and return the court fines and fees for all whose cases were dismissed. The court did not require any acknowledgment of misconduct, where prosecutors did not initially disclose the full extent of the problem with Farak's work.

The system itself has not been held accountable. In Massachusetts, the response was that state police took over the labs, with an increased budget. They doubled the drug-testing staff and added locked storage bins, with video cameras, and added security. "[The lab] is now both nationally accredited and internationally accredited, and we feel confident that the right systems and personnel are in place," said the state attorney general.[52] Is that enough to be confident in the labs? After the Dookhan revelations, officials responded that this was a bad apple situation and could not happen again, and yet shortly afterward, the Farak scandal broke. Few states have created commissions to investigate and report on any errors or negligence at crime labs.[53] As I will describe in chapter 11, labs can implement serious quality controls; if randomly selected cases are retested, analysts cannot so easily falsify the evidence.

Nicole said that as part of her twelve-step path to sobriety she had had to identify and apologize to people she had wronged. She wants the prosecutors who for so long refused to notify people of the scale of the forensics disaster in Massachusetts to do the same thing. An apology would just be a start; as Nicole put it, "I want them to be held accountable like I was held accountable."[54]

10 Crime Scene Contamination

Joe Bryan served thirty years in prison, after he was convicted at two trials, in 1986 and in 1989, for the murder of his wife in Clifton, Texas. A key piece of evidence connecting him to the crime was a flashlight that police found in the trunk of his car. An almost wholly untrained police officer concluded that the flashlight had blood spatter on it, and he made uncannily precise statements in his testimony at trial about how it was held by the shooter, with "high velocity" blood spattering back toward it, forty-six inches from the victim's body, held in the left hand, and at a downward angle. While the officer reached findings on his "experience, knowledge, and training," in fact, he had never done a blood pattern analysis before; he had only taken a single forty-hour course the prior summer. Blood pattern analysis is challenging work and there had been very little research on how blood patterns form. The National Academy of Sciences has explained blood pattern interpretation "in many cases" is "difficult or impossible" to do, given the complexities of overlapping patterns.[1] The Texas Forensic Science Commission examined the case and called the work "unreliable" and "scientifically unsupportable," including because the case also had a contamination problem.[2]

The body of the victim, Joe Bryan's wife Mickey Bryan, was discovered at approximately 8:25 a.m. on October 15, 1985. During a ten-and-a-half-hour period, at least four civilians, more than six law enforcement officers, an entire crime scene lab team, and an unknown number of employees from the local funeral home had entered and potentially contaminated the Bryan house. It had rained that day, and officers had tracked water and mud into the house. Police had stepped on the bloody carpet in the bedroom. Bryan's body was lying on the bed when first responders arrived, but by the time the blood pattern examiner arrived, officers had removed the bedding, and employees of a private funeral home removed the body. It was not until approximately 7 p.m. that evening, over ten and a half hours after the first officer arrived on scene, that this newbie police officer began his analysis of the blood evidence.

The crime scene was contaminated, which makes it impossible to this day to answer key questions about how the murder took place. Despite these problems, Bryan was denied parole for a seventh time in April 2019. Afterwards, my law students and I filed a brief in the Texas Court of Criminal Appeals in support of Bryan's post-conviction motion and detailing the problems with the evidence. The judges dismissed the motion without any explanation.[3] In March 2020, however, Texas officials finally granted Bryan parole, and he was released.

The problem extends beyond shoddy crime scene collection of evidence to non-collection of evidence. A recent study revealed across four urban jurisdictions that some physical evidence was collected in nearly all homicide investigations, but evidence was collected in only 30 percent of assault investigations and only 20 percent of burglary investigations.[4] Large numbers of cases have no evidence collected at all. That problem is extremely pressing. Obviously, police cannot swab every surface or test every object at a crime scene. Yet, all too often, critical evidence in serious cases is not collected and can never be tested.

In this chapter, I will describe how poor crime scene work can cause evidence to be altered, contaminated, or not collected at all. I turn to the special challenges of crime scene DNA, in which minute quantities of evidence can be contaminated. I describe how new and untested "black box" forensic technology is increasingly being rolled out to police, not crime labs, raising even greater concerns about unreliable forensic work in the field. Breath tests used in driving while intoxicated cases, field drug tests, even field DNA tests—all raise enormous reliability problems. Crime labs and scientists should be providing sound guidance on how to collect crime scene evidence and when to collect it. Yet police crime scene units often lack adequate resources and training. Police also often lack adequate resources for preserving evidence so that it can be tested. Indeed, there are few legal consequences if evidence is fabricated, altered, or destroyed. The problem of error in forensics begins at the crime scene.

ALTERING EVIDENCE

Perhaps the most high-profile example of shoddy crime scene evidence collection occurred in the O. J. Simpson case, in which the defense forensic experts pointed out how key evidence was not documented or tracked. Defense attorney Johnnie Cochran called the Los Angeles Police Department lab a "cesspool of contamination." An officer put a vial of blood that police took as a sample from Simpson in his pocket and went to Simpson's home rather than booking it into evidence. Socks found in Simpson's bedroom were never examined for blood until two months later. A technician collected evidence, put it in improper packaging, and left it in a van during a hot summer day. To the extent that evidence was poorly handled, it could have altered the evidence itself. In response, the lab instituted reforms, including using a crime scene manager at scenes and barcodes to track evidence.[5] Those problems highlight how evidence can be altered in any number of different ways, from the crime scene to the laboratory.

One type of alteration is through contamination, in which something is rendered impure or unsuitable through contact with something else. A high-profile example of contamination occurred in the case of Amanda Knox, then an American college student, convicted of murder in Perugia, Italy. Italian police charged Knox and her boyfriend with murder. After officers searching her boyfriend's apartment found a kitchen knife, lab experts claimed that they identified a trace amount of the victim's DNA on it, leading them to suppose it had been used as the weapon. The boyfriend's DNA was also identified, along with that of two unknown males, on the victim's bra-clasp. Videos that the officers took during their investigation, however, showed that they did not wear caps, did not use sterile gloves, dropped items on the floor, and did not change their gloves as they collected items. Gloves, in particular, have been shown to easily transfer low levels of DNA between objects. The bra-clasp had been lying on the floor of the victim's apartment for weeks after the crime and the knife had very small amounts of DNA on it: both could have been contaminated. For these reasons, and due to other flaws in the work, including the potential for lab contamination, unsound testing methods, and errors in the interpretation of the DNA results, appellate judges reversed Knox's conviction in 2015.[6]

DNA AND CONTAMINATION

A fatal shooting in May 2017 occurred in Houston, Texas, after off-duty police responded to a parking lot fight outside a nightclub, only to find a man brandishing an assault rifle. A simple task, like securing a crime scene for forensic testing, has become much more complicated today due to the potential for DNA testing—and DNA contamination. Analysts can now test very small quantities of DNA, which analysts call "trace" DNA, including samples as small as a few cells, transferred through skin contact. When analysts examine such small quantities of evidence, even a small breach of protocol can contaminate the scene. The *Houston Chronicle* posted on its website a slideshow of photos taken of crime scene work in the early morning hours after the shooting. You first see trained crime scene unit staff, walking behind the red and yellow–taped scene, wearing booties, gloves, and face masks to prevent contamination of the evidence.[7] The yellow tape marks where the public may not enter, while the red tape marks where only crime scene staff can enter. You see police officers, not wearing protective gear, standing outside the red tape, but talking to technicians inside the secured area. Next you see earlier photos of uniformed police officers walking through the crime scene. Two officers stand right over the assault rifle, chatting away, and also not wearing any protective gear. We think of DNA testing as the gold standard for forensics, yet precisely because such minute quantities of evidence can be analyzed, even just a few cells, contamination can occur easily. The assault rifle was covered with DNA from the two police officers and any hope of DNA testing may be gone. The scene was contaminated. That photo shows why it is crucial that scientists supervise the crime scene; the culture shift in forensics needs to happen, not just in the lab but in police departments.

The crime scene investigation units that police departments use to collect evidence at crime scenes do not look like television depictions. Crime lab directors complain that almost everything they receive from crime scenes is improperly sealed, if not also poorly labeled, or even contaminated. The backlogs and time pressure in labs are real, but they are magnified by police submitting evidence that will not actually help to catch a culprit, because it is not useful, it is duplicative, or it is badly collected. Whereas quality control at the lab can be terribly inadequate, quality control in the field can be much worse. Often it is police agencies, not crime laboratories, that gather evidence at crime scenes; these roles also may sometimes be mixed.[8]

FIELD TESTING

The pills in her car were vitamins, said a Tampa Bay, Florida, woman who had run out of gas when police arrived. The officer suspected drugs and conducted a field test, using a chemical kit, which said these were oxycodone pills. She was arrested, and her husband could not make the $5,000 bail the judge set. A mother of four with no prior record, she was charged with drug trafficking, and languished in jail for five months before the crime lab did additional tests and found the pills were vitamins. "It felt like my whole life was over. It was terrible. My kids were devastated."[9]

She refused to plead guilty during those months in jail. But one reason we do not know how often basic tests like drug tests go wrong is that so many people face enormous pressure to plead guilty in our criminal justice system. Take the example of field drug testing. In the 1960s, police began to commonly test drugs using inexpensive and simple kits in the field. They put a small amount of the substance in a baggie, with prepackaged chemicals designed to react and change color, depending on the substance. These $2 tests report whether evidence is a controlled substance or not. However, these commercial kits can be of somewhat unknown reliability. Studies have found these kits can have shockingly high error rates. ProPublica has kept a running list of items that result in false positive test results on these kits: "sage, chocolate chip cookies, motor oil, spearmint, Dr. Bronner's Magic Soap, tortilla dough, deodorant, billiards chalk, patchouli, flour, eucalyptus, breath mints, Jolly Ranchers, Krispy Kreme donut glaze, exposure to air and loose-leaf tea."[10] The field tests are supposed to be followed up by a more rigorous lab test, but in the meantime a person may be arrested for drug possession, and people face great pressure to plead guilty, particularly if they are poor, denied bail, and remain in jail waiting for a day in court.

That is what happened in Houston: hundreds of wrongful convictions resulted and almost all of those innocent people pleaded guilty. In Harris County, Texas, an audit by the prosecutor's Conviction Integrity Unit uncovered that 456 cases involving field drug tests were erroneous. In 298 of the cases, there were no controlled substances, and in the other cases it was the wrong drug or wrong weight.[11] The convictions in those cases were all reversed. The Texas Forensic Science Commission, in 2016, said that these field tests are too unreliable to use in criminal cases, and that there should also be a follow-up lab test. In 2017 Houston police banned the use of those field drug tests. What will they use instead? At the time the police chief said that officers have "a wealth of training and experience into what narcotics look like, what they feel like in terms of the packaging, the color, the appearance."[12] The problem of arrests, based on poor judgments and evidence leading to guilty pleas, is not going away.

THE MAGIC BOX

If field test kits for drug testing are not that reliable, and we know it, but they are used anyway, then what will happen when DNA testing is done in the field? They call it the "magic box": rapid DNA testing machines are now available, and they do the types of analyses that are done by large machines in a crime lab, except in a unit the size of a desktop computer. "I barely need a pulse to use this instrument," said a detective in Bensalem,

Pennsylvania, telling a journalist how he just inserts a cheek swab from a motorist into a plastic cartridge, places it in the machine, and gets a reading. He had several hours of training from IntegenX, the manufacturer, and that was it. However, running the results from a single swab through a DNA database is simple. Large machines in crime labs can test a hundred such swabs at the same time.[13] What is far more complex is interpreting crime scene DNA samples, which can contain DNA mixtures from several people. Studies have suggested that these machines can consume or destroy samples, rendering them unusable, and that they make errors. Indeed, the National District Attorneys Association has said that it opposes the use of such machines, unless they are used by experienced DNA analysts. In some police departments, rapid DNA is used as an initial test, somewhat similar to field drug kits, but then sent to a crime lab for a more involved test. Often, however, the evidence is consumed, and it is impossible for the lab to conduct an accurate test. If so, it then raises the same issue as those field drug tests: will a less accurate technique be used to get cheap, quick results, and then produce guilty pleas, before there is a chance to find out what the evidence really means?

This is not hypothetical; already police have falsely arrested and jailed people due to mistaken rapid DNA results. Pop star Harry Styles was falsely connected to a string of unsolved murders in Hawaii by a rapid DNA machine and remained in jail for ten days until the error was uncovered. A state senator in Ohio was falsely connected to a series of child sexual assaults after he was given a rapid DNA test at a possible drunk driving stop and was held in jail for eight days until his lawyers uncovered the error.[14] One wonders how often rapid DNA mistakes occur in cases of people who are not well known and who cannot afford lawyers.

Indeed, rapid DNA testing using these magic boxes is now being used in a pilot program at the U. S. / Mexico border. The machines can identify parentage and sibling relationships, but not other relatives, since they were designed to be used for criminal databases. They do not use the hundreds of thousands of genetic locations that genetic genealogists use. This quick-and-dirty test cannot necessarily identify a half-sibling or an aunt or a grandparent and it could provide false results beyond identifying biological parents.[15] Such tests are highly inappropriate and inaccurate for use in immigration cases.

BREATH TESTS

A woman pleaded guilty in Spring Lake Municipal Court to driving while intoxicated in New Jersey, after the officer who stopped her car found her blood-alcohol level one point over the legal limit. This was her third offense, so she was in prison for a mandatory six-month sentence. Just two weeks into her sentence, her lawyer was informed that the machine used to measure her blood alcohol, the Alcotest, had not been calibrated. The detective whose job it was to calibrate the machines every six months was himself criminally charged with official misconduct and tampering with records, because he skipped the calibration step. The woman sought to take back her guilty plea. Her lawyer also filed a class action, to reverse all of the convictions of people who, like her, were affected—the detective was responsible for the machines in twenty counties. Ultimately, a judge held hearings and concluded that these failings could have led to real errors in a vast number of cases. Over twenty thousand cases were thrown out by the state Supreme Court in late 2018 due to this misconduct.[16] These people may have had jail time, suspended driver's licenses, and fines, all based on tainted test results. The forensic evidence was contaminated, and not in the lab, but by police operating equipment in the field.

The problem of police being asked to carry out reliable blood alcohol testing at the crime scene may be the biggest challenge for modern forensics, and it has never been satisfactorily solved. The scale of enforcement is vast. Each year, over ten thousand deaths are attributed to drunken driving. Almost one and a half million people are arrested for driving while intoxicated in the United States: a huge number of arrests, constituting almost one in two hundred licensed drivers.[17] All states have laws barring driving while under the influence or while intoxicated (abbreviated as DUI or DWI) and all states except Utah, which has a lower limit, define impairment as driving with a blood alcohol concentration of .08 grams per deciliter. That technical definition of driving while impaired did not originally exist.

Before blood testing, evidence of intoxication came from police officers, who described the suspect's behavior and appearance. It was a subjective test. Walk and turn, put a finger to your nose, or stand on one leg: police developed these field sobriety tests to try to make the work more objective.

The tests sound pretty basic and some judges have said these are not scientific and police are not acting as experts. Some judges have said police cannot claim to be using a "test" or using terms like "pass" or "fail" or "points."[18] These field tests have themselves been tested, and they perform terribly. In one test, police used field tests to find almost half of subjects with no alcohol in their system were too intoxicated to drive.[19] Those tests have been "standardized" by the National Highway Traffic Safety Administration, which found only six of fifteen commonly used roadside tests to be useful. In Ohio, after courts barred use of field tests where police did not comply with those standards, legislators passed a law stating that prosecutors can introduce the results of a field sobriety test whether they followed national standards or not.[20]

The solution, like in other areas of forensics, was to move toward more objective measures. Many states added laws with a blood alcohol concentration (BAC)–based definition. That created a new challenge. It is not easy to get a warrant and administer blood tests in the field. Some states, like North Carolina, have mobile trailers—BAT-mobiles, they call them—with a judge on board to issue warrants and a medical professional who can draw blood. Otherwise, it takes time to obtain cause and then later bring a person to a lab setting to draw blood. By then, the amount of alcohol in the blood may have changed.

To try to gather evidence of impairment earlier, in the 1930s, companies developed machines, beginning with the Breathalyzer, a portable unit designed to measure alcohol present in the breath. It was never intended to be definitive. Breath tests have all sorts of problems, including because different people release more alcohol into their breath than others. It can depend on how you breathe. For example, twenty seconds of rapid breathing or hyperventilation can decrease the amount of alcohol in one's breath by 11 percent. A few deep breaths can decrease breath alcohol by 4 percent and holding one's breath can increase it by 12 percent. Changes in a person's body temperature also have a big impact on breath alcohol, as does breath temperature. Finally, lung volume makes a big difference. On average, women and older individuals have less lung volume and may typically show higher breath alcohol.[21] Nevertheless, these devices were seen as so useful that they were widely adopted by police in DUI / DWI cases: as the New York Court of Appeals has put it, these machines are "universally accepted."[22] Indeed, breath testing is commonly used as the basis for DUI prosecutions. Yet like other machines, they can have glitches, they malfunction, they must be calibrated, and their measurements have uncertainty. The manufacturers often do not want to test or disclose problems with machines they sell, but what is more troubling is that police continue to use them and judges continue to allow them to be used without disclosing error rates.

Twenty individuals in New Jersey challenged their convictions for DUI based on the state law, which defines driving under the influence as operating a motor vehicle with a BAC of 0.08 percent or more.[23] New Jersey had an exclusive contract with a company that makes the Alcotest breath analyzer. The Alcotest uses infrared light to assess the amount of alcohol in breath, as well as a fuel cell that measures an electric current generated when exposed to alcohol. However, the fuel cell wears down over time. The designers included an algorithm to adjust for that, but it is incomplete, and the court said that it must be recalibrated every six months.[24] The manufacturer refused to let researchers test the Alcotest, but concerned about reliability issues, the New Jersey Supreme Court asked that a retired judge be appointed to conduct a review. The judge asked for several of the machines for the defense lawyers and prosecutors to examine. They were provided, but Alcotest refused to provide the software source code, saying that its contract with the state declared it a "trade secret." The company resisted any effort to disclose its source code, even after the judge ordered that it do so, but finally, two independent labs were retained to error-check the code. The defense firm found two dozen defects in the code, recommending that the Alcotest "should be suspended from use until the software has been reviewed."[25] The judge, however, ruled that the Alcotest is "scientifically reliable." Ultimately, the New Jersey Supreme Court agreed that the machine could be used, but subject to a number of conditions, including calibrating the machines regularly to be sure that their readings are more accurate. That was not the end of the story: in 2018, twenty thousand cases were reversed because this calibration requirement was not being followed.

The same problems exist in other states. In perhaps the largest-scale exclusion of forensic evidence of all time, 36,000 Alcotest results over eight years were thrown out by the courts in Massachusetts in 2019.[26]

Only one state, Minnesota, has required the company to provide the source code to its breath analyzer.[27] There too, in examining over a thousand pages of source code, the judges found a range of errors in the code for a different machine, the commonly used Intoxilyzer.[28] Indeed, problems with the machines have come to light across the country. In Florida, the new Intoxilyzer 8000 had a software glitch, resulting in the dismissal of hundreds of cases. In response, Florida lawmakers passed a law in 2008 barring the defense from getting technical information about these machines, at least from the government. In a clever bit of drafting, the law says that the defense can get "full information" about a blood alcohol test, but defines "full information" to include basically just the date, time, and results of a test, and specifically not any software or any information in the possession of the machine's manufacturer.[29] After the law was passed, problems continued, and local Florida judges then ordered the manufacturer to disclose source code. The company initially refused and judges then imposed over $100,000 in fines. The company then agreed to very limited "controlled viewing" of the code.[30]

Drunk driving is incredibly dangerous and it is one of our most serious public health problems. But a DUI conviction can result in a serious criminal record, loss of a driver's license, loss of employment, and serious harm to reputation. The very notion that we allow corporations to sell black box machines to police, without telling police how they work or how reliable they are, is astounding. It is shocking that entire states have contracted to buy these machines without rigorously testing them and asking for source code to assure sound functioning. It should be unconstitutional to ever use black box machines, of unknown reliability, to investigate crimes, much less to convict people of crimes.

PRESERVING EVIDENCE

The Pearson Place warehouse that the New York Police Department operates in Long Island City, Queens, is like no other warehouse on earth. It covers vast city blocks. Seized counterfeit goods, shopping carts containing the belongings of homeless people, proceeds from massive drug heists: you can see officers wheeling just about anything seized in the five boroughs of the city into its cavernous interiors. These items are duly logged by the property clerks and then stored. Rooms full of barrels store DNA evidence from sexual assault cases. I visited the warehouse back in 2003, as a young lawyer, to examine the seals on a rape kit from a State Island case, in which DNA tests exonerated a man for a rape that he did not commit. During my visit, I did not know that a neighboring barrel held evidence from the case of Alan Newton.

In 1994 Newton began to make requests that his evidence be pulled from the warehouse for a DNA test. An NYPD sergeant had told Newton that the evidence no longer existed at Pearson Place: it had been destroyed. Newton did not give up and every two years he filed new requests. Every time he made a request to test the evidence, he was told it was gone. Innocence Project lawyers took on the case, and in 2004 the evidence was found in a barrel in the Pearson Place warehouse, right where it should have been all along. Apparently, during all of those years, the officers had never really looked. Newton was exonerated in 2006 and he sued for damages. At a federal civil rights trial, the jurors awarded him over $18 million (although the city fought the award for years and the amount was later reduced on appeal).[31]

HIDING THE FORENSICS

Consider the case of John Thompson, convicted in New Orleans, Louisiana, for a murder he did not commit. Fourteen years after this trial, he was exonerated. At his trial, though, the prosecutors concealed a forensic report that showed that the blood type from the victim's clothing did not match his, among other evidence of innocence. In fact, the New Orleans prosecutors even removed the evidence from the police property room when the defense lawyer inspected the evidence locker, so that the defense would not even know that evidence was tested. The Constitution requires that such evidence be shared with the defense. Police and prosecutors must, under the Supreme Court's 1963 ruling in *Brady v. Maryland,* disclose all material exculpatory evidence, as a matter of fundamental fairness and due process.[32] Here, the prosecutors violated that rule. The Supreme Court justices, in a closely split five-four decision, held that prosecutors still could not be sued for damages, because the issue was so "nuanced" that they should be immune from paying damages. Justice Clarence Thomas wrote that even though there were other similar violations by that office, during the same time period, the violations were not systematic enough. Justice Thomas emphasized that in the Orleans Parish district attorney's office, "junior prosecutors were trained by senior prosecutors who supervised them as they worked together to prepare cases for trial." Thompson was innocent and prosecutors violated his constitutional rights by hiding the forensics, but he received no compensation for his fourteen years in prison.

Even outright misconduct by police or lab analysts may not violate the Constitution, as interpreted by the U. S. Supreme Court. In a 1984 ruling in *California v. Trombetta*, the Court placed the burden on a defendant to show that forensic evidence destroyed by police would have had value in proving innocence. It is hard to know what value it might have had, once the evidence is destroyed.[33] In the case of Larry Youngblood, the Supreme Court held that if police fail to preserve evidence in a manner that permits forensic testing, it is not a violation of due process unless it is done in bad faith.[34] Such bad faith, reasonably available means, and materiality showings are prohibitively difficult to make. Indeed, the defendant Youngblood was later exonerated: he was an innocent man. The very same poorly preserved evidence was later, due to advances in genetic technology, able to be tested using DNA, and it cleared Youngblood and implicated another person.[35]

Judges should be holding police to a higher standard, considering that forensic evidence can be the difference between guilt and innocence. Complicated constitutional rules regulate searches and seizures, the warnings police must give when they question suspects, and so much more that officers do in their daily jobs. Yet, for forensics and scientific evidence, the Constitution has not yet caught up to the work of crime scene analysts or lab analysts. States and localities set the rules on careful evidence collection, documenting evidence, and preserving evidence. To paraphrase Supreme Court Justice William J. Brennan, "[i]f a policeman must know the Constitution," why not a crime scene analyst or a forensic scientist?[36]

None of the improvements in court or at crime labs matters much if there is no quality control for the police officers who collect the evidence:

garbage in, garbage out. This is true of crime scene collection and of police property lockers and warehouses, and it is true as police departments try out new technology, whether it is field drug kits or magic box DNA kits. We need scientists involved at all stages of the process, beginning with crime scene collection. We cannot depend on the outcomes in our labs or in our courtrooms if sound science and quality control are not in place at the crime scene.

PART IV

The Movement to Fix Forensics

11 The Rebirth of the Lab

"Scientific evidence really nails this man to the wall," the Harris County, Texas, prosecutor told the jurors in his closing statements. It really did. In February 1987 two men abducted and raped a fourteen-year-old girl in Houston, Texas. The victim initially identified two brothers and a man named Isidro Yanez, but after several suggestive lineup procedures were used, she instead identified George Rodriguez. At the trial, Rodriguez told the jury that he was innocent. He had a good alibi; he had been working at a factory on the day of the crime. The prosecutor emphasized, however, that the blood typing of the swabs taken from the victim showed Rodriguez did commit the crime, a hair from the crime scene matched his, and the forensics showed that the alternative suspect, Yanez, "could not have committed the offense." Rodriguez was convicted of aggravated kidnapping and sexual assault and sentenced to sixty years in prison. Seventeen years later, the same hair was tested again, but this time using DNA analysis.[1] The results exonerated Rodriguez—and brought down the entire Houston police crime lab. The city shut down one unit, and then the entire lab, with hundreds of cases called into question. Headlines dubbed the Houston lab "the Worst Crime Laboratory in the Country."[2]

HOUSTON HAS A PROBLEM

At Rodriguez's trial, the analyst found the single hair located on the victim's panties to have been "consistent with" those from Rodriguez. That testimony was not totally overstated, but we know more today about how unreliable such hair comparisons can be. Next, the analyst described the blood type of swabs from the rape kit. Blood typing is a simple procedure based on sound research and statistics. This analyst testified, though, that Rodriguez could have left the stains and that Yanez was definitively excluded since "one would predict his genetics would show up as a donor in a sexual assault" and blood of his type was not observed. This was flat-out wrong. In reality, the tests were consistent with the victim's blood type. No person could be either included or excluded. The test results provided nothing that could be linked to Rodriguez, or to anyone else on the planet.

Rodriguez was convicted of rape, largely on the strength of these flawed forensics. He lost his appeals and languished in prison for eighteen years. During that time, the biological evidence in his case was mostly destroyed by the crime lab. Few jurisdictions had rules in place that forensics must be preserved. A single hair had been miraculously saved, though, and by 2003, scientists could conduct mitochondrial DNA testing on it. The Innocence Project at Cardozo Law School in New York City stepped in, secured the DNA tests, and the very hair that the lab analyst found "consistent" at trial now exonerated Rodriguez.

In 2002, just before Rodriguez sought this DNA testing, journalists uncovered errors in the Houston lab DNA unit's work. A man named Josiah Sutton, convicted of rape and kidnapping based on DNA test results, had spent four and a half years in prison. The analyst claimed only one person in 694,000 shared the profile of a semen sample from the backseat of the victim's car. In fact, one in sixteen black men shared that profile. While in prison, Sutton read about DNA testing and wrote a handwritten request to the judge for testing. The judge refused to grant it; Texas had no law permitting post-conviction DNA testing at the time. However, local journalists investigating the lab sent the DNA reports from Sutton's case to University of California Irvine professor William Thompson. Thompson found blatant errors in the reports; he concluded the lab had the statistics wrong. The DNA was retested and the results showed the semen came from a single man, and not Sutton. Sutton was exonerated, and initially, the DNA unit was shut down to allow for a review and retesting of hundreds of other cases. As so often happens, however, the errors were not isolated mistakes made by a few "bad apple" analysts but rather symptoms of a deeper problem. By this time, Rodriguez was similarly cleared by DNA tests. The analyst who presented the blood and hair testimony in Rodriguez's case had been promoted to head the entire lab's serology and DNA units. Since that analyst supervised so much of what the lab had done for years, tens of thousands of forensic tests were called into question.

AUDIT

To their credit, the city ordered a comprehensive audit of the crime lab by an entire team of lawyers and forensic scientists, who would review over 3,500 cases. Michael Bromwich, who headed the FBI hair audit, also headed this effort. The team reviewed hundreds of DNA cases and thousands of serology cases.[3] For six years, the roof over the evidence storage room had leaked, contaminating cases. The head of the DNA unit had no prior experience with DNA. The team learned of other types of problems at the lab, including "dry-labbing," that is, wholly fabricating conclusions when no testing was conducted.

The audit team recommended that hundreds of old cases be reopened and changes to the policies and supervision of the lab. The city shut down the crime lab entirely. When the 2003 *New York Times* headline asked whether Houston was "the Worst Crime Laboratory in the Country," perhaps still more telling was the second part of the headline: "Or Is Houston Typical?" As I described, Houston is far from the only laboratory that has been shut down, due to a pervasive lack of quality control and regulation. How can these scandals be prevented?

A LAB REBORN

Today, the Houston crime lab is a totally different place—not the worst, and perhaps the best. Taking the elevators upstairs, you enter a different world. The lab, reopened in 2014 and renamed the Houston Forensic Science Center (HFSC), is now run by scientists, headed by Peter Stout, the visionary head of the lab, and no police can be seen.

When I first visited the lab in 2018, I entered the lobby of the Houston Police Headquarters. Past the security check, I walked by the police museum, with old squad cars, a helicopter, SWAT gear, uniforms, banners of police badges, and a Wall of Honor memorial for fallen officers. Yet up on the twenty-sixth floor, the lab was a model for forensics work independent of law enforcement (and it has since moved to a new location). No longer were lab analysts "cops in lab coats," as law professor Sandra Guerra Thompson memorably put it in her wonderful book describing this transformation.[4] No lab in the world is quite like the Houston lab. There have been private, for-profit labs in the United States, ever since DNA testing became available, with paying customers, including people with paternity cases. However, law enforcement operates the bulk of the crime labs in the United States, and in addition, most labs will only test evidence if law enforcement requests it. In 2012 the Houston lab was renamed and separately incorporated as the HFSC using a Texas law that had been used to set up corporations for highway construction projects. Peter Stout is not a lab director but rather the president and CEO. His boss is a nine-member board of directors that represents the diverse constituencies of the lab, including prosecutors, police, defense lawyers, law professors, scientists, and an exoneree, Anthony Graves, who spent nearly twenty years, half on death row, for a murder that he did not commit.[5]

The lab is gigantic by crime lab standards, with about 200 employees and about 30,000 requests for testing per year, and a $27 million budget. Stout created a quality division with seven people whose full-time jobs are to prevent and detect errors in the lab.[6] Most labs, Stout observes, may have a lab director, who also doubles as the quality manager, and "also the plumber and the janitor, and everything else." The goal of this unit is no less than testing the entire system operating in the lab. I have talked about how proficiency tests can be a good thing. Proficiency tests, however, often just test how well examiners analyze evidence. The HSFC's goal is to test every stage in the process, from how the evidence comes into the lab to how conclusions are reported out.

BLINDS

Sociologist Henry Landsberger conducted experiments at the Hawthorne Works, a Western Electric factory outside Chicago, Illinois, studying whether workers were more productive when the factory provided more lighting. Even small changes in the lighting resulted in real improvements in productivity, but so did other minor changes, like cleaning worksta-tions. Landsberger suspected that the workers knew they were being watched. The workers may have also known what the observers wanted to find. The term "Hawthorne effect" now describes the notion that people being observed may behave differently.

Peter Stout is trying to create a giant Hawthorne effect by running experiments constantly on an entire crime laboratory. The Case Management Division of the lab receives evidence from law enforcement and creates a firewall between police and lab analysts. This also makes it possible to run a blind quality control program, where the lab sends fake test cases to analysts. Stout started his career in the military, and was familiar with the National Laboratory Certification program, which had used blind testing for decades. A Marine Corps aircraft crashed into the deck of the aircraft carrier USS Nimitz in May 1981, killing fourteen peo-ple and injuring forty-two. The Navy investigation resulted in the first large blind proficiency testing program in the United States. The Navy dis-covered that six of the ten deck crew who had died had used illegal drugs in the past month. The Navy began mass screening of all servicemembers, and the labs quickly found themselves overwhelmed with truckloads of urine samples. In the first year of this drug testing program, over a thou-sand disciplinary actions against Navy sailors were reversed due to botched tests. The chief of naval operations responded by instituting a series of quality controls, including the placing of blind tests among the samples to be drug tested. The federal government adopted these procedures for all labs, which in 1988 became the modern National Laboratory Certification Program.[7]

A crime lab can do the same thing, but none had tried before Stout. To roll out blind testing, "you have to have somebody firmly behind it." The goal is to test the entire system, day in and day out, as "a giant Hawthorne effect experiment." All of the analysts at the lab know that any case that they work on might be a test, across all of the seven disciplines: toxicology, controlled substances, digital evidence, DNA, firearms, toolmarks, and latent prints.[8] As this program was ramping up, in December 2018, I visited the quality division, where they make the blind tests. As part of my work with a federally funded consortium, the Center for Statistics and Applications in Forensic Evidence (CSAFE), my colleagues and I supported this quality work to create blinds. This work was done at the time in an obscure room with no sign on the door; we had to switch between three elevator banks to find it. The analysts who did firearms work down the hall likely had no idea what was happening. Inside the narrow room was a freezer with hundreds of vials of samples to test in drug toxicology cases. Blind testing is easiest to do for drug testing, or toxicology; every lab uses the same gray-topped tubes for testing. Fingerprint blinds are harder to construct, because the prints have to be created on the standard lift cards police use. Shelves have a variety of mugs and tools and other objects they use to create latent prints. The analysts would be able to pick out blinds readily if they see a series of cases with fingerprints all left on the same type of mug. Sheets taped to the walls included contact information for police officers who are "in" on the tests. Stout explains that when analysts have spotted blind tests, it is usually because of the packaging. When "the handwriting is too neat, and there were no spelling errors," then the analyst guesses that it just "can't be a cop." The specialists learned to practice writing backward or behind their back. For the fingerprint blinds, analysts only spotted one in the first hundred.[9] Overall, 51 of the first 901 blinds were detected.[10]

The blinds in digital evidence were hardest to construct. Digital evidence is increasingly important to forensics; there are now more digital phones in the world than there are people, and our phones leave a digital trail everywhere people go. A smartphone may have a terabyte of data on it that must be downloaded, without altering it, and analyzed. The system that police often use, called a Cellebright kiosk, can bypass lock screens and passwords to extract data from a device. However, if used improperly, it can also lose or alter data. Manufacturers release dozens of new devices every day, with new specifications and updates: it is an arms race for digital forensics specialists to keep up. Similarly, to analyze video evidence, there may be proprietary programs and drivers for each device. The

Houston lab conducts digital evidence blinds by sending staff to pawn-shops to buy old tablets or cheap "burner phones." Then, people in the lab text the device at random times, including in the middle of the night, using phrases suggesting they are working, say, on a drug deal. They can test the digital evidence staff on whether they preserve all of that evidence, and locate the key incriminating evidence.

Stout has a standing bet with the staff that if they identify a case as a blind and they are right, he has a Starbucks card for them. If they say call out a blind and are wrong, they owe him a dollar. Last I checked, Stout reported that he was "up two dollars." Today, 5 percent of all cases in the lab are blind tests.[11] Stout put it this way: "Some bald-headed lunatic," meaning Stout, "keeps saying, 'I want to target 5 percent of the work flow going through there.'" Where does the 5 percent goal come from? "It is enough that everybody has an expectation they are going to see them, but it's not so small that they never think they are going to see one." No other labs do this at such a scale. A few labs have done two or three blinds a year. The Toronto lab has done two or three cases a year over a ten-year period, as does the Defense Forensic Science Center. Houston, formerly the worst lab in the country, is showing the world how it can be done.

VERIFICATION

Forensics work can be safeguarded by including a second quality check: to require that the work in a case is checked by another analyst—that is, veri-fication. Verification traditionally just involved looking over someone else's work and seeing what a co-worker concluded, without conducting an inde-pendent analysis. A blind verification, though, requires a second person to do a separate analysis, without knowing who the first examiner was, what the case details are, or what conclusion the first examiner reached. The FBI instituted blind verification, in cases involving single fingerprints, after the Mayfield error. The Houston lab is also rolling out blind re-verifi-cation of a fixed percentage of cases. So far, it is not a big program. The Virginia Department of Forensic Sciences does the same in randomly selected cases. Such approaches can be easily done more broadly.

What happens if any analyst makes an error in a blind proficiency test or a verification? Is the analyst "ruined," as a fingerprint examiner put it at a conference I held at Duke? After all, the defense could question the analyst on the stand about failing a test. Peter Stout's response is that errors will occur and they will be disclosed publicly, but analysts will not be "ruined." In a healthy organization, human errors happen, but they are detected and remedied. This question—whether an examiner is ruined or burned after making an error on a blind test—can itself be tested. With psychologists Jeff Kukucka and William Crozier, we gave 1,400 mock jurors, recruited online from across the county, different versions of testimony from a fingerprint examiner, based on testimony in real trials. We found that blind proficiency testing mostly helps. Experts who describe a blind testing to the jury, and report that they pass their tests, obtained more guilty votes than experts who do not say anything about proficiency. The jurors voted to convict less when they heard from low-proficiency experts. When the lawyer cross-examined the expert about the subjectivity of fingerprint analysis, the jurors convicted even less for a low-proficiency expert. Jurors really do care about proficiency, but they are fairly forgiving of experts, if the blind testing is routine.[12]

TRANSPARENCY

How can you tell what work a forensic analyst did and whether they did it correctly? Even if you have the lab reports, you may have no way of knowing whether the expert followed procedures. Often next to nothing is known about what the procedures are for a lab. The Houston lab posts all of its policies, validation tests, protocols, audits, and reviews online for the public to see. Most crime laboratories do not do that, and even when the policies are shared, they may not explain what the forensic analysts actually do. In 2018 the Department of Justice announced that transparency is a "core value," and stated all federal crime labs will now post all policies, procedures, and protocols, quality management systems documents, and internal validation studies online.[13] Hopefully more labs will follow suit.

NEXT-GENERATION CRIME LABS

It took a "hard, bloody, bare-knuckled fight" to re-create the Houston lab as the independent HSFC, as Stout likes to say. All labs can run like the Houston lab. In fact, the same investments in quality that can detect potential errors have also made work more efficient. The lab is now better at tracking and prioritizing work. All of these changes cost something, but consider the cost of untested or poorly tested evidence. False negatives, where no correct match is made, are the most common forensic errors, according to some studies. Failure to link fingerprints to hundreds of burglaries, or failure to link fingerprints to a single homicide, could result in crime that costs Houston residents millions of dollars in harm. There are three hundred homicides a year in Houston, and failure to link forensic evidence to just one of them would cause terrible harm. Or take George Rodriguez's wrongful conviction. You can never return the years of his life taken away; in his civil rights case, the jury awarded him $5 million and the case later settled for $3.1 million, with another $1 million from the state of Texas. That would pay for years of quality control at the lab.

The costs of errors are not normally factored into the management of a crime lab, such as they would be for a hospital. Stout asks: How accurate do you need to be? Is a system that makes an error 1 in a 100 times good enough? Given the stakes, Stout aims for a 1 in 10,000 system, to prevent both costly crimes and wrongful convictions. What if federal grants required every lab to develop a 1 in 10,000 system to catch and prevent errors? Forensic science is not like medicine: it is not a trillion-dollar industry but a three- to four-billion-dollar industry. The quality controls we desperately need, though, are not that expensive. If the former "worst lab in the country" can do it, then every lab can and must adopt sound quality controls.

12 Big Data Forensics

Willie Allen Lynch, convicted of drug charges, is serving an eight-year sentence largely based on a blurry cellphone photo. Undercover detectives in Jacksonville, Florida, conducted a $50 crack purchase, and while they did not make an arrest at the time, one did pretend to make a call on his phone and used it to take a photo of the seller (see photo). The undercover officers had no leads. They came across Lynch after he was identified by a facial recognition algorithm that searched a database of driver's license and other police photos. The local police in Jacksonville accessed the FBI's data. The FBI's facial recognition unit, which runs the aptly named Facial Analysis, Comparison, and Evaluation (FACE) services, has access to 641 million photos (almost double the U. S. population). Just eight days before trial, Lynch's lawyers learned he was identified using such facial recognition. Apparently, four other faces were also identified. His photo was given a "one star" rating. Lynch's lawyers were not informed what that single star meant, or what the other four faces looked like. Even at trial, the judge did not allow the defense any access to the forensics database or to the complete results.[1]

That is why Lynch, the first in the country to do so, asked the judge to bar the facial identification in his case, and argued that at the very least,

Willie Lynch facial recognition image. Courtesy of Ben Conarck and
the *Florida Times-Union*.

he should be able to see the photos of the four other people that the database search turned up. The software had never been tested. The
Jacksonville police, like many others, had no policies for how to use such
facial recognition programs, nor did they disclose how they used it. Plus,
there were specific reasons for concern in Lynch's case. A lab analyst
showed a detective who had observed the drug transaction a single photo
of Lynch, asking if he was the one. That was very suggestive: they did not
use a proper police lineup, with a group of photos. The analyst also told
the detectives that she knew Lynch's criminal history, which included
prior convictions for drug sales.[2]

These judges explained that the prosecutors were not required to turn
the evidence over to Lynch, because "he cannot show that the other photos
the database returned resembled him." He could make that showing if the
prosecutors disclosed the photos. This Catch-22 reasoning was still more
unfair because the five photos must have resembled each other to some
degree, since after all, the database chose each of them for that reason.
Lynch, who is black, also argued the database may make more errors when
searching black faces, since most facial recognition databases have been
shown to do so. The trial judge should not have allowed the facial recognition expert to testify, without substantial evidence of the reliability of the
method.[3] In 2019 the Florida Supreme Court declined to hear the case, so
Lynch is still serving an eight-year sentence.

Why can't you smile in a passport photo or, in states with "no smile" laws, in a driver's license photo? The reason why has to do with the challenge Lynch brought in his case. The DMV employee taking your photo will instruct you not to smile, and not because they want you to look serious. The reason is that, this very moment, a federal agent may be using your driver's license photo in a facial recognition algorithm, or passport photo, or any federal identification photo. When a person smiles, it changes the distances between facial features, which can throw off the algorithm. That is why the federal REAL-ID act imposes standards calling for identification photos without smiles. Super-ID cards are coming next: international agreements increasingly call for enhanced identification, including with chips or barcodes that share more biometric data at border checkpoints.

Officers are definitely using my photo. I have a North Carolina driver's license, and my state shares all of its driver's license photos with the Federal Bureau of Investigation (FBI). A little-known exception to the Driver's Privacy Protection Act allows states to share photos with the FBI. The FBI has photos from massive federal databanks but also from twenty-one states and the District of Columbia.[4] Police have conducted hundreds of thousands of these FACE searches. Yet none of us agreed, when we had our driver's license photos taken, to have our faces used by the FBI or by the police. The FBI created this program "in the shadows with no consent," said House Oversight Committee chairman Elijah E. Cummings.[5] When the FBI began using these photos in criminal investigations, in 2011, it did not ask for permission. In fact, for five years after it began using all of this personal information, the FBI did not conduct the legally required privacy reviews to explain what they were doing.[6]

These face searches can link innocent people to crimes. After all, hundreds of millions of faces are in the databases. In a 2019 General Accountability Office report, examiners found that the FBI did not properly audit the accuracy of the facial recognition algorithm used on this massive database. Most troubling, the FBI admitted it had never checked how often a person's photo might be incorrectly matched. That was a stunning admission: the FBI had never checked its error rate and it still has not tested it. Instead, the FBI noted that searches located a photo of a face known to be in the database as much as 86 percent of the time, but only when running searches in which the system was able to return at least fifty photos. Errors can also be caused by how a photo is edited, the analysis of the search results, and the criteria used to decide if it is a "match," as well as any law enforcement follow-up.

If you have been to an airport, if you have a passport, if your face is available on social media, or if you have a driver's license, then your biometric information is probably in one of these massive databases that police and the FBI search. Half of all adults in the United States had their faces included by 2016, and many more have their faces added each year. The Georgetown Law School Center on Privacy and Technology, the first to report this, called it a "perpetual lineup."[7] Police have even used face searches on faces of people at rallies. Moreover, the algorithm may be biased, based on race, gender, or other characteristics. An MIT study of Amazon's facial recognition software, increasingly used by law enforcement, found that it was less accurate in simply identifying a person's gender if a person is female or darker-skinned.[8]

We have to worry about contamination of crime scene evidence; for instance, if the officer handling evidence did not wear gloves. Today, we must also worry about contamination through connections officers make using interlocking databases, with evidence from hundreds of millions of innocent people. Welcome to our dystopian world of big data forensics. Bringing data into forensics can be a good thing, but without any assessment of reliability, new technology can create new dangers, just like with the untested FACE program. Police and labs increasingly use fingerprint databases, risk assessments, facial recognition systems, and rapid DNA kits. Some of these computer programs or systems are owned by for-profit private companies, who do not share how their systems work. This should not be allowed. When any scientific methods are used, whether it is a checklist, a complex algorithm, or big data, it must be disclosed and validated by researchers, examined for potential bias and inaccuracy, and made transparent, including to the defense. Lawyers and scientists must wage new battles to uncover and test the wave of black box forensics being used to send people to prison.

STATISTICS AND DNA MIXTURES

Researchers increasingly use algorithms to analyze the complex mixtures that raise the most difficult challenges for DNA testing. Sometimes police know that they have a single-source sample, such as when they take a swab of a convict to enter that person's DNA profile in a DNA databank. Samples in sexual assault cases often involve a simple mixture of material from two people, and analysis can isolate any male contribution to a sample. Crime scene DNA is different. The lab analysts may have no way of knowing how many people's DNA may be present. The DNA test may reflect the genetic profile of one, or two, or dozens of people. Small quantities, down to just a few cells, can now be tested using extraordinarily sensitive equipment, but just a few cells from people who come into contact with a sample can turn it into a mixture.

A complex mixture, with more than two contributors to a sample, is "inherently difficult" to analyze, as the White House PCAST report put it.[9] Even if a suspect's profile can be observed within a mixture, what is the probability that the suspect really contributed to the sample? For example, if you use the entire bag of Scrabble pieces with letters from the alphabet, it is easy to rearrange the tiles and make out your own name. If you only draw seven tiles, though, the changes are low. Developers of computer algorithms increasingly claim they can make sense of complex DNA mixtures with three, four, five, or more contributors. The concern is that, in effect, they are looking for names using the entire bag of Scrabble pieces. Subjective interpretation of such complex DNA mixtures risks error, and studies like those by Itiel Dror and Greg Hampikian show how such interpretation can be biased.[10] In a troubling Virginia case, the DNA analyst interpreted a mixture and reported only 1 in 1.1 billion people would, like the defendant, share the DNA profile. However, professor William Thompson later reexamined the evidence and concluded that actually one in *two people* might actually share the profile.[11]

In Texas, the Department of Public Safety asked that DNA mixture evidence be reexamined in 2015, in response to errors in the FBI's population data used to calculate results. They found grave errors in the DNA mixture statistics used in criminal trials, including a case where the report stated that the DNA would be randomly shared by 1 in 1.4 billion people, when it was in fact 1 in 36 people, or another case in which the DNA was totally inconclusive. They initiated, with the Texas Forensic Science Commission, a review of tens of thousands of cases in which DNA mixture evidence was presented.[12]

Yet computer algorithms have additional problems. There are at least eight such programs available, and some of them remain "black box" and proprietary—that is, the developers will not share the details of how they work. In one case, there was a battle of the algorithms. The two algorithms were called STRmix, which was developed by researchers at a company in New Zealand, and TrueAllele, which was created by an American company called Cybergenetics. The defendant, charged with the murder of a twelve-year-old boy, sought to contest DNA tests of scrapings taken from under the victim's fingernails. Most of that material was consistent with the boy's DNA, but there was a small quantity of additional DNA. The expert using STRmix software said that the result included the defendant. The expert using TrueAllele software said that the results were inconclusive.[13] The judge ultimately ruled that none of this competing DNA evidence was admissible.[14]

How much DNA is needed before the method can even be used? The PCAST report found that there should be serious scientific research and validation done of any DNA mixture algorithms before they are to be used in criminal cases.[15] Yet they are still being used in criminal cases. So far, no other judge has raised questions concerning the software.

SEARCH

Databases have transformed forensics, making new connections possible and making work more efficient, but also in ways that raise deep new cause for concern. Before the mid-1990s, a forensic analyst could only search by hand. Latent fingerprints lifted from a crime scene would sit on a shelf, with no reason to look at it unless one had a suspect in mind, and located the evidence on that shelf. Until recently, spent shell casings or bullets from a crime scene would languish. Unless the police seized a suspect's gun, they had nothing to compare those shells or bullets to. Similarly, sexual assault kits and other biological evidence would often sit untested, or would be thrown away after time passed. Without a suspect, there was not much one could do with stale evidence. Many crimes remained unsolved.

Forensic databases introduced big data searches to criminal investigations. Fingerprint databases can automatically search against large archives of suspects. National DNA databanks, in efforts to close unsolved crimes, search against archives of millions of DNA samples. The Combined DNA Index System (CODIS), the set of DNA databanks, is run by the FBI, as permitted by federal law and generously funded by Congress. The National Integrated Ballistic Information Network (NIBN) database maintained by the Bureau of Alcohol, Tobacco and Firearms (ATF) allows spent shell casings and bullets to be searched, to potentially match them to those from other crime scenes. Facial recognition software attempts to compare features of faces from crime scene photos or video footage. If you have ever walked in an airport, or in downtown Washington, DC, then your face has been scanned and stored in these databanks. "That is just how it is," as a local crime lab deputy put it to my students, suggesting that there is nothing one can do about it: we all now live in a surveillance society.

There are benefits to the automation that these databases and accompanying computer programs provide. They can save time and make work more accurate. Programs can auto-extract prints, for example, meaning they do an initial markup of the prints, saving an analyst from having to laboriously hand-mark the evidence. Fingerprint analysts will tell you that although this auto-extract function is a time saver and the algorithms have improved, they are still quite inaccurate; hopefully they will improve. Another benefit of relying more on machines is that they can, if we design them to do so, create a better record of the analysis. For example, automated systems, such as the MIDEO system used at some labs, can create a digital record of what features were identified and compared, together with any changes made during the process in what was identified and relied upon to reach conclusions. Still better are systems that record the entire examination and decision-making process. That said, other systems, like the black box algorithms just described, create no record of what they do to make comparisons and assign probabilities. No one working in crime labs knows how the NIBN database searches casings, or how an AFIS system searches fingerprints, or how FACE facial algorithms operate. They remain a black box.

CLOSED ACCESS

These databases are typically proprietary, meaning that while crime labs and lab analysts can access them, the analysts themselves may not know how the computer programs or algorithms that search and analyze these data operate. This is true of forensic technology created by private companies, but also of government programs; as noted, the FBI has never audited or error-tested its facial recognition algorithm. The FBI's culture of secrecy, which extends back to Hoover's era of "Do Not File" memos and secret files with paperwork on public figures, now surrounds its high-tech databanks and algorithms. While criminal investigations demand some degree of secrecy, scientific endeavors demand some degree of transparency in data collection and analysis, including through peer review and replication of research.

DNA provides a case study of how forensics becomes widely adopted, when it helps to convict the guilty, and not so much when it could help to free the innocent. When DNA testing was developed in the 1980s, state and federal lawmakers and judges moved quickly to allow DNA to be used by law enforcement and in court to provide powerful evidence of guilt. Congress passed in 1993 the DNA Identification Act, which allowed the FBI to assemble DNA samples in a national databank, the CODIS.[16] Each state collects DNA profiles, which can then be accessed and searched by the FBI software, with any resulting "matches" then provided to the law enforcement agency. The 1996 Anti-Terrorism and Effective Death Penalty Act (AEDPA) and the 2000 DNA Act provided the FBI with authority to add to CODIS the DNA profiles of federal offenders. The 2004 Justice for All Act expanded DNA collection to all federal felons, and 2005 federal legislation permitted arrestee DNA to be entered into CODIS.[17] The CODIS now contains over eleven million profiles, and it continues to expand. The FBI reported that as of October 2019 it "has produced over 488,318 hits assisting in more than 477,812 investigations."[18] Although the federal legislation creating the database states that DNA results may be made available to law enforcement, judicial proceedings, and for criminal defense purposes, few of those states allow defense lawyers access to the databases for searches that might show clients' innocence.[19]

The federal law creating the DNA databanks provides for access by the scientific community, including for "identification research and protocol development."[20] Despite those statutes, the FBI has almost entirely restricted research access, and as a result the statistics used to calculate a "match" in the CODIS remain opaque; we do not even know the racial or ethnic composition of the DNA databases.[21] With the increase in the size of these databanks, and as partial samples are increasingly run in them, there is an increasing (but undisclosed) chance of "adventitious" or coincidental matches. While concerns had been registered for years, in May 2015 the FBI admitted it made basic mathematical errors in the tables used by DNA analysts—not just at the FBI but in crime labs generally—to calculate statistics for CODIS matches. In some cases, these errors could make an enormous difference. For example, in a Galveston County case, one of the first to be reexamined, the lab originally calculated that the odds that a person in the population would be expected to randomly match the DNA found on a piece of evidence was 1 in 290 million. After the DNA probabilities were recalculated in response to the FBI announcement, the lab revised its result in that case, and the new random match probability was very, very different: it was just 1 in 38.[22]

As compared to the aggressive use of federal funding to turbo-charge the DNA databanks that are intended to identify potential culprits, the use of DNA testing to free the innocent moved at a snail's pace. In the 1990s only two states, New York and Illinois, had statutes providing a right for convicts to access post-conviction DNA testing to potentially provide innocence. Many of the people freed by DNA tests waited for years to obtain those tests. Today, all fifty states have enacted statutes providing access to DNA and post-conviction relief. However, many of those statutes contain sharp restrictions on access to DNA testing, including barring access to testing if the defense lawyer made a mistake by not asking for testing at trial, limits on access to persons convicted of certain felonies, and bars to testing of persons who pleaded guilty or did not litigate the issue of identity at their trials.[23]

"It's over finally," said Joseph Buffey, on the steps of the Harrison County, West Virginia courthouse, in fall 2016. Buffey was free after fifteen years in prison, and yet, that entire time, DNA excluded him. Buffey had been convicted in 2002 of a rape and robbery of an eighty-three-year-old woman, in Clarksburg, West Virginia, who was the mother of a Clarksburg police officer.[24] He had told his lawyers that he was innocent, but when his lawyers asked for the prosecutors' evidence, they never received the lab report that showed Buffey was not the source of the DNA from the victim. Six weeks after the prosecutors received that DNA report, Buffey then took the advice of his lawyers: he took a plea. His lawyer thought he would get a ten-year sentence, but Buffey was sentenced to seventy years in prison. By 2010 Buffey tried again to proclaim his actual innocence and secure a DNA test. The prosecutor's expert, however, now claimed Buffey could not be completely excluded. A more modern DNA test was done, and this test was conclusive: it was not Buffey's DNA.

Over the next eighteen months, Buffey's lawyers fought to search the DNA databank, to locate the actual culprit. However, the local prosecutors refused access and refused to support his release. The prosecutor said, "Why would someone plead guilty and say they were sorry several months later if they really had no participation in it?" The prosecutor suggested that perhaps there was a second rapist who left the DNA, despite the fact that the victim had always said there was a single culprit. Innocence Project co-director Barry Scheck countered: "This state was more interested in covering up what happened here than in finding the person who committed a vicious rape of an old woman and could have been on the streets committing more of them." More problematic still, the prosecutors argued that the judge had no power to order a DNA test. In fact, the national system of interconnected DNA databanks, maintained by the FBI, is wholly one-sided. Every state shares DNA profiles with the FBI, but very few states, and West Virginia was not one of them, have a law that allows defense lawyers to access database results. The prosecutors argued that the defense lacked a right to access the database to potentially locate the culprit of a crime. Only the police could do that, they argued, and only the prosecutor could approve such a search.[25] The Innocence Project offered to have a certified lab run the search, but the prosecutor rejected the idea, saying there was "no good reason" to do it. The judge finally ordered the prosecutors to run the test. The prosecutors refused initially, but a month later, finally capitulated.

The database search resulted in a cold hit to another inmate: a man, incarcerated in another West Virginia prison, with a history of sexual assaults: the victim's paperboy. Yet it still took more time to free Buffey, since he had pleaded guilty. His lawyers argued that it violated due process to conceal forensics from him. While the DNA tests excluded Buffey, the state maintained he would have pleaded guilty anyway, the results did not matter, and the results did not rule out his involvement. Eventually, the West Virginia Supreme Court concluded in a landmark ruling that prosecutors are obligated to provide exculpatory forensic evidence to the defense during plea negotiations. The court held that the *Brady v. Maryland* due process right entitles a defendant, even during plea negotiations, to have access to such potentially exculpatory evidence, and that none of those arguments "detract from the exculpatory nature of the evidence of DNA testing or its materiality." The court reversed Buffey's conviction.[26] In 2015, when Buffey finally obtained DNA tests and a database search, he was exonerated. Yet his case showed how neither the law nor the U.S. Constitution offers much protection for criminal suspects and defendants who seek to question or obtain evidence from forensics databases.

Not just DNA but other forensic databases, like fingerprint databases, are one-sided: law enforcement can use them but not defendants. Archie Williams was released in March 2019 after spending thirty-six years in prison in Louisiana. He initially wrote to the Innocence Project in New York in 1995; he was their longest-running client. During Williams's original trial over three decades earlier, it was known that fingerprints from the crime scene did not belong to him. The prosecutor claimed they might have come from "[t]he air-conditioning man, people who clean your carpets, [or] the little girl home from school." Beginning in 1999, Williams tried to have the prints compared with the national database, but prosecutors opposed the analysis, and Louisiana had no law that offered access to post-conviction testing. Later, in 2009, the state ran the prints through the national database without notifying Williams or his lawyers, but the results of the analysis were not consistent with anyone. In 2014 the former technique used for database searches was replaced with newer technology called Next Generation Identification (NGI). Yet the FBI's policy has remained, as with other databases, that only law enforcement can access this database. Only after the state judge threatened to order it did the prosecutors agreed to run an NGI search. Within hours, there was a finding that the crime scene prints were consistent with the fingerprints of a man who committed four more rapes while Williams was in prison, and who was arrested after attempting a fifth in 1986. Williams languished in prison, an innocent man, for years because there was no right to access the fingerprint database. His lawyer commented: "There was technology out there that would lead to the truth, that would give him his innocence—and we were blocked from it."[27]

PRIVACY

The explosion of forensics databases raises real privacy concerns. We think of crime labs as crime solvers, but we should think of them, in large part, as data hoarders. A growing percentage of what crime labs do is process samples from people arrested and convicted of crimes, to add to this growing system of databases. In the last federal survey of crime labs, 36 percent of requests to state labs and 39 percent of requests to federal labs were DNA testing for database samples: generous federal funding has pushed that expansion.[28] All of these forensic databases are increasingly linked. The Department of Homeland Security maintains the Automatic Biometric Identification System (IDENT), which includes "digital fingerprints, photographs, iris scans, and facial images," linked with "biographic information."[29] We do not know what quality controls exist in these databases. There are no public rules for how the databases are used. The government has our information and it can do what it wants with it.

In 2019 the largest maker of police body cameras, Axon (formerly called Taser International), convened an independent ethics board to examine whether it should use facial recognition technology. The report recommended against using the technology for body cameras, stating: "Even if face recognition works accurately and equitably—and we stress in detail that at present it does not—the technology makes it far easier for government entities to surveil citizens and potentially intrude into their lives." [30] The company decided that were it ever to use facial recognition in the future, it would do so only within an ethical framework and with oversight from the relevant communities. Only one city, San Francisco, California, has banned the use of facial recognition software. Others, like Detroit, Michigan, have hired companies to operate systems of facial recognition used to monitor hundreds of cameras throughout the city, and other cities, like Orlando, Florida, have piloted real-time facial recognition systems. Even if laws are passed, they may not be followed. The state of Washington passed a law barring facial recognition searches using driver's license photos without a court order. Yet, in 2019, Georgetown Law School researchers uncovered that federal Immigrations and Customs Enforcement officials had been secretly running facial recognition algorithms on driver's licenses in several states, including Washington, without a court order.[31]

The Supreme Court had a chance to step in to protect forensic data privacy rights in the case of *Maryland v. King*. The Court held that taking DNA from an arrestee in order to run it in the CODIS DNA databank to check whether the person is wanted for other crimes is a form of identity verification during "booking" that imposes only a minimal invasion of privacy. Now officers will ask for "License, Registration, and Cheek Swab, Please," as law professor Erin Murphy puts it.[32] Already, states have expanded DNA collection programs beyond just "serious" crimes to minor and even juvenile crimes. Justice Antonin Scalia memorably dissented in the *King* case and deplored the "genetic panopticon" that could result.[33] Today, the panopticon is not just genetic but also biometric and digital, with information increasingly aggregated from government records, biometrics, and social media. In theory, these data could allow the government to track our lives, our actions, and even our thoughts and feelings, online and in the physical world.

As one judge put it, when complaining about the use of poorly explained risk assessments, "our law does not allow mere conclusions to be mounted on spikes and paraded around our courtrooms without statistical context."[34] Machines will not solve all of the problems in forensics; they have already created new ones. Data scientists and statisticians entered forensics as the myth-busting researchers who would replace "match" statements with risk assessments, probabilities, and machine learning. However, statistical approaches must be validated and transparent. New types of automation shroud forensic work in secrecy, and also threaten to push forensic testing out of the lab and into police stations, using expensive proprietary devices that people do not understand. Our crime labs, our judges, and ultimately our lawmakers and communities must rise to the challenge.

One solution is the "Justice in Forensic Algorithms Act," which lawmakers introduced in Congress in fall 2019, a law that would require source code be made available to criminal defendants in all cases in which such algorithms are used.[35] The act would protect a criminal defendant's due process rights by prohibiting the use of trade secrets privileges to prevent access and challenges to such evidence. The act would provide that the National Institute of Standards and Technology (NIST) be directed to establish new programs to assess any computer programs or forensic algorithms before approving them for use by federal law enforcement. The act should be passed, and further, forensics should be vetted not only by the government but also by independent researchers. We need far more serious regulation of the use of algorithms and data before we allow them to be used by police, crime labs, or in court.

13 Fixing Forensics

"There should be some kind of regulation. There should be some way that experts have to meet a bar. A very high bar. Because you end up ruining people's lives," Keith Harward explained to the National Forensic Science Commission. Despite the lessons learned from tragic wrongful convictions like Harward's, judges continue to lower the bar in our courtrooms. To this day, we have almost no legal regulation of crime labs or of forensics. The commissioners, all leading scientists, forensics professions, and lawyers convened by the Department of Justice (DOJ) and the National Institute of Standards and Technology (NIST), had been meeting regularly since 2013. Shortly after Harward's remarks, with the new presidential administration assuming office in January 2017, the U. S. attorney general abruptly shut them down. The commission members reported they had "provided an essential forum . . . to improve the forensic sciences." Although they had issued many recommendations, the members had to stop their work, despite the fact that "there is still work to be done."[1]

Keith Harward knows something about patiently waiting for the truth to emerge; he was sixty years old when DNA cleared him, having spent more than half of his life in prison. Harward told my law students how as a young sailor in the Navy, he had dreams of living in the Blue Ridge mountains when he left the service, caring for his parents in their old age, and opening a mechanic's business. Instead, he last saw his parents begging the jury to spare his life; both died while he was in prison, and he was not allowed to attend their funerals. None of the dentists whose bite mark testimony convicted him have apologized or even commented on his case. None have been disciplined, much less investigated, by a professional board.

Despite the recommendations of leading scientists, most judges still allow testimony just like that which sent Harward to prison. Only one state, Texas, bans bite mark testimony. In a sign of change, though, a Georgia appellate judge, in a March 2020 ruling in the case of Sheila Denton, concluded that bite mark evidence was so unreliable that her conviction should be reversed. The judge was "aware of the many, and increasing, exonerations of people wrongly convicted based on bite mark evidence." Where today, the most dentists can say is that a defendant "cannot be excluded as the biter," the judge found that such testimony has little value, and regardless, the bite mark evidence in Denton's case "has been proven to be unreliable."[2]

Given the stubborn resistance to change, what is the path forward for forensics? Real CSI is not like what you see on TV, where glamorous lab analysts call up instant and dramatic results on large computer screens. We are obsessed with new technology transforming our lives. Willingly or not, we share data online, including our images, browsing history, and even our DNA. All of that information can be searched by police and linked to crime scene evidence by technicians in crime labs. Yet, inside our crime labs, the reality is often not hi-tech. Analysts still make comparisons, Mr. Peanut–style, by peering through a magnifying glass. That being said, a culture shift has been building.

In this chapter, I set out a vision for forensics that brings science into the crime lab to address each of the main problems set out in this book. First, we need to replace definitive conclusions with real error rates, to clearly set out the limits of forensic methods. Second, we must require forensic experts to disclose that information in their reports and in carefully limited court testimony. Third, they must be tested for their proficiency, so that we all know how accurate they are. Fourth, firewalls must be built to prevent cognitive bias from harming the accuracy of forensic work. Fifth, a system of quality control must comprehensively regulate crime labs. Sixth, police evidence collection should be supervised by scientists. Seventh, judges should rethink their role as gatekeepers and how they should make sure jurors really hear about the limits of forensic evidence.

The lessons from each of the sources of error that I have described in the previous chapters all point toward the same conclusion: we need national regulation of forensics. The quality controls implemented in the Houston Forensic Science Center show how reform is possible today, but one lab is not enough. Nor should labs monitor themselves; we need independent inter-laboratory testing. We need rules to regulate the forensics system, from police crime scene units, to crime labs, to coroners, to our courtrooms. We need bold national action. I hope reading this book helps you to join the effort to push forensics reform beyond the boiling point.

A BLUEPRINT FOR FIXING FORENSICS

First, we need to open the black box on error rates. Would you have believed that fingerprint conclusions could be wrong one in a million times, much less one in three hundred or one in eighteen times, until you read this book? Would you have believed that for most forensics, we have no idea what the error rates are, because they have not been tested? The era of the categorical conclusion must end: no technique is foolproof and all evidence is probabilistic. If we do not know how reliable a method is, it should not be used. We should discard error-prone techniques like bite mark comparison, along with discredited techniques such as bullet lead and hair comparison evidence.

Second, we must require forensic experts to disclose error rate information in their reports and in court. Relatedly, categorical and unqualified terms like "identified" or "individualized" should not be used, because they can convey the misleading impression that evidence was 100 percent certain to have come from the suspect. In the past, forensic expert used terms like "match," "consistent with," "identical," "similar in all respects tested," and "cannot be excluded as the source of." Such terms, even those that may sound more modest, like "reasonable scientific certainty," have no accepted scientific meaning and should not be used. Scientists in disciplines outside of forensics have standards, templates, and protocols for reporting. Scientists recognize an ethical responsibility to assist nonscientists to understand their findings before they are used as decision aids.[3] It is high time that forensic experts followed those basic ethical and scientific rules.

Third, we should not allow people to serve as experts if we do not know how reliable they are. Labs must regularly assess how examiners use their experience, skill, and judgment to make decisions using proficiency testing. An accredited organization is normally required to conduct annual proficiency testing, but the tests are not rigorous, testing conditions are not realistic or monitored, and examiners know they are being tested. If blind proficiency testing is required then we can end the era of the self-proclaimed expert.

Fourth, firewalls must be built to prevent cognitive bias from harming the accuracy of forensic work. We are all biased. However, in criminal cases, we need scientific experts and not cops in lab coats. Forensic experts routinely receive all sorts of biasing and irrelevant information from police or prosecutors. Further, a forensic examiner's work should be documented and transparent, with all information about methods used and conclusions reached shared with lawyers and the court.

Fifth, a system of quality controls must comprehensively regulate crime labs. The quality assurance at crime labs looks nothing like at a hospital or a clinical lab. All agencies should adopt quality controls such as blind testing, random audits, and documentation requirements. Any errors, including nonconformities or misconduct, should be corrected as part of any sound quality control process. Labs must notify lawyers and the court of all errors.

Sixth, police evidence collection should be supervised by scientists. Far too often, police contaminate crime scenes because they lack resources and training. Far too often, forensic evidence remains uncollected or untested. And far too often, police adopt unreliable field tests, rather than wait for more rigorous testing in a lab.

Seventh, our judges need to step up. "Albert Einstein could rise from the dead, come into the courtroom, say it is not science," and still judges would let the forensics in, argued Innocence Project lawyer Chris Fabricant at a conference I held in spring 2019. The scientists, forensic practitioners, and lawyers in the room all nodded in agreement. Over time, though, judges have started to become more receptive to flaws in forensics. Judges must rethink their role as gatekeepers. Further, where most criminal cases do not have a trial and are plea-bargained, it is crucial that defense lawyers understand what forensic evidence means and how strong it is when they consider what bargain is appropriate for their client. Judges must ensure full discovery so that prosecutors and defense lawyers both have complete information.

Finally, judges should make sure that the jurors really hear about the limits of forensic evidence. In recent years, six states have passed laws to allow judges to reopen cases based on a new understanding of the science used to convict a person: California, Connecticut, Texas, Michigan, Nevada, and Wyoming.[4] Each of those states has had many wrongful convictions caused by flawed forensics come to light. In the past, judges would cite to the interest of finality in refusing to grant relief to people who pointed out errors in forensic tests. Judges must be open to reopening old cases, and they need more: tools for conducting systematic reviews when mass forensic disasters occur, such as in Massachusetts and other states. To better conduct such audits, a different system is needed: national regulation.

THE SHORT-LIVED COMMISSION

"Injustice anywhere is a threat to justice everywhere," said Judge Harry Edwards, quoting Martin Luther King, Jr.'s "Letter from a Birmingham Jail" to the group assembled in 2013. Judge Edwards was speaking to the National Commission on Forensic Science, created by the DOJ and NIST, to review standards for forensics. During its existence, we had a national body on forensics with at least the authority to recommend if not actually regulate. The members issued forty-nine recommendations, binding only on the federal government, including that the same detailed discovery should be given to the defense in a criminal case as would occur in a civil case. They required that federal law enforcement only use evidence from accredited laboratories and that all federal laboratories must follow the same code of ethics. They recommended doing away with misleading language like "reasonable scientific certainty." What they did not reach was consensus on what more should be said in reports, including what should be said about error rates in forensics.

Ten years after the 2009 National Academy of Sciences report, crucial recommendations have been adopted piecemeal, with no single national agency to regulate forensics. There is more of a research culture in forensics and more research is being done. There is a new focus on standards for reports and testimony, although progress has been painfully slow. There is more public awareness of the problems with forensics. Even comedian John Oliver has quoted the key sentence in the NAS report, in an episode on forensics, noting that many forensic sciences do not meet the "fundamental requirements of science." Yet there has been very little legislation. For the most part, little has changed in the courts. And there are plenty of forensic analysts who refuse to believe the NAS report got it right, not to mention those who have *never heard* of the report.

Until there is some type of national regulation, oversight by state and local scientific advisory boards can provide guidance to police agencies and crime laboratories as they make decisions that implicate scientific and technical knowledge. The Texas Forensic Science Commission not only conducts trainings; it can make recommendations to state laboratories, investigate the validity of forensic techniques in use, and investigate allegations of professional negligence or misconduct by forensic professionals.[5] "Undetermined," concluded the Texas Forensic Science Commission in its blockbuster report in April 2011. Cameron Todd Willingham had been sentenced to death in 1991, and executed in 2004, for setting off a fire that killed his three children in his home in Corsicana, Texas. Firefighters from the Corsicana Fire Department responded to the scene and the fire marshal arrived a few days later to investigate the cause of the fire. They concluded that it was arson. They had no written procedures or standards. Arson investigators relied upon "process of elimination" and the training from their mentors to decide whether a fire was set on purpose. There had been few experiments done to research causes of fires, and the few studies done suggest very high error rates.[6]

Why did these investigators conclude that the fire was set on purpose? The deputy fire marshal had testified: "So this area right here are what I call burn trailers. Burn trailers is like a trailer, you know, like a little path, a burnt path." He contended: "A pour pattern, which is a pattern like somebody put some liquid on the floor or wherever and, of course, when you pour liquid, then it creates a puddle." Fire investigators thought, in the early 1990s, that fire always moved up. That if you pour flammable liquid on the floor, you will see "pour patterns" that make unusual burn patterns on the floor. They thought this was "nearly proof alone" that a fire was caused by arson. The fire investigator said that irregular patterns like this cannot be caused by an accidentally caused fire. We now know that synthetic carpet pads, like the ones in Willingham's home, can melt or turn to liquid when they burn, making patterns just like the ones they observed. Other sources for such patterns include flaming debris, drop-down burning from synthetic mattresses and bedding, and "flashover" conditions that are common as a fire spreads through a home.[7]

The investigators reported that there were "V-patterns" in the hallway in Willingham's house. The deputy fire marshal testified at trial that this indicated where the fire came from: the center hallway, which was a place where you would not expect a fire to start by accident. Yet fire scientists now know that this was completely faulty; a V-pattern can be made anywhere something is burning during a fire, and not necessarily where the fire originally started.[8] They made many other claims that today we know were false.

National coverage described how Willingham may have been executed for a crime that he did not commit—and for a crime that may not have occurred at all, as the fire may have been completely accidental. The commission issued a detailed report laying out how the arson science had been presented in a misleading manner. Texas lawmakers created the commission in May 2005, with nine members tasked with investigating, "in a timely manner," any allegation of negligence or misconduct that could "substantially affect the integrity of the results of a forensic analysis." By 2010 the commission had staff and could investigate complaints. They hired a fire scientist, Craig L. Beyler, to conduct a full review of Willingham's case and obtained written comments from other independent fire science experts. The commission's work led to new standards in Texas for how to investigate and present arson conclusions. The commission was accomplishing its central role. After all, "One of the ways to lose faith in the criminal justice system is to convict innocent people . . . using evidence that is unreliable, unscientific and pure junk science," said State Senator Juan Hinjosa.[9] The commission also oversees all Texas crime labs.[10]

The idea that states should regulate forensic science was not new. In 1994, New York was the first state to create a commission to oversee and regulate crime laboratories.[11] The New York commission gives the state inspector general the power to investigate problems in labs.[12] Today, thirteen states and Washington, DC, have created such bodies. In response to concerns regarding forensic science work, the Virginia legislature also separated the Department of Forensic Science from law enforcement and created a Forensic Science Board and a Scientific Advisory Committee.[13] Most recently, Maine and Michigan have considered creating commissions.[14] The Texas commissioners have ordered sweeping audits of the use of hair evidence, DNA evidence, and bite mark evidence.[15] They have issued new policies for the state: after reviewing the science, they concluded that bite mark evidence should not be used in Texas. They developed trainings and standards. Few of the other commissions actually conduct oversight of forensic methods and work. Most are advisory bodies that meet infrequently.

Other states have done very little in response to serious forensics problems. For example, California convened a series of task forces to review the state of its crime labs. One task force made recommendations in 2009 that a new body be created to provide oversight over crime labs, but in 2010 the task force was disbanded, with professor William Thompson noting that the group was "dominated by laboratory managers" who opposed new regulations.[16] Similarly, an effort by reformers to create a commission in Arizona failed due to opposition from labs, although the state does have a Forensic Science Advisory Committee, convened by the state attorney general. Many of these commissions have not been very active, meeting irregularly or doing little more than convening occasional trainings.[17]

Nor has federal regulation added much oversight. Crime labs in all fifty states receive federal funding from the Coverdell DNA testing program, and the law requires that any lab receiving the grants retain an independent auditor who has the power to conduct an investigation of any quality control problems of the lab.[18] A subsequent investigation uncovered that many labs did not provide the required certification, or when the supposed auditor was contacted, they had no idea that they were supposed to be conducting independent investigations at a lab.[19] Yet the federal authorities imposed no consequences for labs violating the rules. The National Institute for Justice only provided labs with examples of how they could meet the requirement in the future.[20] Although the federal government provides so much funding to crime labs at the state and local levels, it has yet to insist on accountability.

When leading lights in science and law, assembled by the National Academy of Sciences, finished their hearings, their study of the scientific research, and then presented their conclusions in their 2009 report, they made one central recommendation: Congress should fund the creation of a new national agency to tackle the problem of forensic science, a National Institute of Forensic Science (NIFS), along the lines of the National Institutes of Health (NIH). This was not simply one among the list of proposals in a lengthy report; the committee called NIFS "the greatest hope for success." They noted that all of the "remaining recommendations ... are crucially tied to the creation of NIFS."[21] The proposal to create NIFS was applauded by many academics and some in the forensic science community—and attacked by some in the law enforcement community even before the report was released.[22] Congress did not create an agency to comprehensively regulate forensics across the country, and that may help to explain why change has been so slow.

Instead, members of Congress quickly focused on NIST as a source for research.[23] NIST specializes in the science of measurement, to develop and assess standards for science and technology. It seemed like the best agency for the job. However, it is not a regulatory agency. It cannot impose rules on crime labs. Still, NIST began to do more to address problems in forensics, producing new research reports on human factors and cognitive bias issues in forensics. NIST convened a large group of scientists and practitioners to develop standards for all of the forensic disciplines, called the Organization of Scientific Area Committees (OSAC). That process has so far proceeded fairly slowly and resulted in few standards, which must be approved by yet another body.[24] Moreover, when statisticians have raised concerns over accuracy of standards, they have been outvoted. For example, the first standard to come through OSAC was on the obscure topic of glass comparisons, and which it stated had an error rate of "less than .1%." Statisticians Karen Kafadar and Karen Pan countered that when one actually analyzes existing data, the error rates are far larger, and may be anywhere from 1 to 11 percent. Nevertheless, the OSAC standard still includes an inaccurate 0.1 percent error rate and implies glass can be conclusively "matched" or found not distinguishable.[25]

If new research cannot find a way to make the technique more reliable, then we should stop using it. The FBI stopped using bullet lead comparisons and voice comparisons following critical reports from the scientific community. These types of forensics can be discarded. Indeed, many labs have already done just that. Most big labs, like the Houston lab, do not conduct comparisons of paint chips, glass pieces, tape, or fibers. They do not do shoeprint comparisons. Such techniques are marginal, they do not come up often, and serious labs with quality controls do not bother with them. The workhorse forensic techniques are latent fingerprint comparison, toxicology, controlled substances testing, DNA, and, increasingly, digital evidence. Here is the good news: federal research funding has mounted. People working in a multi-university group of researchers, the Center for Statistics and Applications in Forensic Evidence (CSAFE), of which I am a part, use statistics to develop ways to analyze everything from fingerprints to bullet casings. A new generation of researchers is bringing statistics to forensics.

After reading this book, if you are selected to serve on a jury in a criminal case, you will have many questions that you will want the experts to answer. Did the expert claim to be able to "identify" the source of the evidence? Did the expert explain the limits of the analysis? How reliable is the forensic technique, or do we even know? What are the error rates? What is the expert's own proficiency? Did the expert take blind proficiency tests? Did the expert receive potentially biasing information from police, prosecutors, or colleagues? Did the defense get all of the expert's documentation and data? Did the defense get an expert? What quality controls did the lab maintain? Did the expert use a forensic database and if so, how reliable are the computer programs used to search the databases? We do not need to be given complicated statistics, but we do need to be told the whole truth about the quality of the forensic evidence, in terms that we can understand.

As jurors, we focus our attention on the strength of the evidence in a criminal case. We must decide whether the state has proved, beyond a reasonable doubt, that a defendant committed the crime. Yet for decades, we have been misled about the strength of forensic evidence. Forensic experts claimed to be infallible superheroes, which made for great drama but also tragic wrongful convictions of innocent people. We can solve these problems. In fact, as citizens, if we bring skepticism to the jury box, then forensic experts will change the way that they talk. They will not patronize us with terms like "same source" and "identification" if we know better and if we demand better evidence. Judges and lawyers will have to make sure that our questions are answered. The next generation of forensics research will help to ensure that those questions can be answered.

Today, Brandon Mayfield, whose story introduced this book, still lives in Oregon, where his daughter, Sharia Mayfield, is now also a lawyer. He has spoken at national forensics conferences about what can go wrong in forensics, including at NIST, where I first met him. Mayfield has commented that forensic experts often tell him they are "personally sorry" for what happened to him, representing a culture change that is "a sign of what's right in this country."[26] For far too long, faulty forensics has created terrible injustices, far too few of which have ever been corrected. We will never know how many innocent people were arrested, fined, pleaded guilty, tried, wrongly convicted, or imprisoned, based on flawed science. We can never fully compensate them for their loss. We will never know how many culprits continued to act with impunity, with forensics contaminated or botched. Yet there is cause for optimism. Slowly but surely, a new culture of science and statistics is replacing the myth of infallible forensics. After the autopsy of the crime lab, a rebirth of forensics is finally under way.

Acknowledgments

This book benefited from invaluable comments on the manuscript by Kerry Abrams, Jeff Bellin, Adam Benforado, Curtis Bradley, Sarah Chu, Simon Cole, William Crozier, Itiel Dror, Heidi Eldridge, Brett Gardner, Adam Gershowitz, Paul Giannelli, Lisa Griffin, Larry Helfer, Eisha Jain, Lee Kovarsky, Sandra Levick, Dan Medwed, Alexandra Natapoff, Peter Neufeld, Sarah Olson, Vikrant Reddy, Chris Slobogin, and Rebecca Wexler. I am grateful for feedback from Amanda Knox, Brandon and Sharia Mayfield, and Betty Anne Waters, who read the parts of the book that told their stories, as well as Peter Stout, who read portions discussing the transformation of the Houston Forensic Science Center, and Pamela Colloff, who read portions that describe Joe Bryan's case. I am so grateful to Duke law student research assistants Hunter Albritton and Nicholas Lynch, who provided invaluable help editing chapters and checking citations. I am also grateful to the detailed comments by the two peer reviewers whose feedback improved the manuscript enormously.

Several chapters benefited from work published in law reviews and peer-reviewed journals, beginning with my work with Peter Neufeld studying the role that forensic evidence played in DNA exoneration cases. Many chapters also benefited from work focused on how jurors evaluate forensic evidence. My long-term collaboration with Greg Mitchell on mock jury studies deeply changed how I understand the role forensic evidence plays in the courtroom. That work, and other work examining forensic evidence, including collaboration with statisticians, especially Karen Kafadar, with psychologists William Crozier, Jeff Kukucka, and Nicholas Scurich, and with crime lab staff such as Peter Stout and the Houston Forensic Science Center, was supported by the Center for Statistics and Applications in Forensic Evidence (CSAFE), which is in turn supported by the National Institute of Standards and Technology (NIST).

For years, I taught a forensic science colloquium with John Monahan at the University of Virginia School of Law, which was as much an education for me as for my students. I have also taught several times a forensics litigation course with Kate Philpott, in which law students and practicing lawyers litigate a mock trial with a fingerprint examiner. More recently, at Duke Law, Nita Farahany and I taught both the forensic science colloquium and an amicus lab course, in which our students co-authored amicus briefs raising forensic science issues in appellate cases.

I was very grateful for comments by participants at a criminal justice books-in-progress conference that I organized at Duke Law, as well as comments on chapters presented at a roundtable conference at UNC School of Law, a presentation at University of Glasgow School of Law, a presentation at Berkeley Law, and a keynote speech at a conference organized by Public Defender Services in Washington, DC. This book benefited from informal conversations with and comments by many of my wonderful colleagues at Duke University School of Law. I have also presented versions of this book and the underlying research to a wide array of different public defense and prosecution offices and associations, and their practical insight has been extremely valuable.

I thank Maura Roessner at University of California Press for her thoughtful guidance throughout the publication process, as well as the two peer reviewers for their insightful comments and Paul Tyler for his expert copyediting. I thank my agent, James Levine, for expertly shepherding the manuscript to an ideal publisher.

My greatest thanks, as always, are to my wife, Kerry Abrams, who is a lovely and brilliant partner in all things.

APPENDIX Suggested Resources

PART I. THE CRISIS IN FORENSICS

The introduction to this book begins with the story of Brandon Mayfield's wrongful detention based on fingerprint evidence. To learn more about the federal investigation of what went wrong, I recommend that you read the 2006 report by the U. S. Department of Justice, Office of the Inspector General.[1]

In chapter 1, I tell the story of Keith Harward. Well over half of the people now exonerated by DNA testing were originally wrongly convicted based on flawed forensics. I created a resource website that includes the actual testimony of forensic experts at the trials of these DNA exonerees.[2] After his exoneration, Harward left Virginia and moved to North Carolina, not far from where I live and teach. In spring 2019, Keith spoke at Duke to my law students about his DNA exoneration, the problems with bite mark testimony, and how he will continue to speak out for forensic science reform; you can watch an online video of his talk. His case was featured in the third episode of the Netflix documentary series *The Innocence Files*.[3]

In chapter 2, I describe how the National Academy of Sciences 2009 report set the stage for a new understanding of the limitations of forensics, including all of the non-DNA methods used to link evidence to particular suspects. The report includes sections describing the limitations of a wide range of forensic methods and I strongly recommend reading it. The report is available online at no cost.[4] The 2016 White House report that followed offered more pointed criticism of the

209

underlying lack of validation of several techniques, including firearms comparisons. That report is also available for free online.[5]

PART II. FLAWED FORENSICS

In chapter 3, I explore how a forensic method like fingerprinting can be vulnerable to error. I focus on the Brandon Mayfield story. Brandon and Sharia Mayfield co-wrote a powerful book about the experience of falsely being subjected to surveillance, arrest, and national security detention.[6] I also encourage you to read Simon Cole's *Suspect Identities,* which provides a wonderfully detailed history of fingerprinting, including experts' claims of infallibility and the denial that there is any possibility of error.[7]

In chapter 4, I begin with the story of Kenny Waters, wrongly convicted despite hidden fingerprint evidence that excluded him, and his sister Betty Anne Waters, who fought for years to free him. I recommend watching the 2010 major motion picture *Conviction,* starring Hilary Swank, which dramatized Betty Anne's role. The case highlights how little we hear in court about errors, including outright evidence of a specific person's innocence, as well as evidence of error rates in general.

The PCAST report does a great job of laying out how little had been done to measure error rates at that time. For firearms comparisons, only a single adequate study by the Ames Laboratory had been done, which found a false positive error rate of only 1.01 percent, but if one included inconclusive errors, the error rate increased dramatically to 34.76 percent.[8] Two studies existed in the area of latent fingerprint comparison, with the FBI study finding false positive rates as high as 1 in 306, and a Miami-Dade study as high as 1 in 18.[9] Those estimates included some clerical errors and did not include inconclusive errors. While two studies are not enough to sufficiently understand how reliable such work is, they provide a much-needed corrective. People assume forensic error rates are very low. Professor Jay Koehler found that jurors estimated the error rate for fingerprint comparison was 1 in 5.5 million, and for bite mark comparison and hair comparison jurors estimated 1 in a million.[10] Telling jurors the actual error rates can make a difference. Professor Gregory Mitchell and I did a mock juror study where the fingerprint examiner admitted a possibility of error. After hearing that concession of fallibility, jurors gave markedly less weight to the evidence.[11]

In chapter 5, I begin with the overstated testimony in hair comparison cases in Washington, DC, that led to a national FBI audit. Journalist Spenser Hsu of the *Washington Post* wrote a series of stories that helped to break this scandal.[12] The FBI itself produced a report, available online, with the results of its audit of 2,900 cases, 96 percent of which involved overstated testimony.[13] I also recommend the American Statistical Association's short guidance on how forensic conclusions should be phrased.[14] The U. S. Department of Justice announced new guidelines for several forensic disciplines in 2019, such as that experts should not bolster their conclusions by citing their years of experience, but the guidelines also explicitly allow the use of the potentially misleading term "source identification."[15]

In chapter 6, I ask what really makes an expert qualified. Unfortunately, credential and education programs in forensics have long been lacking. Frontline and ProPublica, in a documentary titled *The Real CSI*, showed just how easy it was for a person with no background or ability at all in forensics to be certified as a "forensic consultant."[16] Even an experienced person with impressive credentials, though, can be error prone. Indeed, many forensic experts make errors on the routine tests—called proficiency tests—that they are given. Greg Mitchell and I collected results of thirty-nine different tests on fingerprint comparisons from 1995 to 2016 and we found widely varying error rates.[17] We also studied how jurors consider information about the proficiency of an individual expert. Not surprisingly, jurors consistently gave less weight to the evidence when an expert performed less well on proficiency tests.[18]

In chapter 7, on hidden bias, I explore how researchers have uncovered the role that cognitive biases play in forensics. I recommend that a reader interested in learning more start with Itiel Dror's work, beginning with his study in which he told fingerprint examiners that they were examining the print from the Brandon Mayfield case; his website also includes his lengthy list of publications.[19] The U. K. authorities conducted a detailed investigation into the Shirley McKie fingerprint error in Scotland, highlighting the role of circular reasoning and biasing information.[20] I also recommend the article by psychologist Daniel Murrie and colleagues, who have shown in a series of studies how there is a strong "allegiance effect" among forensic psychologists that tends to skew their results in favor of the defense or the prosecution.[21] Finally, in the U. K., detailed government guidance from the Forensic Science Regulator recommends use of debiasing techniques for forensic labs, to be sure that the forensic practitioner "only has the information about the case that is relevant to the analysis."[22]

In chapter 8, I turn to the role that judges have played in allowing forensics in court despite lack of evidence of reliability. I strongly recommend reading the flip-flop in the two decisions that I describe by Judge Louis Pollak in the *Llera Plaza* case.[23] Professor Simon Cole has described how judges have typically "grandfathered" forensic evidence, based on precedent, avoiding ruling on its reliability.[24] Chris Fabricant and I examined hundreds of state court rulings on forensics, finding that judges almost always ruled that the forensic evidence was property admitted and rarely said anything about its reliability.[25] Law professor Paul Giannelli has also detailed in an article that many judges have permitted labs to refuse to share documents like the underlying notes detailing forensic analysis.[26]

III. FAILED LABS

Turning in chapter 9 to the larger failures in the regulation of crime labs, I describe a series of lab scandals. I strongly recommend that you read Sandra Guerra Thompson's book *Cops in Lab Coats* to learn more about how crime labs can be better regulated and run.[27] The story of the Massachusetts lab scandal is depicted in the Netflix documentary *How to Fix a Lab Scandal*.

The crime scene, where evidence collection begins, affects any forensics work done afterwards. I begin chapter 10 by describing the blood spatter evidence in the case of Joe Bryan, including how the crime scene itself was contaminated. Journalist Pam Colloff wrote a powerful ProPublica series, "Blood will Tell," describing Bryan's ordeal.[28] The *New York Times* wrote a story in 2019 with a compelling overview of problems with blood alcohol testing in the field.[29]

IV. THE MOVEMENT TO FIX FORENSICS

Turning toward how to improve forensics, in chapter 11 I describe how to fix crime labs, beginning with the rebirth of the Houston Forensic Science Center. For further reading, I again strongly recommend Sandra Guerra Thompson's *Cops in Lab Coats*. The Houston Forensic Science Center celebrated its tenth anniversary, as Peter Stout, the head of the Houston lab, continues to launch new quality improvement initiatives. The lab continues to expand its blind proficiency testing program and Stout continues to tout such quality programs to other labs.[30]

Big data has the potential to both improve forensics and create new sources for error and invasion of privacy, as I describe in chapter 12. I begin by describing problems with facial recognition. You can check to see which government agencies may have your face in their facial recognition databases at a website created by the Electronic Frontier Foundation.[31] I also recommend reading reports on facial recognition by the Georgetown Law School Center on Privacy and Technology that first reported on the "perpetual lineup."[32]

The book concludes, in chapter 13, by discussing a range of reforms that can improve forensic science. I describe how a number of states have created forensic science commissions. Arkansas, Delaware, Maryland, Minnesota, Missouri, Montana, New York, New Mexico, North Carolina, Rhode Island, Texas, Virginia, Washington, and Washington, DC, have created such bodies.[33] For particularly impressive commission work, I recommend reading the report of the Texas Forensic Science Commission on the Cameron Todd Willingham case.[34] The final report of the National Commission of Forensic Science, before it was discontinued in January 2017 by the Department of Justice, summarized the work of that group and noted the additional work that is still needed at the national level.[35]

Judge Harry Edwards continues to speak forcefully about the legal system's inadequate response to the problems identified in the National Academy of Sciences report. Judge Edwards said: "Perhaps most critically, we still do not know what we do not know." Ten years later, we still "need better scientific studies and standards to shape the work of forensic practitioners and regulate the admission of forensic evidence." We still need top scientists to "engage in research on forensic methods and appear in court to explain the evidence." He summed it up: "much remains to be done."[36]

Notes

INTRODUCTION

1. *CSI: Miami,* season 7, episode 9, "Power Trip," directed by Joe Chappelle, written by Anthony Zuiker, Ann Donahue, Carol Mendelsohn, Matthew Partney, and Corey Evett, featuring Adam Rodriguez, aired January 24, 2008, CBS.

2. Steven T. Wax, *Kafka Comes to America: Fighting for Justice in the War on Terror—A Public Defender's Inside Account* (New York: Other Press, 2008), 212–13.

3. U. S. Department of Justice, Office of the Inspector General, *A Review of the FBI's Handling of the Brandon Mayfield Case,* March 2006, 99, 111; https://oig.justice.gov/special/s0601/final.pdf.

4. Brandon L. Garrett, *Convicting the Innocent: Where Criminal Prosecutions Go Wrong* (Cambridge, MA: Harvard University Press, 2011), 9.

5. National Research Council, *Strengthening Forensic Science in the United States: A Path Forward* (Washington, DC: National Academies Press, 2009) [hereafter NAS Report], 107–8.

CHAPTER ONE. THE BITE MARK CASE

1. Frank Green, "'Bite Mark' Testimony Questioned in 1982 Newport News Rape and Murder Case," *Richmond Times-Dispatch,* March 27, 2016.

2. C. Michael Bowers, "Identification from Bitemarks," in *Modern Scientific Evidence: The Law and Science of Expert Testimony,* ed. David Faigman et al. (West Group 2010).

3. People v. Marx, 54 Cal. App. 3d 100 (1975).

4. Gerry L. Vale et al., "Unusual Three-Dimensional Bite Mark Evidence in a Homicide Case," *Journal of Forensic Science* 21 (1976): 642.

5. Michael Saks et al., "Forensic Bitemark Evidence: Weak Foundations, Exaggerated Claims," *Journal of Law and the Biosciences* 3 (2016): 538.

6. Andre Moenssens et al., *Scientific Evidence in Civil and Criminal Cases,* 4th ed. (New York: Foundation Press 1995), 985.

7. Paul Giannelli, "Bite Mark Evidence," *Public Defender Reporter* 9, no. 5 (June 1986): 3–4.

8. Trial Transcript, 506, Commonwealth v. Harward, No. 9489-83 (Circuit Court, Newport News, March 6, 1982) [hereafter Harward Trial Transcript].

9. NAS Report, 175.

10. NAS Report, 174–75; see also Bowers, "Identification from Bitemarks," 538, 549–50 (reviewing "less than persuasive" literature and concluding "[t]he demonstration of uniqueness is a blend of art and opinion").

11. President's Council of Advisors on Science and Technology Report, "Forensic Science in Criminal Courts: Ensuring Scientific Validity of Feature-Comparison Methods," Executive Office of the President, September 2016 [hereafter PCAST Report], 84–85, 174.

12. Giannelli, "Bite Mark Evidence," 4.

13. Brandon L. Garrett and Peter J. Neufeld, "Invalid Forensic Science Testimony and Wrongful Convictions," *Virginia Law Review* 95, no. 1 (March 2009): 68.

14. Harward Trial Transcript, 559.

15. Stanley L. Brodsky, Tess M. S. Neal, Robert J. Cramer, and Mitchell H. Ziemke, "Credibility in the Courtroom: How Likeable Should an Expert Witness Be?", *Journal of the American Academy of Psychiatry and the Law* 37 (2009): 525; and Stanley L. Brodsky, *Coping with Cross Examination and Other Pathways to Effective Testimony* (Washington, DC: American Psychological Association, 2004).

16. Jonathan Koehler, N. J. Schweitzer, Michael Saks, and Dawn McQuiston, "Science, Technology, of the Expert Witness: What Influences Jurors' Judgments about Forensic Science Testimony," *Psychology, Public Policy and Law* 22 (2016): 401.

17. Frank Green, "Keith Harward Lashes Out at Field of Dentistry That Helped Wrongly Convict Him," *Richmond Times-Dispatch*, February 13, 2017.

18. Garrett and Neufeld, "Invalid Forensic Science Testimony," 69–70.

19. Green, "Keith Harward Lashes Out."

20. American Board of Forensic Odontology, *Standards and Guidelines for Evaluating Bitemarks*, accessed February 2018, http://abfo.org/wp-content /uploads/2012/08/ABFO-Standards-Guidelines-for-Evaluating-Bitemarks-Feb-2018.pdf.

21. Aura Bogado, "Here's How ICE Sent Children Seeking Asylum to Adult Detention Centers, *Reveal News*, May 3, 2018; and Mimi Dwyer, Belle Cushing, and Antonia Hylton, "The U. S. Is Checking Immigrant Kids' Teeth to See if They Actually Belong in Adult Detention," *Vice News*, October 11, 2018.

22. Green, "Keith Harward Lashes Out."

CHAPTER TWO. THE CRISIS IN FORENSICS

1. Testimony of Mr. John Grisham, Senate Committee on Commerce, Science and Transportation, "Turning the Investigation on the Science of Forensics," December 7, 2011.

2. U. S. Senate, Hearing Before the Committee on Commerce, Science, and Transportation, "Turning the Investigation on the Science of Forensics," December 7, 2011.

3. Harry T. Edwards, "Solving the Problems That Plague the Forensic Science Community," *Jurimetrics* 50, no. 1 (Fall 2009): 5, 7.

4. Brandon L. Garrett, "Judging Innocence," *Columbia Law Review* 55 (2008): 108.

5. "About NAS: Membership Overview," National Academy of Sciences, accessed March 9, 2020, www.nasonline.org/about-nas/membership/.

6. "Short Tandem Repeats (STRs)," DNA Diagnostics Center, accessed July 9, 2019, www.forensicdnacenter.com/dna-str.html.

7. Jay D. Aronson, *Genetic Witness: Science, Law, and Controversy in the Making of DNA Profiling* (New Brunswick, NJ: Rutgers University Press, 2007), 15, 17.

8. Adapted from Kerry Abrams and Brandon L. Garrett, "DNA and Distrust," *Notre Dame Law Review* 91, no. 2 (February 2016): 774–75.

9. Eric S. Lander, "DNA Fingerprinting on Trial," *Nature* 339 (1989): 501.

10. National Research Council, *DNA Technology in Forensic Science* (Washington, DC: National Academies Press, 1992); and National Research Council, *The Evaluation of Forensic DNA Evidence* (Washington, DC: National Academies Press, 1996).

11. Brandon L. Garrett, *Convicting the Innocent: Where Criminal Prosecutions Go Wrong* (Cambridge, MA: Harvard University Press, 2011).

12. NAS Report, 44–45.

13. John Grisham, "Why the Innocent End Up in Prison," *Los Angeles Times*, March 11, 2018.

14. These data are available at *Convicting the Innocent, DNA Exonerations Database,* Duke Law: Center for Science and Justice, www.convictingtheinnocent .com.

15. Paul C. Giannelli and Edward J. Imwinkelried, *Scientific Evidence,* 4th ed. (LexisNexis 2007), chaps. 14, 18, 21.

16. Paul Coverdell National Forensic Sciences Improvement Act of 2000, Pub. L. No. 106–561, 114 Stat. 2787 (2000) (codified at 42 U.S.C. § 3797(j) et seq.); and Erin Murphy, "What 'Strengthening Forensic Science' Today Means for Tomorrow: DNA Exceptionalism and the 2009 NAS Report," *Law, Probability and Risk* 9 (2010): 21–22.

17. Donald Kennedy, editorial, "Forensic Science: Oxymoron?," *Science* 302, no. 5651 (December 2003): 1625.

18. Honorable Harry T. Edwards, Presentation at the Superior Court of the District of Columbia Conference on the Role of the Court in an Age of Developing Science and Technology, "The National Academy of Sciences Report on Forensic Sciences: What It Means for the Bench and Bar," Washington, DC, May 6, 2010, 8.

19. Ibid.

20. Garrett, *Convicting the Innocent,* 94–95; see also Brandon Garrett and Peter Neufeld, *Improper Use of Forensic Science in the First 200 Post-Conviction DNA Exonerations,* https://sites.nationalacademies.org/cs/groups/pgasite /documents/webpage/pga_049970.pdf.

21. Sue Ballou, "The NAS Report: Ten Years of Response," *Journal of Forensic Sciences* 64, no. 1 (2019): 6–9.

22. NAS Report, 4–5.

23. Ibid., 12.

24. Ibid., 19.

25. Jonathan J. Koehler, "Forensic Science Reform in the 21st Century: A Major Conference, A Blockbuster Report and Reasons to be Pessimistic," *Law, Probability & Risk* 9 (2010): 1–6, doi: 10.1093/lpr/mgp029; and Jennifer L. Mnookin et al., "The Need for a Research Culture in the Forensic Sciences," *UCLA Law Review* 58 (2011): 725–79.

26. Melendez-Diaz v. Massachusetts, 557 U.S. 305 (2009).

27. Paul Giannelli, "The 2009 NAS Forensic Science Report: A Literature Review," *Criminal Law Bulletin* 48, no. 2 (2012): 378–93.

28. *Strengthening Forensic Science in the United States: Hearing Before the S. Comm. on the Judiciary,* 111th Cong. 1 (2009) (statement of Senator Jefferson Sessions).

29. NAS Report, 176.

30. Judicial Conference Advisory Committee on Evidence Rules, "Symposium on Forensic Expert Testimony, *Daubert,* and Rule 702," October 17, 2017. Transcript available in *Fordham Law Review* 86 (2018): 1463–550.

31. PCAST Report, 87.

32. Federal Bureau of Investigation, *Comments On: President's Council of Advisors on Science and Technology Report to the President*, September 20, 2016, www.fbi.gov/file-repository/fbi-pcast-response.pdf.

33. President's Council of Advisors on Science and Technology, *An Addendum to the PCAST Report on Forensic Science in Criminal Courts*, Executive Office of the President, January 6, 2017, 2–3, https://obamawhitehouse.archives.gov /sites/default/files/microsites/ostp/PCAST/pcast_forensics_addendum_finalv2 .pdf.

34. Judicial Conference Advisory Committee, "Symposium."

35. National District Attorneys Association, "National District Attorneys Association Slams President's Council of Advisors on Science and Technology Report," press release, September 2, 2016.

36. Harold Ruslander, *IAI Response to the Report to the President "Forensic Science in Criminal Courts Ensuring Scientific Validity of Feature-Comparison Methods" Issued by the President's Council of Advisors on Science and Technology (PCAST) in September 2016*, International Association for Identification, accessed July 14, 2019, https://theiai.org/docs/8.IAI_PCAST_Response.pdf.

37. National Research Council, *On the Theory and Practice of Voice Identification* (Washington, DC: National Academies Press, 1979).

38. National Research Council, *Forensic Analysis: Weighing Bullet Lead Analysis* (Washington, DC: National Academies Press, 2004).

39. Cliff H. Spiegelman and Karen Kafadar, "Data Integrity and the Scientific Method: The Case for Bullet Lead Data as Forensic Evidence," *Chance* 19, no. 2 (2006): 17–25.

40. Seth Augenstein, "Deputy AG: Forensic Science Is Not Only Numbers, Automation," *Forensic Magazine*, August 8, 2018, www.forensicmag.com /news/2018/08/deputy-ag-forensic-science-not-only-numbers-automation.

41. Brief of the New England Journal of Medicine, the Journal of the American Medical Association, and Annals of Internal Medicine as Amici Curiae in Support of Respondent, Daubert v. Merrell Dow Pharm., Inc., 509 U. S. 579 (1993), January 19, 1993.

CHAPTER THREE. FALSE ID

1. Vindu Goel, "That Fingerprint Sensor on Your Phone Is Not as Safe as You Think," *New York Times*, April 10, 2017; and "About Touch ID Advanced Security Technology," Apple, accessed July 14, 2019, https://support.apple.com /en-us/HT204587.

2. ABS Group, "Root and Culture Cause Analysis of Report and Testimony Errors by FBI MHCA Examiners," August 2018, 67, 79.

3. "The Fingerprint Inquiry Report" (Edinburgh: APS Group Scotland, 2011), accessed July 14, 2019, www.thefingerprint inquiryscotland.org.uk/inquiry /3127-2.html.

4. H. Cummins and C. Midlo, *Fingerprints, Palms, and Soles: An Introduction to Dermatoglyphics* (New York: Dover, 1943), 12–13 (quoting J. C. A. Mayer, *Anatomical Copper-plates with Appropriate Explanations* [1788]).

5. Simon A. Cole, *Suspect Identities: A History of Fingerprinting and Criminal Identification* (Cambridge, MA: Harvard University Press, 2002), 173.

6. "Fingerprinting Evidence Is Used to Solve a British Murder Case," *History .com*, November 13, 2009, last updated July 27, 2019, www.history.com/this-day-in-history/fingerprint-evidence-is-used-to-solve-a-british-murder-case.

7. Cole, *Suspect Identities*, 181.

8. Mark Twain, *The Tragedy of Pudd'nhead Wilson* (Hartford, CT: American, 1894), 185.

9. Arthur Conan Doyle, *The Sign of the Four* (Philadelphia: Lippincott's Magazine, 1891), 7.

10. David Sedaris, *Holidays on Ice* (Boston, MA: Little Brown, 1997).

11. The image comes from a Department of Justice report on the Brandon Mayfield case. Office of the Inspector General Report (Unclassified and Redacted), "A Review of the FBI's Handling of the Brandon Mayfield Case," Department of Justice, March 2006 [hereafter 2006 OIG Report].

12. 2006 OIG Report, 189.

13. Ibid., 132.

14. Ibid., 132.

15. Ibid., 135–37.

16. Ibid., 144.

17. Andres Cediel and Lowell Bergman, "The Real CSI," *Frontline*, PBS, April 17, 2012, www.pbs.org/wgbh/frontline/film/real-csi/transcript/.

18. Ibid.

19. For a timeline of these events, see 2006 OIG Report, 2–3.

20. Alicia Rairden, Brandon L. Garrett, Daniel Murrie, Sharon Kelley and Amy Castillo, "Resolving Latent Conflict: What Happens When Latent Print Examiners Enter the Cage?" *Forensic Science International* 215 (2018): 289.

21. Ibid.

22. Brandon Garrett and Gregory Mitchell, "How Jurors Evaluate Fingerprint Evidence: The Relative Importance of Match Language, Method Information, and Error Acknowledgment," *Journal of Empirical Legal Studies* 10, no. 3 (September 2013): 484–511. In another study, 84.3 percent responded in the same way; Gregory Mitchell and Brandon Garrett, "The Impact of Proficiency Testing on the Weight Given to Fingerprint Evidence," *Behavioral Sciences and the Law* 37 (2019): 195–210.

23. Katsuhiro Kikuchi, Keiji Higuchi, Takao Kameda, and Akira Yamashita, "A Global Classification of Snow Crystals, Ice Crystals, and Solid Precipitation Based on Observations from Middle Latitudes to Polar Regions," *Atmospheric Research* 460 (2013): 132.

24. NAS Report, 141–44.

25. Christian Sheckler and Ken Armstrong, "The Questionable Conviction, and Reconviction, of Ricky Joyner," ProPublica, July 19, 2019.

26. Ryan Gabrielson, "The FBI Says Its Photo Analysis Is Scientific Evidence; Scientists Disagree," ProPublica, January 17, 2019.

27. Bureau of Justice Statistics, "Nonfatal Firearm Violence, 1993–2011, Special Tabulation from the Bureau of Justice Statistics' National Crime Victimization Survey" (2011), www.nij.gov/topics/crime/gun-violence/pages/welcome.aspx.

28. Bonnie Lanigan, "Firearms Identification: The Need for a Critical Approach to, and Possible Guidelines for, the Admissibility of 'Ballistics' Evidence," *Suffolk Journal of Trial & Appellate Advocacy* 17 (2012): 54.

29. United States v. Monteiro, 407 F. Supp. 2d 351, 361 (D. Mass. 2006).

30. Association of Firearms and Tool Mark Examiners, "Theory of Identification as It Relates to Toolmarks," *AFTE Journal* 30, no. 1 (1998): 86.

31. National Research Council, *Ballistic Imaging* (Washington, DC: National Academies Press, 2008).

32. NAS Report, 155.

33. United States v. Tibbs, No. 2016 CF1 19431, 46 (D. C. Super. Ct.); United States v. Glynn, 578 F. Supp. 2d 567, 572 (S. D. N. Y. 2008); United States v. Romero-Lobato, 379 F. Supp. 3d 111, 1121 (D. Nev. 2019); and United States v. Green, 405 F. Supp. 2d 104, 114 (D. Mass. 2005).

34. For an overview, see Brandon L. Garrett, Nicholas Scurich, and William Crozier, "Firearms Testimony and Jurors' Evaluation of Firearms Testimony" (draft on file with author).

35. U. S. Department of Justice, "Approved ULTR for the Forensic Firearms /Toolmarks Discipline—Pattern Match," January 24, 2019, www.justice.gov/olp /page/file/1083671/download.

36. Federal Bureau of Investigation (FBI), "The Science of Fingerprints" (Washington, DC: Justice Dept., Federal Bureau of Investigation, 1984), iv.

37. Seth Augenstin, "DOJ's Fingerprint Uniform Language Is Part of 'Constant Evolution,' Says IAI," *Forensic Magazine*, March 1, 2018, www .forensicmag.com/news/2018/03/dojs-fingerprint-uniform-language-part-constant-evolution-says-iai.

38. U. S. Department of Justice, "Approved Uniform Language for Testimony for the Forensic Latent Print Disciplines," February 2018, www.justice.gov /file/1037171/download.

39. Heidi Eldridge, "'I Am 100% Certain of My Conclusion.' (But Should the Jury be Certain?)," *Evidence Technology Magazine*, March–April 2012.

40. Simon Cole, Valerie King, and Henry Swofford, poster presentation, "Survey of Fingerprint Examiners on Probabilistic Reporting Standards," CSAFE All Hands Meeting, June 2019.

CHAPTER FOUR. ERROR RATES

1. The National Registry of Exonerations, "Kenny Waters," www.law.umich .edu/special/exoneration/Pages/casedetail.aspx?caseid = 3722.
2. The Innocence Project, "Kenny Waters," at www.innocenceproject.org /cases/kenny-waters/.
3. Interview with Betty Anne Waters, January 10, 2020.
4. Decca Aitkenhead, "Betty Anne Waters: 'We Thought Kenny Was Coming Home,'" *The Guardian,* December 10, 2010.
5. The Innocence Project, "Troy Webb," www.innocenceproject.org/cases /troy-webb/.
6. Frank Green, "Blood-Typing Error Alleged to Have Contributed to Wrongful Murder Convictions," *Richmond Times-Dispatch,* April 6, 2016.
7. Federal Bureau of Investigation, *The Science of Fingerprinting: Classification and Uses* (Washington, DC: U. S. Government Printing Office, 1985), iv.
8. Simon A. Cole, *Suspect Identities: A History of Fingerprinting and Criminal Identification* (Cambridge, MA: Harvard University Press, 2001), 182.
9. United States v. Byron Mitchell, 365 F.3d 215 (3d Cir. 2004).
10. Simon A. Cole, "More Than Zero: Accounting for Error in Latent Fingerprint Identification," *Journal of Criminal Law and Criminology* 990, no. 27 (2005): 95.
11. Robert Epstein, "Fingerprints Meet Daubert: The Myth of Fingerprint 'Science' Is Revealed," *Southern California Law Review* 75 (March 2002): 605-57.
12. Andres Cediel and Lowell Bergman, "The Real CSI," *Frontline,* PBS, April 17, 2012, www.pbs.org/wgbh/frontline/film/real-csi/transcript/.
13. Max M. Houck and Bruce Budowle, "Correlation of Microscopic and Mitochondrial DNA Hairs Comparisons," *Journal of Forensic Sciences* 47, no. 5 (September 2002): 1-4.
14. The Honorable Fred Kaufmann, *The Commission on Proceedings Involving Guy Paul Morin* (Ontario: Commission on Proceedings Involving Guy Morin, 1998), 324.
15. The Honorable Douglas M. Lucas, *Report on Forensic Science Matters to the Commission of Inquiry re: James Driskell,* August 17, 2006, 24.
16. Kristopher L. Arheart and Iain A. Pretty, *Results of the 4th ABFO Bitemark Workshop—1999,* Forensic Science International 104 (December 2001): 124; and Michael Bowers et al., "Forensic Bitemark Identification: Weak Foun-

dations, Exaggerated Claims," *Journal of Law and Biosciences* 3 (2016): 538-75.

17. PCAST Report, 86.

18. Sherie A. Blackwell et al., "3-D Imaging and Quantitative Comparison of Human Dentitions and Simulated Bite Marks," *International Journal of Legal Medicine* 121 (January 2007): 9.

19. Robert Garrett, IAI President, "Letter to All Members," International Association for Identification, February 19, 2009.

20. Parisa Dehghani-Tafti and Paul Bieber, "Folklore and Forensics: The Challenges of Arson Investigation and Innocence Claims," *West Virginia Law Review* 119 (January 2017): 549-619; and John J. Lentini, "The Evolution of Fire Investigation and Its Impact on Arson Cases," *Criminal Justice* 27, no. 1 (Spring 2012): 12.

21. U. S. Fire Administration, "Fire Investigation: Essentials R0206," accessed August 19, 2019, https://apps.usfa.fema.gov/nfacourses/catalog/details/38.

22. P. A. Pizzola et al., "Blood Droplet Dynamics—I," *Journal of Forensic Science* 31 (1986): 36, 37.

23. NAS Report, 179.

24. Michael Taylor et al., "Reliability of Pattern Classification in Bloodstain Pattern Analysis, Part I: Bloodstain Patterns on Rigid Non-absorbent Surfaces," *Journal of Forensic Science* 64 (2016): 922, 926-27.

25. NAS Report, 23.

26. Paul Giannelli, "Forensic Science: Why No Research?", *Fordham Urban Law Journal* 38, no. 2 (January 2011): 502-18.

27. Jonathan J. Koehler, "Intuitive Error Rate Estimates for the Forensic Sciences," *Jurimetrics Journal* 57 (2017): 153-68.

28. PCAST Report, 6.

29. Ibid., 11-12.

30. Joseph B. Kadane, "Fingerprint Infallibility" (draft on file with author, 2020).

31. Bradford T. Ulery, R. Austin Hicklin, JoAnn Buscaglia, and Maria Antonia Roberts, "Accuracy and Reliability of Forensic Latent Fingerprint Decisions," *Proceedings of the National Academy of Sciences* 118 (2011): 7733.

32. United States v. Tibbs, No. 2016 CF1 19431, 42 (D. C. Super. Ct. 2019).

33. Itiel E. Dror and Glenn Langenburg, " 'Cannot Decide': The Fine Line between Appropriate Inconclusive Determinations Versus Unjustifiably Deciding Not to Decide," *Journal of Forensic Science* 64 (2019): 10, 11.

34. Alicia Rairden, Brandon L. Garrett, Daniel Murrie, Sharon Kelley, and Amy Castillo, "Resolving Latent Conflict: What Happens When Latent Print Examiners Enter the Cage?" *Forensic Science International* 289 (2018): 215.

35. Bradford T. Ulery, R. Austin Hicklin, JoAnn Buscaglia, and Maria A. Roberts, "Repeatability and Reproducibility of Decisions by Latent Fingerprint Examiners," *PLoS ONE* 7, no. 3 (2012).

36. Brandon Garrett and Gregory Mitchell, "How Jurors Evaluate Fingerprint Evidence: The Relative Importance of Match Language, Method Information, and Error Acknowledgment," *Journal of Empirical Legal Studies* 10, no. 3 (September 2013): 484–511.

37. Jonathan Koehler, "If the Shoe Fits They Might Acquit: The Value of Forensic Science Testimony," *Journal of Empirical Legal Studies* 8 (2011): 21.

38. Brandon L. Garrett, William Crozier, and Rebecca Grady, "Likelihood Ratios, Error Rates, and Jury Evaluation of Forensic Evidence," *Journal of Forensic Sciences* (2020).

39. Trial Transcript, 84, State v. Pacheco (Cal. Super. Ct. Dec. 2016), 7–8.

40. Ibid., 101–2.

41. Ibid., 129.

42. Paul Flahive, "Experts Call for CSI Reform at San Antonio Forensics Event," Texas Public Radio, August 6, 2018.

43. Nicole Wetsman, "Fingerprint Analysis Could Finally Get Scientific, Thanks to a New Tool," *Gizmodo*, May 15, 2018.

44. Ibid.

45. FrStat Software, at www.forensicxpert.com/frstat/.

46. Jonathan J. Koehler, "Error and Exaggeration in the Presentation of DNA Evidence at Trial," *Jurimetrics Journal* 34 (1993): 21.

47. Ibid.

48. William Thompson and Edward L. Schumann, "Interpretation of Statistical Evidence in Criminal Trials: The Prosecutor's Fallacy and the Defense Attorney's Fallacy," *Law & Human Behavior* 11 (1987): 167.

49. Ted R. Hunt, "Agenda Materials on 'Overstatement' in Forensic Science," Advisory Committee on the Federal Rules of Evidence, April 29, 2019.

CHAPTER FIVE. OVERSTATEMENT

1. Brandon L. Garrett, "Donald Eugene Gates," *Convicting the Innocent: DNA Exonerations Database*, www.convictingtheinnocent.com/exoneree/donald-eugene-gates/.

2. U. S. Department of Justice, Office of the Inspector General, "Part Five: Findings and Recommendations Concerning Individuals," *The FBI Laboratory: An Investigation into Laboratory Practices and Alleged Misconduct in Explosives-Related and Other Cases*, April 1997, https://oig.justice.gov/special/9704a/index.htm.

3. John F. Fox, Jr., "The Birth of the FBI's Technical Laboratory—1924 to 1935," *Federal Bureau of Investigation*, accessed August 5, 2019, www.fbi.gov/about-us/history/highlights-of-history/articles/laboratory.

4. Geoff Earle, "Discredited Ex-FBI Agent Hired Back as Private Contractor Years Later," *New York Post,* July 21, 2014.

5. National Academy of Sciences, *Needs of the Forensic Science Community: The Perspective of the FBI Laboratory and Other Federal Crime Laboratories,* accessed August 5, 2019, https://sites.nationalacademies.org/cs/groups/pgasite/documents/webpage/pga_049712.pdf.

6. Sir Arthur Conan Doyle, "A Case of Identity," in *The Adventures of Sherlock Holmes* (Mineola, NY: Dover, 2009).

7. Laboratory Division of Federal Bureau of Investigation, "Proceedings of the International Symposium on Forensic Hair Comparisons," June 1985.

8. John W. Hicks, Special Agent, *Microscopy of Hairs: A Practical Guide and Manual, Federal Bureau of Investigation,* U. S. Department of Justice, January 1977, 41.

9. NAS Report, 5–25.

10. Richard E. Bisbing, *Forensic Hair Comparisons: Guidelines, Standards, Protocols, Quality Assurance and Enforcement,* presentation to the National Academy of Sciences, April 24, 2007.

11. Richard E. Bisbing, "Forensic Identification Subspecialities: Hair Evidence," in *Modern Scientific Evidence: The Law and Science of Expert Testimony,* ed. David Faigman et al. (West Group, 2010–11).

12. Government Brief, 8–9, Donald Gates v. United States, No. 82.1529 (D. C. Court of Appeals).

13. Federal Bureau of Investigation, *Microscopic Hair Analysis,* November 9, 2012, accessed August 5, 2019, www.mtacdl.org/attachments/CPE/Nelson/FBI_Limits_of_Science__%20Microscopic_Hair_Comparison.pdf.

14. Brandon L. Garrett and Peter J. Neufeld, "Invalid Forensic Science Testimony and Wrongful Conviction," 95 *Virginia Law Review* 1, 47 (2009).

15. Trial Transcript, 2838, People v. Kharey Wise, No. 4762 / 89 (N. Y. Supreme Ct. Nov. 13, 1990).

16. People v. Campbell, 516 N.E.2d 1364, 1369 (Ill. App. 4 Dist. 1987).

17. State v. Melson, 638 S.W.2d 342, 349 (Tenn. 1982).

18. Bivins v. State, 433 N.E.2d 387, 389–390 (Ind. 1982).

19. State v. Stouffer, 721 A.2d 207, 209 n.1 (Md. 1998).

20. American Academy of Forensic Science, "Code of Ethics and Conduct, Article II" (2019); American Board of Criminalistics, *Code of Ethics,* §§ 9–10, reprinted in Peter D. Barnett, *Ethics in Forensic Science: Professional Standards for the Practice of Criminalistics* (Boca Raton, FL: CRC Press, 2001), 125.

21. Status Hearing Transcript, 20, Donald E. Gates v. United States, F-6602–81 (D. C. Superior Court November 3, 2009).

22. Spencer S. Hsu, "Convicted Defendants Left Uninformed of Forensic Flaws Found by Justice Dept.," *Washington Post,* April 16, 2012.

23. U. S. Department of Justice, Office of the Inspector General, "The FBI Laboratory: An Investigation into Laboratory Practices and Alleged Misconduct in Explosives-Related and Other Cases" (April 1997) [hereafter 1997 OIG Report].

24. Ibid.

25. Earle, "Discredited Ex-FBI Agent Hired Back."

26. 1997 OIG Report, 5.

27. U. S. Department of Justice, Office of the Inspector General, "The FBI Laboratory One Year Later: A Follow-Up to the Inspector General's April 1997 Report on FBI Laboratory Practices and Alleged Misconduct in Explosives-Related and Other Cases" (June 1998).

28. U. S. Department of Justice, Office of the Inspector General, "An Assessment of the 1996 Department of Justice Task Force Review of the FBI Laboratory," July 2014.

29. Ibid., 52.

30. U. S. Department of Justice, "Letter to Chief Judge Lee F. Satterfield," November 15, 2010; and U. S. Department of Justice, "Letter to Chief Judge Lee F. Satterfield," December 16, 2010.

31. Carrie Johnson, "Justice Delayed: After Three Decades, An Apology," *NPR All Things Considered,* July 10, 2012.

32. 1997 OIG Report, 5.

33. Ibid.

34. Federal Bureau of Investigation Criminal Justice Information Services Division, "FBI / DOJ Microscopic Hair Comparison Analysis Review," accessed March 21, 2020, www.fbi.gov/services/laboratory/scientific-analysis/fbidoj-microscopic-hair-comparison-analysis-review.

35. ABS Group, "Root and Culture Cause Analysis of Report and Testimony Errors by FBI MHCA Examiners," August 2018, 12–13, 77, 120, 126, 222, 226.

36. Seth Augenstin, "DOJ's Fingerprint Uniform Language Is Part of 'Constant Evolution,' Says IAI," *Forensic Magazine,* March 1, 2018, www.forensicmag.com/news/2018/03/dojs-fingerprint-uniform-language-part-constant-evolution-says-iai.

37. Federal Bureau of Investigation, "Root Cause Analysis for Microscopic Hair Comparison Completed," press release, August 14, 2019.

38. American Statistical Association, *American Statistical Association Position on Statistical Statements for Forensic Evidence,* presented under the guidance of the ASA Forensic Science Advisory Committee, January 2, 2019, 1, www.amstat.org/asa/files/pdfs/POL-ForensicScience.pdf.

39. Spencer S. Hsu, "D. C. Police Framed Man Imprisoned 27 Years for 1981 Murder, U. S. Jury Finds," *Washington Post,* November 18, 2015.

40. Beatrice Gitau, "D. C. to Pay Tennessee Man $16.65 Million over Wrongful Conviction," *Christian Science Monitor,* November 20, 2015.

41. Spenser S. Hsu, "Judge Orders D. C. to Pay $13.2 Million in Wrongful FBI Hair Conviction Case," *Washington Post*, February 28, 2016.

CHAPTER SIX. QUALIFICATIONS

1. Collaborative Testing Services, a leading provider, used a test like this in 2019. Firearms Examination, Test No. 19–526 Summary Report, https://cts-forensics.com/reports/19-526_Web.pdf.

2. Spencer S. Hsu and Keith L. Alexander, "Forensic Errors Trigger Reviews of D. C. Crime Lab Ballistics Unit, Prosecutors Say," *Washington Post*, March 24, 2017.

3. Keith Alexander, "FBI, Federal Prosecutors Investigate District's Forensic Firearms Lab," *Washington Post*, January 30, 2020.

4. Hearing Transcript, 34, State of North Carolina v. Daniels, No. 17-CRS-54689, 18-CRS-5391 (Sup. Ct. North Carolina, July 24, 2019).

5. Ibid., 11.

6. Ibid., 36–39.

7. Eric Bradner and Rene Marsh, "Acting TSA Director Reassigned after Screeners Failed Tests to Detect Explosives, Weapons," *CNN*, June 2, 2015.

8. Jim Fisher, *Forensics under Fire: Are Bad Science and Dueling Experts Corrupting Criminal Justice?* (New Brunswick, NJ: Rutgers University Press, 2008), 242.

9. NAS Report, 232.

10. National Commission on Forensic Science, *Proficiency Testing in Forensic Science*, Views Document, February 25, 2016.

11. New York State Unified Court System, Language Access and Court Interpreters, accessed March 19, 2020, ww2.nycourts.gov/COURTINTERPRETER/ExamInformation.shtml.

12. 42 U. S. C. § 263a(b).

13. U. S. Department of Justice, Office of the Inspector General, "Combined DNA Index System, Operational and Laboratory Vulnerabilities," May 2006, vi, 11, 55.

14. Hugh J. Hansen et al., "Crisis in Drug Testing, Results of CDC Blind Study," *Journal of the American Medical Association* 253 (April 1985): 2382–87.

15. National Commission on Forensic Science, "Views of the Commission, Optimizing Human Performance in Crime Laboratories through Testing and Feedback," May 27, 2016.

16. Jonathan J. Koehler et al., "The Random Match Probability (RMP) in DNA Evidence: Irrelevant and Prejudicial?" *Jurimetrics Journal* 35 (Winter 1995): 201–19.

17. Brandon L. Garrett and Greg Mitchell, "The Proficiency of Experts," *University of Pennsylvania Law Review* 166 (2018): 915–16.

18. Ibid. See also Simon A. Cole, "Grandfathering Evidence: Fingerprint Admissibility Ruling from Jennings to Llera Plaza and Back Again," *American Criminal Law Review* 41 (2004): 1189, 1213.

19. Brett O. Gardner, Sharon Kelley, and Karen D. Pan, "Latent Print Proficiency Testing: An Examination of Test Respondents, Test-Taking Procedures, and Test Characteristics," *Journal of Forensic Sciences* 64 (2019) 1–7.

20. Brandon L. Garrett and Gregory Mitchell, "The Impact of Proficiency Testing Information and Error Aversions on the Weight Given to Fingerprint Evidence," *Behavioral Sciences and Law* 37, no. 1 (2019).

21. Jennifer McMenamin, "Police Expert Lied about Credentials," *Baltimore Sun*, March 9, 2007.

22. *In re* Renewed Investigation of the State Police Crime Lab., Serology Div., 438 S.E.2d 501, 514–20 (W. Va. 1993).

23. Andres Cediel and Lowell Bergman, "The Real CSI," *Frontline*, PBS, April 17, 2012, www.pbs.org/wgbh/frontline/film/real-csi/transcript/.

24. NAS Report, 210–11.

25. Ibid., 237.

26. Mike Bowers, "Bitemarkers Double-Down With a 'Pay-to-Play' Membership Drive," *CSI DDS*, February 15, 2017, https://csidds.com/2017/02/15/bitemarkers-double-down-with-a-pay-to-play-membership-drive-aafs2017/; and ABFO, *Qualifications and Application*, February 2017, http://abfo.org/wp-content/uploads/2012/08/APPLY-Intro-v.-Feb-2017.pdf.

27. Garrett and Mitchell, "Impact of Proficiency Testing Information," 915–16.

28. 42 U.S.C. § 263a (2012).

29. Walt Bogdanich, "Lax Laboratories: The Pap Test Misses Much Cervical Cancer through Labs' Errors," *Wall Street Journal*, November 2, 1987, A1.

30. See, e.g., Okla. Stat. Ann. tit. 74, § 150.37.

31. NAS Report, 208–9.

32. U.S. v. Lewis, 220 F. Supp. 2d 548, 554 (S. D. W. V. 2002).

CHAPTER SEVEN. HIDDEN BIAS

1. Maria Godoy, "The Judgment of Paris: The Blind Taste Test That Decanted the Wine World," *NPR*, May 24, 2016.

2. Daniel Kahneman and Amos Tversky, "On the Psychology of Prediction," *Psychological Review* 80, no. 4 (July 1973).

3. Sue Russell, "Bias and the Big Fingerprint Dust-Up," *Pacific Standard*, June 18, 2009.

4. Itiel E. Dror, David Charlton, and Ailsa E. Peron, "Contextual Information Renders Experts Vulnerable to Making Erroneous Identifications," *Forensic Science International* 156 (2006): 74–78.

5. Andres Cediel and Lowell Bergman, "The Real CSI," *Frontline*, PBS, April 17, 2012, www.pbs.org/wgbh/frontline/film/real-csi/transcript/.

6. Itiel E. Dror and R. Rosenthal, "Meta-Analytically Quantifying the Reliability and Biasability of Forensic Experts," *Journal of Forensic Sciences* 53, no. 4 (July 2008): 900–903.

7. "The Fingerprint Inquiry Report" (Edinburgh: APS Group Scotland, 2011), accessed July 14, 2019, www.thefingerprintinquiryscotland.org.uk/inquiry/3127-2.html.

8. Itiel E. Dror and Greg Hampikian, "Subjectivity and Bias in Forensic DNA Mixture Interpretation," *Science & Justice* 204 (2011).

9. Paul Bieber, "Measuring the Impact of Cognitive Bias in Fire Investigation," in *Proceedings of the International Symposium on Fire Investigation Science and Technology* (Sarasota, FL: National Association of Fire Investigators, 2012), 3–17.

10. Larry S. Miller, "Procedural Bias in Forensic Examinations of Human Hair," *Law and Human Behavior* 11 (1987): 157; and Paul Bieber, "Fire Investigation and Cognitive Bias," in *Wiley Encyclopedia of Forensic Science*, ed. Allan Jamieson and Andre Moenssens (New York: Wiley, 2014).

11. Saul M. Kassin, Itiel E. Dror, and Jeff Kukucka, "The Forensic Confirmation Bias: Problems, Perspectives, and Proposed Solutions," *Journal of Applied Research in Memory & Cognition* 2 (2013): 43, 45.

12. Brandon Garrett, "The Substance of False Confessions," *Stanford Law Review* 62, no. 4 (April 2010): 1051–119.

13. Daniel C. Murrie, Marcus T. Boccaccini, Lucy A. Guarnera, and Katrina A. Rufino, "Are Forensic Experts Biased by the Side That Retained Them?" *Psychological Science* 24, no. 10 (2013): 1889–97; and Daniel C. Murrie and Marcus T. Boccaccini, "Adversarial Allegiance Among Expert Witnesses," *Annual Review Law Social Science* 11 (2015): 37–55.

14. Gregory Mitchell and Brandon L. Garrett, "Creating Reasonable Doubt in Fingerprint Identification Cases: Substantive and Methodological Rebuttals by Defense Experts" (under submission).

15. Itiel E. Dror, Christophe Champod, Glenn Langenburg, David Charlton, Heloise Hunt, and Robert Rosenthal, "Cognitive Issues in Fingerprint Analysis: Inter- and Intra-expert Consistency and the Effect of a 'Target' Comparison," *Forensic Science International* 208 (May 2011): 1–3.

16. "Fingerprint Inquiry Report," 638.

17. Itiel E. Dror, William C. Thompson, Christian A. Meissner, I. Kornfield, Dan Krane, Michael Saks, and Michael Risinger, "Context Management Toolbox: A Linear Sequential Unmasking (LSU) Approach for Minimizing Cognitive

Bias in Forensic Decision Making," *Journal of Forensic Sciences* 60, no. 4 (July 2015): 1111–12.

18. U. S. Department of Justice, Office of the Inspector General, "A Review of the FBI's Progress in Responding to the Recommendations in the Office of the Inspector General Report on the Fingerprint Misidentification in the Brandon Mayfield Case," June 2011, 5, 27.

19. Itiel E. Dror and Jennifer Mnookin, "The Use of Technology in Human Expert Domains: Challenges and Risks Arising from the Use of Automated Fingerprint Identification Systems in Forensics," *Law, Probability and Risk* 9, no. 1 (January 2010): 47–67. See also Itiel E. Dror, Kasey Wertheim, Peter Fraser-Mackenzie, and Jeff Walajtys, "The Impact of Human-Technology Cooperation and Distributed Cognition in Forensic Science: Biasing Effects of AFIS Contextual Information on Human Experts," *Journal of Forensic Sciences* 57, no. 2 (March 2012): 343–52.

20. Brett Gardner, Sharon Kelley, Daniel Murrie, and Kellyn Blaisdell, "Do Evidence Submission Forms Expose Latent Print Examiners to Task-Irrelevant Information?" *Forensic Science International* 297 (April 2019): 236–42.

21. National Commission on Forensic Science, "Ensuring That Forensic Analysis Is Based upon Task-Relevant Information," 2015, www.justice.gov/archives /ncfs/page/file/641676/download.

22. Emily Pronin, Daniel Y. Lin, and Lee Ross, "The Bias Blind Spot: Perceptions of Bias in Self Versus Others," *Personality and Social Psychology Bulletin* 28, no. 3 (March 2002): 369–81.

23. Kassin, Dror, and Kukucka, "Forensic Confirmation Bias."

24. NAS Report, 177–78.

25. Michael Taylor et al., "Reliability of Pattern Classification in Bloodstain Pattern Analysis, Part I: Bloodstain Patterns on Rigid Non-absorbent Surfaces," *Journal of Forensic Science* 64 (2016): 922, 926–27.

26. D. M. Albert, J. W. Blanchard, and B. L. Knox, "Ensuring Appropriate Expert Testimony for Cases Involving the 'Shaken Baby,'" *Journal of the American Medical Association* 308, no. 1 (2012): 39–40.

27. Debra Rosenberg and Evan Thomas, "I Didn't Do Anything," *Newsweek*, November 9, 1997; and Commonwealth v. Woodward, 694 N.E.2d 1277, 1281 (Mass. 1998).

28. Stephen T. Goudge, "Inquiry into Pediatric Forensic Pathology in Ontario" (Toronto: Ontario Ministry of the Attorney General, 2008), 531.

29. For an estimate of 1,500 diagnoses and 200 convictions a year, see Deborah Tuerkheimer, "The Next Innocence Project: Shaken Baby Syndrome and the Criminal Courts," *Washington University Law Review* 87, no. 1 (January 2009).

30. Brief of Amici Curiae, State v. McPhaul, No. 421PA17 (N. C. July 30, 2018).

31. State v. McPhaul, 808 S.E.2d 294 (2017).

32. Alicia Rairden, Brandon L. Garrett, Daniel Murrie, Sharon Kelley, and Amy Castillo, "Resolving Latent Conflict: What Happens When Latent Print Examiners Enter the Cage?" *Forensic Science International* 289 (June 2018): 215–22.

33. Michael D. Risinger, "The NAS / NRC Report on Forensic Science: A Glass Nine-Tenths Full (This Is about the Other Tenth)," *Jurimetrics* 50, no. 1 (2009–10): 21; and NAS Report, 191.

34. Forensic Science Regulator, "Cognitive Bias Effects Relevant to Forensic Science Examinations," FSR-G-217, no. 1 (2015).

35. Melissa K. Taylor et al., *Latent Print Examination and Human Factors: Improving the Practice Through a Systems Approach*, U. S. Department of Commerce, National Institute of Standards and Technology, February 2012.

36. Ibid., 182.

CHAPTER EIGHT. GATEKEEPERS

1. Henry T. Greely and Judy Illes, "Neuroscience-Based Lie Detection: The Urgent Need for Regulation," *American Journal of Law and Medicine* 33 (2007): 385.

2. Frye v. United States, 293 F. 1013 (D. C. Cir. 1923).

3. National Research Council, *The Polygraph and Lie Detection* (Washington, DC: National Academies Press, 2003), 8.

4. United States v. Scheffer, 523 U. S. 303 (1998).

5. Daubert v. Merrell Dow Pharmaceuticals Inc., 509 U. S. 579 (1993).

6. Jed Rakoff, "Judging Forensics," keynote address, *Virginia Journal of Criminal Law* 6 (2018): 35.

7. Daubert, 509 U. S. 579, 590.

8. Barry C. Scheck, "DNA and Daubert," *Cardozo Law Review* 15 (2004): 1959.

9. Randolph N. Jonakait, "The Meaning of Daubert and What That Means for Forensic Science," *Cardozo Law Review* 15 (2004): 2117.

10. United States v. Starzecpyzel, 880 F. Supp. 1027 (S. D. N. Y. 1995).

11. Williamson v. Reynolds, 904 F. Supp. 1529, 1554 (E. D. Okla. 1995), *rev'd* Williamson v. Ward, 110 F.3d 1508, 1523 (10th Cir. 1997).

12. Kumho Tire Co., Ltd. v. Carmichael, 526 U. S. 137 (1999).

13. U. S. v. Llera Plaza, 188 F. Supp. 2d 549, 550 (E. D. Pa. 2002).

14. U. S. v. Llera Plaza, 179 F. Supp. 2d 492 (E. D. Pa. 2002).

15. U. S. v. Llera Plaza, 188 F. Supp. 2d 549 (E. D. Pa. 2002).

16. Ibid., 565.

17. Ibid., 556.

18. Ibid., 558.

19. See, e.g., United States v. Crisp, 324 F.3d 261, 269–73 (4th Cir. 2003); United States v. Havvard, 260 F.3d 597 (7th Cir. 2001); United States v. George, 363 F.3d 666, 672–73 (7th Cir. 2004); and United States v. John, 597 F.3d 263, 275 (5th Cir. 2010).

20. See United States v. Bonds, No. 15 CR 573-2, 2017 WL 4511061, at 4 (N. D. Ill. October 10, 2017).

21. Oliver Wendell Holmes, "The Path of the Law," *Harvard Law Review* 10 (1897): 457.

22. Peter Neufeld, "The (Near) Irrelevance of Daubert to Criminal Justice and Some Suggestions for Reform," *American Journal of Public Health* 95 (2005): S107.

23. State v. O'Connell, No. 2010CF012600, 2015 WL 10384608, at 4 (Fla. Cir. Ct. 2015).

24. Simon A. Cole, "Grandfathering Evidence: Fingerprint Admissibility Ruling from Jennings to Llera Plaza and Back Again," *American Criminal Law Review* 41 (2004): 1195–97.

25. Johnson v. Com., 12 S.W.3d 258, 262 (Ky. 1999).

26. Meskimen v. Com., 435 S.W.3d 526 (Ky. 2013)

27. Ibid., 534–36.

28. United States v. Llera Plaza, Nos. CR. 98–362-10, CR. 98–362-11, CR. 98–362-12 (E. D. Pa. Jan. 7, 2002).

29. Transcript of Trial, Day Three at 114–15, United States v. Mitchell, No 96–407 (E. D. Pa. July 9, 1999).

30. United States v. Havvard, 117 F. Supp. 2d 848, 854 (S. D. Ind. 2000).

31. *60 Minutes,* "Fingerprints: Infallible Evidence," aired January 5, 2003, CBS.

32. Kay Stephens, "Judge Permits Bite Mark Evidence for Ross Retrial: District Attorney Can Use Testimony about Mark during Ross Murder Retrial," *Altoona Mirror,* March 9, 2017.

33. Gen. Elec. Co. v. Joiner, 522 U. S. 136 (1997).

34. Johnson v. Commonwealth, 12 S.W.3d 258 (Ky. 1999).

35. State v. Favela, 323 P.3d 716, 718 (Ariz. Ct. App. 2014).

36. Brandon Garrett and Chris Fabricant, "The Myth of the Reliability Test," *Fordham Law Review* 86 (2018): 121.

37. Rakoff, "Judging Forensics."

38. Ibid.

39. State v. Rose, Case No. K06–0545, 25 (Md. Cir. Ct. Oct. 19, 2007); U. S. v. Rose, No. CCB-08–0149 (D. Md. Dec. 8, 2009).

40. U. S. v. Monteiro, 407 F. Supp. 2d 351, 355 (D. Mass. 2006).

41. U. S. v. Willock, 696 F. Supp. 2d 536 (D. Md. 2010).

42. Gardner v. U. S., 140 A.3d 1172 (D. C. 2016).

43. Brandon L. Garrett, Nicholas Scurich, and William Crozier, "Firearms Testimony and Jurors' Evaluation of Firearms Testimony," *Law and Human Behavior* (forthcoming, 2020).

44. Fed. R. Crim. P. 16 (Advisory Committee's Note, 1975).

45. National Commission on Forensic Science, "Recommendations to the Attorney General Regarding Pretrial Discovery," July 12, 2015.

46. Paul C. Giannelli, "Scientific Evidence: Bench Notes & Lab Reports," *Criminal Justice* 22, no. 2 (2007): 50–51.

47. Paul C. Giannelli, "Criminal Discovery, Scientific Evidence, and DNA," *Vanderbilt Law Review* 44 (1991): 791, 808.

48. Procedural Order: Trace Evidence 1 (D. Mass. Mar. 2010), www.mad .uscourts.govboston/pdf/ProcOrderTraceEvidenceUPDATE.pdf.

49. State v. Proctor, 347 S. C. 587 (Ct.App. 2001); *rev'd* State v. Proctor 358 S. C. 417 (2004).

50. Brandon L. Garrett, "Constitutional Regulation of Forensic Evidence," *Washington & Lee Law Review* 73 (2016): 1147, 1181.

51. Dist. Attorney's Office for Third Judicial Dist. v. Osborne, 557 U. S. 52, 55 (2009).

52. Garrett, "Constitutional Regulation of Forensic Evidence," 1183.

53. Melendez-Diaz v. Massachusetts, 557 U. S. at 318 (2009).

54. Williams v. Illinois, 132 S. Ct. 2221 (2012).

55. Jennifer Mnookin and David Kaye, "Confronting Science: Expert Evidence and the Confrontation Clause," *Supreme Court Review* 4 (2012): 99.

56. David Alan Sklansky, "Hearsay's Last Hurrah," *Supreme Court Review* 1 (2009): 73–74.

57. Fed. R. Evid. 706 (Advisory Committee Notes to 1972 Proposed Rules).

58. Jones v. United States, No. 15-CO-1104 (D. C. Cir. 2017).

59. Gretchen Gavett, "The Real CSI: Judge Harry T. Edwards: How Reliable Is Forensic Evidence in Court?" *Frontline*, April 17, 2012.

CHAPTER NINE. FAILED QUALITY CONTROL

1. Petition Appendix, 18, Commonwealth v. Cotto, Indictment No. 2007770, 2017 WL 4124972 (Sup. Ct. Mass. June 26, 2017), n. 15.

2. Commonwealth of Massachusetts, Office of the Attorney General, "Investigative Report Pursuant to *Commonwealth v. Cotto*, 471 Mass. 97 (2015)," April 1, 2016, 22–23 [hereafter Farak Report].

3. Farak Report, 9.

4. Ibid., 14.

5. Affidavit, Petition Appendix, 183.

6. Ibid., 184; see also Committee for Public Health Services v. Attorney General (Sept. 20, 2017), Complaint, 14, www.courthousenews.com/wp-content/uploads/2017/09/mass-farak.pdf.

7. Eric S. Lander, "DNA Fingerprinting on Trial," *Nature* 339 (1989): 501, 505.

8. Sandra Guerra Thompson, *Cops in Lab Coats: Curbing Wrongful Convictions through Independent Forensic Laboratories* (Durham, NC: Carolina Academic Press, 2015), 52–61.

9. Murray Weiss, "Criminal Errors," *New York Post,* December 4, 2007; Jaxon Van Derbeken, "SFPD Drug-Test Technician Accused of Skimming," *San Francisco Chronicle,* March 10, 2010, A1; and Steve Mills and Maurice Possley, "Report Alleges Crime Lab Fraud: Scientist Is Accused of Providing False Testimony," *Chicago Tribune,* January 14, 2001.

10. Ben Schmitt and Joe Swickard, "Troubled Detroit Police Crime Lab Shuttered: State Police Audit Results 'Appalling,' Wayne County Prosecutor Declares," *Detroit Free Press,* September 26, 2008, 1; and Lianne Hart, "DNA Lab's Woes Cast Doubt on 68 Prison Terms," *Los Angeles Times,* March 31, 2003, A19.

11. Michael Kranish, "Crime Lab Scandal Rocked Kamala Harris's Term as San Francisco District Attorney," *Washington Post,* March 6, 2019.

12. Rick Anderson, "The Fallibility of Forensic Science," *Criminal Legal News,* January 2019.

13. New State Ice Co. v. Liebmann, 285 U.S. 262, 311 (1932) (Brandeis, J., dissenting).

14. John F. Fox, Jr., FBI Historian, "The Birth of the FBI's Technical Laboratory—1924 to 1935," www.fbi.gov/about-us/history/highlights-of-history/articles/laboratory.

15. Paul Giannelli, "Forensic Science: Why No Research?", *Fordham Urban Law Journal* 38 (2010): 503.

16. See John I. Thornton, "Criminalistics: Past, Present and Future," *Lex et Scienta* 11 (1975): 23.

17. Matthew R. Durose, Kelly A. Walsh, and Andrea M. Burch, *Census of Publicly Funded Forensic Crime Laboratories, 2009,* Bureau of Justice Statistics (August 2012), 1, www.bjs.gov/content/pub/pdf/cpffcl09.pdf.

18. Max Blau, "As New and Lethal Opioids Flood U.S. Streets, Crime Labs Race to Identify Them," *Stat,* July 5, 2017, www.statnews.com/2017/07/05/opioid-identification-analogs/.

19. See, for example, Arash Khamooshi, "Breaking Down Apple's iPhone Fight with the U.S. Government," *New York Times,* March 21, 2016.

20. Matthew R. Durose and Connor Brooks, Bureau of Justice Statistics, *Census of Publicly Funded Forensic Crime Laboratories, 2014,* Bureau of Justice Statistics (2015), 1; Durose et al., *Census of Publicly Funded Forensic Crime Laboratories, 2009.*

21. John Stith, "Judge Makes the Call on DNA Fee: Even if Defendant's DNA Is in State Databank, Some Judges Require the Fee Be Paid Again," *Post-Standard* (Syracuse), April 8, 2007; and Kirsten D. Levingston, "The Cost of Staying Out of Jail," *New York Times,* April 2, 2006.

22. Human Rights Watch, "Testing Justice: The Rape Kit Backlog in Los Angeles City and County," March 31, 2009.

23. Tina Daunt, "LAPD Blames Faulty Training in DNA Snafu," *Los Angeles Times,* July 31, 2002, B3.

24. Innocence Project, "Cody Davis," www.innocenceproject.org/cases /cody-davis/.

25. U. S. Department of Justice, *Notice Regarding the Solicitation "Paul Coverdell Forensic Science Improvement Grants Program—Formula,"* April 19, 2018, www.nij.gov/funding/documents/solicitations/nij-2018-13760.pdf.

26. Durose and Brooks, *Census of Publicly Funded Forensic Crime Laboratories, 2014,* Appendix Table 9.

27. Michael Connelly, "Making L. A. Come Alive—With a Little Help from Cal State L. A.," *Today Magazine,* Spring 2015, www.calstatela.edu/univ/ppa/today /city-detective-and-crime-lab.

28. Trial Testimony, 134–44, *In re* Minor (March 2017), www.documentcloud .org/documents/5765041-Seavers-Redacted-2.html#document/p73/a485948.

29. Nicole Westman, "CPD Police Fingerprint Work Undermines Chicago Property Crime Cases," *Chicago Reporter,* March 12, 2019.

30. Katie Mettler, "How a Lab Chemist Went from 'Superwoman' to Disgraced Saboteur of More Than 20,000 Drug Cases," *Washington Post,* April 21, 2017.

31. NAS Report, 134.

32. Loene M. Howes et al., "Forensic Scientists' Conclusions: How Readable Are They for Non-scientist Report-Users?" *Forensic Science International* 231 (2013): 102.

33. National Commission on Forensic Science, *Recommendation to the Attorney General: National Code of Professional Responsibility for Forensic Science and Forensic Medical Service Providers,* 2015, 3.

34. Farak Report, 9.

35. Ibid., 11–12.

36. Ibid., 13–14.

37. Ibid., 16–17.

38. Ibid., 16.

39. Ibid., 20.

40. Petition Appendix 9–11, Committee for Public Counsel Services v. Attorney General of Massachusetts, No. SJ-2017 (September 20, 2017).

41. International Standard, "General Requirements for the Competence of Testing and Calibration Laboratories," ISO / IEC 17025:2017(E), 3rd ed., 2017, 8.7.1. (ISO / IEC 17025:2017).

42. NAS Report, 14.

43. National Commission on Forensic Science, *Universal Accreditation*, 2016, 1, www.justice.gov/archives/ncfs/page/file/624026/download.

44. See Okla. Stat. Ann. tit. 74, § 150.37 (2004); N. Y. Exec. § 995b (McKinney 2003) (requiring accreditation by the state Forensic Science Commission). Like New York, Texas created a Forensic Science Commission; Tex. Crim. Proc. Code art. 43 38.01 (2007).

45. Andrea M. Burch et al., *Publicly Funded Forensic Crime Laboratories: Quality Assurance Practices, 2014*, Bureau of Justice Statistics (2016), www.bjs .gov/content/pub/pdf/pffclqap14.pdf.

46. Wendy J. Koen and C. Michael Bowers, eds., *Forensic Science Reform: Protecting the Innocent,* (London: Academic Press, 2017), 257–60.

47. Mandy Locke and Joseph Neff, "Inspectors Missed All SBI Faults," *News and Observer,* August 26, 2010.

48. ANSI National Accreditation Board, "Forensic Accreditation," www.anab .org/forensic-accreditation (last visited February 25, 2020)

49. ISO / IEC 17025:2017(E), 7.7.1–2.

50. Bridgeman v. District Attorney for the Suffolk District, 471 Mass. 465 (2015).

51. Bridgeman v. District Attorney for the Suffolk District, 476 Mass. 298, 309 (2017).

52. Karen Brown, "After Scandals, Officials Say Mass. Drug Labs Have Improved—Concerns Linger," *New England Public Radio,* May 23, 2016.

53. Massachusetts S. B. 2371, Michigan House Bill No. 6 (2018).

54. Joe Pelletier, "Drug Lab Scandal Will Drop More Than 376 Convictions in Plymouth, Bristol and Norfolk Counties," *The Enterprise,* November 30, 2017.

CHAPTER TEN. CRIME SCENE CONTAMINATION

1. NAS Report, 177.

2. Texas Forensic Science Commission, "Report on Investigation of Complaint Filed by Walter M. Reaves, Jr. on Behalf of Joe D. Bryan, Concerning Bloodstain Pattern Analysis, Serology and Trace Evidence," 2018, 11.

3. Brief of Amici Curiae of Scholars, State v. Bryan, No. WR089, 339–01 (2019).

4. Joseph Peterson and Ira Sommers, *The Role and Impact of Forensic Evidence in the Criminal Justice Process,* CSU–LA, School of Criminal Justice and Criminalistics, June 10, 2010, www.ncjrs.gov/pdffiles1/nij/grants/231977 .pdf.

5. Tami Abdollah, "OJ Simpson Case Taught Police What Not to Do at a Crime Scene," *Associated Press,* June 8, 2014.

6. Peter Gill, "Analysis and Implications of the Miscarriages of Justice of Amanda Knox and Raffaele Sollecito," *Forensic Science International: Genetics* 23 (2016): 9.

7. Margaret Kadifa and Andrew Kragie, "Police Shoot Man Brandishing Assault Rifle outside Houston Night Club," *Houston Chronicle*, May 17, 2017, www.chron.com/news/houston-texas/houston/article/Police-shoot-man-brandishing-assault-rifle-11152187.php.

8. Frank Horvath and Robert T. Meesig, *A National Survey of Police Policies and Practices Regarding the Criminal Investigation Process: Twenty-Five Years after Rand*, November 2001, 76, www.ncjrs.gov/pdffiles1/nij/grants/202902 .pdf.

9. Howard Cohen, "She Told Cops They Were Vitamins. But Botched Test Kept Florida Mom in Jail for Months," *Miami Herald*, March 10, 2018, www .miamiherald.com/news/state/florida/article204511844.html.

10. ProPublica, Facebook, March 13, 2018, www.facebook.com/propublica /posts/a-running-list-of-items-that-have-resulted-in-false-positives-on-these-\field-tes/10156305427129445/ (sharing Radley Balko, "Opinion: Why Are Police Still Using Field Drug Tests?" *Washington Post*, March 13, 2018).

11. Texas Forensic Science Commission, *Report in Compliance with HB-34*, December 4, 2018.

12. Ryan Gabrielson, "Houston Police End Use of Drug Tests That Helped Produce Wrongful Convictions," ProPublica, July 14, 2017.

13. Heather Murphy, "Coming Soon to a Police Station Near You: The DNA 'Magic Box'," *New York Times*, January 21, 2019.

14. Erin Murphy, "DNA in the Criminal Justice System," *UCLA Law Review in Discourse*, November 2, 2016.

15. Megan Molteni, "How DNA Testing at the US-Mexico Border Will Actually Work," *Wired*, May 2, 2019.

16. Sergio Bichao, "20,000 SWI Cases in NJ Closer to Possibly Bring Thrown Out," *New Jersey 101.5*, October 20, 2017; and Steve Janowski and Lindy Washburn, "20,000 Alcohol Breath Tests Cannot be Used as Evidence in Drunken Driving Cases," *North Jersey Record*, November 13, 2018.

17. See Centers for Disease Control and Prevention, "Impaired Driving: Get the Facts, Centers for Disease Control and Prevention," https://perma.cc/4EXE-63ZJ; and National Highway Traffic Safety Administration (NHTSA), "Facts and Statistics: Alcohol-Impaired Driving," Insurance Information Institute, www.iii.org /fact-statistic/facts-statistics-alcohol-impaired-driving (citing 2017 data).

18. State v. Ferrer, 95 Hawai'i 409, 23 P.3d 744 (Haw. Ct. App. 2001) ("the majority of courts that have addressed the issue generally consider psychomotor FSTs to be nonscientific evidence").

19. Simon Cole and Ronald Nowaczyk, "Field Sobriety Tests: Are They Designed for Failure?" *Perceptual and Motor Skills Journal* 79 (1994): 99.

20. R. C. 4511.19(D)(4)(b); see also State v. Nutter, 811 N.E.2d 185, 186–87 (Ohio Mun. 2004).

21. Mark Denbeaux et al., "The Untestable Drunk Driving Test," Seton Hall University School of Law, Center for Policy & Research, March 25, 2019, https:// ssrn.com/abstract = 3360029.

22. People v. Gower, 366 N.E.2d 69, 71 (1977).

23. N. J. Stat. 39:4–50.

24. State v. Chun, 194 N. J. 54 (N. J. 2008).

25. Denbeaux et al., "Untestable Drunk Driving Test," 28–29.

26. Stacy Cowley and Jessica Silver-Greenberg, "These Machines Can Put You in Jail. Don't Trust Them," *New York Times*, November 2019.

27. Charles Short, "Guilt by Machine," *Florida Law Review* 61 (2009): 177; *In re* Commissioner of Public Safety, 735 N.W.2d 706 (Minn. 2007).

28. In re Source Code Evidentiary Hearings in Implied Consent Matters, 816 N.W.2d 525, 529 (Minn. 2012).

29. See Fla. Stat. § 316.1932(4) (2008) (stating that full information about scientific tests that a defendant is entitled to request does not include "manuals, schematics, or software of the instrument used to test the person or any other material that is not in the actual possession of the state").

30. See Todd Ruger, "Fines Rise in DUI Software Fight," *Sarasota Herald Tribune*, March 9, 2007, BCE1; and Todd Ruger, "CMI's Refusal to Disclose Software Source Code Has Stalled DUI Cases," *Sarasota Herald Tribune*, October 6, 2007.

31. "Inside the Forensic Files: NYPD Shows PIX11 How It's Tracking Evidence," *Pix11*, May 5, 2015, https://pix11.com/2015/05/05/inside-the-forensic-files-nypd-shows-pix11-how-its-tracking-evidence/.

32. Brady v. Maryland, 373 U. S. 83 (1963).

33. California v. Trombetta, 467 U. S. 479, 489 (1984).

34. Arizona v. Youngblood, 488 U. S. 51, 56–58 (1988).

35. Brandon L. Garrett, *Convicting the Innocent: Where Criminal Prosecutions Go Wrong* (Cambridge, MA: Harvard University Press, 2011), 196.

36. San Diego Gas & Elec. Co. v. City of San Diego, 450 U. S. 621, 661 n.26 (1981) (Brennan, J., dissenting) (asking "why not a planner").

CHAPTER ELEVEN. THE REBIRTH OF THE LAB

1. Adam Liptak and Ralph Blumenthal, "New Doubt Cast on Testing in Houston Police Crime Lab," *New York Times*, August 5, 2004, A19.

2. Adam Liptak, "Worst Crime Lab in the Country—Or Is Houston Typical?" *New York Times*, March 11, 2003.

3. Michael R. Bromwich, *Final Report of the Independent Investigator for the Houston Police Department Crime Laboratory and Property Room* (June 13, 2007), 54–57, www.hpdlabinvestigation.org/reports/070613report.pdf.

4. Sandra Guerra Thompson, *Cops in Lab Coats: Curbing Wrongful Convictions through Independent Forensic Laboratories* (Durham, NC: Carolina Academic Press, 2015), 52–61.

5. "About Us," Board of Directors, Houston Forensic Science Center, www.houstonforensicscience.org/about-us.php.

6. Callan Hundl, Maddisen Neuman, Alicia Rairden, Preshious Rearden, and Peter Stout, "Implementation of a Blind Quality Control Program in a Forensic Laboratory," *Journal of Forensic Science* 1 (2019).

7. Thomas H. Maugh, II, "Navy Viewed as Setting Drug-Testing Standard," *Los Angeles Times*, October 29, 1986.

8. Houston Forensic Science Center, "HFSC Begins Blind Testing in DNA, Latent Prints, National First," press release, November 17, 2016.

9. For an overview, see Hundl et al., "Implementation," 6.

10. Ibid., 5.

11. Ibid., 4–5.

12. Brandon L. Garrett, Jeff Kukucka, and William Crozier, "Juror Appraisals of Forensic Evidence: Effects of Blind Proficiency and Cross-Examination," *Forensic Science International* 315 (2020).

13. U. S. Department of Justice, Justice News, "Deputy Attorney General Rosenstein Delivers Remarks at the American Academy of Forensic Sciences," February 21, 2018, www.justice.gov/opa/speech/deputy-attorney-general-rosenstein-delivers-remarks-american-academy-forensic-sciences.

CHAPTER TWELVE. BIG DATA FORENSICS

1. Jack Karp, "Facial Recognition Technology Sparks Transparency Battle," *Law360*, November 3, 2019.

2. Ben Conark, "Police Surveillance Technology under Fire in Appeal," *Florida Times Union*, March 12, 2018.

3. Ben Conark, "Florida Court: Prosecutors Had No Obligation to Turn over Facial Recognition Evidence," *Florida Times Union*, January 23, 2019.

4. U. S. Government Accountability Office, *Face Recognition Technology: DOJ and FBI Have Taken Some Actions in Response to GAO Recommendations to Ensure Privacy and Accuracy, But Additional Work Remains*, GAO-19-579T, June 4, 2019, 4, www.gao.gov/assets/700/699489.pdf.

5. Drew Harwell, FBI, "ICE Find State Driver's License Photos Are a Gold Mine for Facial-Recognition Searches," *Washington Post*, June 7, 2019.

6. U. S. Government Accountability Office, *Face Recognition Technology*, 11.

7. Stephen Gains and Sara Williams, "The Perpetual Lineup: Unregulated Police Facial Recognition in America," Center on Privacy and Technology at Georgetown Law, October 18, 2016.

8. James Vincent, "Gender and Racial Bias Found in Amazon's Facial Recognition Technology (Again)," *The Verge*, January 5, 2019.

9. PCAST Report, 21.

10. Itiel Dror and Greg Hampikian, "Subjectivity and Bias in Forensic DNA Mixture Interpretation," *Science & Justice* 51, no. 4 (2011).

11. William Thompson, "Painting the Target around the Matching Profile: The Texas Sharpshooter Fallacy in Forensic DNA Interpretation," *Law, Probability and Risk* 8, no. 3 (2009): 257–76.

12. PCAST Report, 77.

13. President's Council of Advisors on Science and Technology, "An Addendum to the PCAST Report on Forensic Science in Criminal Courts," September 2017, 8, https://perma.cc/VQ32-J6RB.

14. Jesse McKinley, "Potsdam Boy's Murder Case May Hinge on Minuscule DNA Sample from Fingernail," *New York Times*, July 25, 2016.

15. PCAST Report, 79–81.

16. DNA Identification Act, Pub. L. No. 103–322, 108 Stat. 2065 (1994) (codified at 42 U. S. C. § 14132).

17. See USA PATRIOT Act of 2001, Pub. L. No. 107–56, § 503, 115 Stat. 272, 364 (codified at 42 U. S. C. § 14135a(d)(2)); see also Regulations under the DNA Analysis Backlog Elimination Act of 2000, 68 Fed. Reg. 74855 (December 29, 2003); Justice for All Act of 2004, Pub. L. No. 108–405, § 203(b), 118 Stat. 2260, 2270 (codified at 42 U. S. C. § 14135a(d)); and DNA Sample Collection from Federal Offenders under the Justice for All Act of 2004, 70 Fed. Reg. 4763, 4764 (January 31, 2005).

18. FBI, "CODIS—NDIS Statistics" (as of January 2020).

19. 42 U. S. C. 14133 (a)(1).

20. 42 U. S. C. 14133 (b)(2).

21. Erin E. Murphy, *Inside the Cell: The Dark Side of Forensic DNA* (New York: Bold Type Books, 2015), 146–47; and Erin Murphy, "DNA in the Criminal Justice System: A Congressional Research Service Report* (*From the Future)," *UCLA Law Review In Discourse*, November 2, 2016.

22. Gabrielle Banks, "Texas Reviewing Thousands of DNA Cases That Used Outdated Method for Calculating Odds," *Dallas News*, January 31, 2016.

23. Brandon Garrett and Lee Kovarsky, *Federal Habeas Corpus: Executive Detention and Post-Conviction Litigation* (New York: Foundation Press, 2013), 164.

24. Kate White, "Joseph Buffey Agrees to Plea Deal, Freed after 15 Years in Prison," *Charleston Gazette-Mail*, October 11, 2016.

25. Ethan Bronner, "Lawyers, Saying DNA Cleared Inmate, Pursue Access to Data," *New York Times*, January 3, 2013.

26. Buffey v. Ballard, 782 S.E.2d 204, 216 (W. Va. 2015).

27. Thomas Fuller, "He Spent 36 Years behind Bars: A Fingerprint Database Cleared Him in Hours," *New York Times*, March 21, 2019.

28. Matthew R. Durose and Connor Brooks, Bureau of Justice Statistics, *Census of Publicly Funded Forensic Crime Laboratories, 2014*, Bureau of Justice Statistics (2015), 1.

29. Kenneth Gantt, U. S. Department of Homeland Security, "Privacy Impact Assessment for the Automated Biometric Identification System (IDENT)," December 7, 2012, 2.

30. Axon Enterprise Inc., *First Report of the Axon AI and Policing Technology Ethics Board*, June 2019.

31. Catie Edmondson, "ICE Used Facial Recognition to Mine State Driver's License Databases," *New York Times*, July 7, 2019.

32. Murphy, *Inside the Cell*, 153.

33. Maryland v. King, 569 U. S. 435, 482 (2013) (Scalia, J., dissenting).

34. Iowa v. Guise, No. 17–0589, 10 (Iowa Ct. App. 2018).

35. Justice in Forensic Algorithms Act of 2019, H. R. 4368, 116th Cong. (2019–2020).

CHAPTER THIRTEEN. FIXING FORENSICS

1. National Commission of Forensic Science, "Reflecting Back—Looking toward the Future," National Institute of Standards and Technology, April 11, 2017.

2. State v. Sheila Denton, No. 04R-330 (Ga. Sup. Ct. Ware County 2020).

3. Loene M. Howes et al., "Forensic Scientists' Conclusions: How Readable Are They for Non-Scientist Report-Users?," *Forensic Science International* 231 (2013): 102.

4. Cal. Penal Code § 1473 (West 2017); 2018 Conn. Pub. S. B. 509 Acts No. 18–61 (Reg. Sess.); Mich. Ct. R. 6.502(g)(2); 2019 Nev. Stat. 356 (2019); Tex. Code Crim. Proc. Ann. art 11.073(b) (West 2015); Wyo. Stat. Ann. § 7-12–403 (West 2018).

5. See Tex. Code Crim. Proc. Ann. art. 38.01; Juan Hinojosa and Lynn Garcia, "Improving Forensic Science through State Oversight: The Texas Model," *Texas Law Review* 91 (2012): 19, 20; and Brandi Grissom, "Bill, Budget Expand Authority of Forensic Science Commission," *Texas Tribune*, May 25, 2013, www.texastribune.org/2013/05/25/reforms-expand-forensic-science-commission-authori.

6. *Report of the Texas Forensic Science Commission, Willingham/Willis Investigation*, April 15, 2011, www.fsc.state.tx.us/documents/FINAL.pdf.

7. Ibid., 24.

8. Ibid., 23.

9. Forensic Technology Center of Excellence, *Final Report, State Forensic Science Commissions* 2016, 4, www.txcourts.gov/media/1440436/forensic-technology-center-of-excellence-report-on-state-forensic-science-commissions.pdf.

10. Tex. Code Crime. Proc. Ann. art. 38.01 (West 2015).

11. N. Y. Exec. Law § 995-a(1)(b), (2) (McKinney 1996).

12. Joseph Fisch, N. Y. Office of the Inspector General, "Report of Investigation of the Trace Evidence Section of the New York State Police Forensic Investigation Center," 2009, 10–11.

13. "About DFS," Virginia Department of Forensic Science, www.dfs.virginia .gov/about/index.cfm; and Paul C. Giannelli, "Wrongful Convictions and Forensic Science: The Need to Regulate Crime Labs," *North Carolina Law Review* 86 (2007): 163, 194–95.

14. Massachusetts S. B. 2371, Michigan House Bill No. 6 (2018).

15. See Texas Forensic Science Commission, Fourth Annual Report, 2015, 15–22.

16. California Crime Laboratory Review Task Force, "An Examination of Forensic Science in California," November 2009, 47; Letter from William Thompson et al. to Members, California Crime Laboratory Review Task Force, June 25, 2010.

17. Larry A. Hammond, "The Failure of Forensic Science Reform in Arizona," *Judicature* 93 (2010): 227, 228.

18. Office of Justice Programs, National Institute of Justice, FY2010 Paul Coverdell National Forensic Science Improvement Act Report to Congress: Funding Table (2010).

19. U. S. Department of Justice, Office of the Inspector General, Review of the Office of Justice Programs' Paul Coverdell Forensic Science Improvement Grants Program, 2008, 7, www.justice.gov/oig/reports/OJP/e0801/final.pdf.

20. U. S. Department of Justice, National Institute of Justice, "Solicitation: Paul Coverdell Forensic Science Improvement Grants Program, 2020, 5–8, www.ncjrs.gov/pdffiles1/nij/sl000921.pdf.

21. NAS Report, 177–78.

22. See, e.g., Paul C. Giannelli, "Daubert and Forensic Science: The Pitfalls of Law Enforcement Control of Scientific Research," *Illinois Law Review* 2011 (2011): 53; and Quintin Chatman, "How Scientific Is Forensic Science?" *The Champion,* August 2009, at 36, 37–38.

23. Strengthening Forensic Science in the United States: The Role of the National Institute of Standards and Technology: Hearing Before the Subcommittee on Technology and Innovation of the House Commission on Science and Technology, 111th Congress, March 10, 2009, 3–4 (2009).

24. National Institute of Standards and Technology, "Forensic Science Standards Effort Takes Shape as NIST Appoints Scientific Area Committees Members," September 3, 2014, www.nist.gov/forensics/sac-members-announcement .cfm.

25. Karen D. Pan and Karen Kafadar, "Statistical Modeling and Analysis of Trace Element Concentrations in Forensic Glass Evidence," *Annals of Applied Statistics* 21 (2018): 788.

26. David Sarasohn, "Brandon Mayfield, 11 Years Later," *Oregonian*, September 22, 2015.

APPENDIX

1. U. S. Department of Justice, Office of the Inspector General, *A Review of the FBI's Handling of the Brandon Mayfield Case*, March 2006, 99, 111, https:// oig.justice.gov/special/s0601/final.pdf.

2. *Convicting the Innocent, DNA Exonerations Database*, at www.convicting theinnocent.com.

3. *Getting Forensics Right*, March 6, 2019, https://web.law.duke.edu/video /tags/keith-harward/; and Netflix, *The Innocence Files*, season 1, episode 3, "The Evidence: The Duty to Correct" (2020), www.netflix.com/title/80214563.

4. NAS Report.

5. PCAST Report.

6. Sharia Mayfield and Brandon Mayfield, *Improbable Cause: The War on Terror's Assault on the Bill of Rights* (Salem, NH: Divertir, 2015).

7. Simon A. Cole, *Suspect Identities: A History of Fingerprinting and Criminal Identification* (Cambridge, MA: Harvard University Press, 2002).

8. United States v. Tibbs, No. 2016 CF1 19431, 42 (D. C. Super. Ct. 2019).

9. PCAST Report, 11–12.

10. Jonathan J. Koehler, "Intuitive Error Rate Estimates for the Forensic Sciences," *Jurimetrics Journal* 57 (2017): 153–68.

11. Brandon Garrett and Gregory Mitchell, "How Jurors Evaluate Fingerprint Evidence: The Relative Importance of Match Language, Method Information, and Error Acknowledgment," *Journal of Empirical Legal Studies*, 10, no. 3 (September 2013): 484–511.

12. Spencer S. Hsu, "Convicted Defendants Left Uninformed of Forensic Flaws Found by Justice Dept.," *Washington Post*, April 16, 2012.

13. Federal Bureau of Investigation, Criminal Justice Information Services Division, "FBI / DOJ Microscopic Hair Comparison Analysis Review," www.fbi .gov/services/laboratory/scientific-analysis/fbidoj-microscopic-hair-comparison-analysis-review.

14. *American Statistical Association Position on Statistical Statements for Forensic Evidence 1* (January 2, 2019), www.amstat.org/asa/files/pdfs/POL-ForensicScience.pdf.

15. U. S. Department of Justice, "Approved ULTR for the Forensic Firearms /Toolmarks Discipline—Pattern Match," January 24, 2019, www.justice.gov/olp /page/file/1083671/download.

16. Andres Cediel and Lowell Bergman, "The Real CSI," *Frontline*, PBS, April 17, 2012, www.pbs.org/wgbh/frontline/film/real-csi/transcript/.

17. Brandon L. Garrett and Greg Mitchell, "The Proficiency of Experts," *University of Pennsylvania Law Review* 166 (2018): 915–16.

18. Gregory Mitchell and Brandon Garrett, "The Impact of Proficiency Testing on the Weight Given to Fingerprint Evidence," *Behavioral Sciences and the Law* 37 (2019): 195–210.

19. Itiel E. Dror, David Charlton, and Ailsa E. Peron, "Contextual Information Renders Experts Vulnerable to Making Erroneous Identifications," *Forensic Science International* 156 (2006): 74–78; see also Dr. Itiel E. Dror, www.ucl.ac .uk/~ucjtidr/.

20. "The Fingerprint Inquiry Report" (Edinburgh: APS Group Scotland, 2011), accessed July 14, 2019, www.thefingerprint inquiryscotland.org.uk /inquiry/3127-2.html.

21. Daniel C. Murrie, Marcus T. Boccaccini, Lucy A. Guarnera, and Katrina A. Rufino, "Are Forensic Experts Biased by the Side That Retained Them?" *Psychological Science* 24, no. 10 (2013): 1889–97; and Daniel C. Murrie and Marcus T. Boccaccini, "Adversarial Allegiance among Expert Witnesses," *Annual Review Law Social Science* 11 (2015): 37–55.

22. Forensic Science Regulator, "Cognitive Bias Effects Relevant to Forensic Science Examinations," FSR-G-217, 1 (2015).

23. U. S. v. Llera Plaza, 179 F. Supp. 2d 492 (E. D. Pa. 2002); *rev'd* 188 F. Supp. 2d 549 (E. D. Pa. 2002).

24. Simon A. Cole, "Grandfathering Evidence: Fingerprint Admissibility Ruling from Jennings to Llera Plaza and Back Again," *American Criminal Law Review* 41 (2004): 1195–97.

25. Brandon Garrett and Chris Fabricant, "The Myth of the Reliability Test," *Fordham Law Review* 86 (2018): 121.

26. Paul C. Giannelli, "Scientific Evidence: Bench Notes & Lab Reports," *Criminal Justice* 22, no. 2 (2007): 50–51.

27. Sandra Guerra Thompson, *Cops in Lab Coats: Curbing Wrongful Convictions through Independent Forensic Laboratories* (Durham, NC: Carolina Academic Press, 2015), 52–61.

28. Pamela Colloff, "Blood Will Tell: Investigating a Forensic Science," ProPublica, July 24, 2018, www.propublica.org/series/blood-will-tell.

29. Stacy Cowley and Jessica Silver-Greenberg, "These Machines Can Put You in Jail: Don't Trust Them," *New York Times,* November 2019.

30. For an example of a podcast in which Stout discusses the lab's work, see, for example, Just Science, "Blind Proficiency Testing," January 2019, www.ncjrs.gov/App/Publications/abstract.aspx?ID = 274792.

31. The Electronic Frontier Foundation, "Who Has Your Face?," at https://whohasyourface.org/#.

32. Stephen Gains and Sara Williams, "The Perpetual Lineup: Unregulated Police Facial Recognition in America," Center on Privacy and Technology at Georgetown Law, October 18, 2016.

33. Ark. Code 2015, § 12–12–302; D. C. Law § 5–1501.01 et seq. (creating Science Advisory Board and Stakeholder Counsel to supervise crime lab); Delaware Code tit. 29, ch. 47, § 4714 (2015); Md. Code Ann., Health-Gen. § 17–2A–02 (LexisNexis 2009) (establishing oversight of forensic science laboratories in Maryland); Minn. Stat. Ann. § 299C.156 (West 2007); Mo. Ann. Stat. § 650.059.1 (West Supp. 2011); N. C. Gen. Stat. ch. 11, art. 9, § 114–61; R. I. Gen. Laws §§12–1.2–1 to -7 (2002 & Supp. 2010) (Rhode Island State Crime Laboratory); Forensic Science Laboratory Advisory Board, Mont. Department of Just., www.doj.mt.gov/enforcement/crimelab/#advisoryboard; N. M. Stat. Ann. § 29–16–5 (Supp. 2004) (DNA Oversight Committee); R. I. Gen. Laws § 12–1-1–3 (2002) (State Crime Laboratory Commission); Va. Code Ann. § 9.1–1110(A)(1), (4) (2006); Wash. Rev. Code Ann. § 43.103.030 (2007) (Washington State Forensic Investigations Council).

34. *Report of the Texas Forensic Science Commission, Willingham/Willis Investigation,* April 15, 2011, www.fsc.state.tx.us/documents/FINAL.pdf.

35. National Commission of Forensic Science, "Reflecting Back—Looking toward the Future," National Institute of Standards and Technology, April 11, 2017.

36. Statement of Judge Harry T. Edwards, February 21, 2019, www.innocenceproject.org/judge-edwards-nas-statement/.

Index

Founded in 1893,
UNIVERSITY OF CALIFORNIA PRESS
publishes bold, progressive books and journals
on topics in the arts, humanities, social sciences,
and natural sciences—with a focus on social
justice issues—that inspire thought and action
among readers worldwide.

The UC PRESS FOUNDATION
raises funds to uphold the press's vital role
as an independent, nonprofit publisher, and
receives philanthropic support from a wide
range of individuals and institutions—and from
committed readers like you. To learn more, visit
ucpress.edu/supportus.